T

Writing Europe

This book may be recalled before the above date.

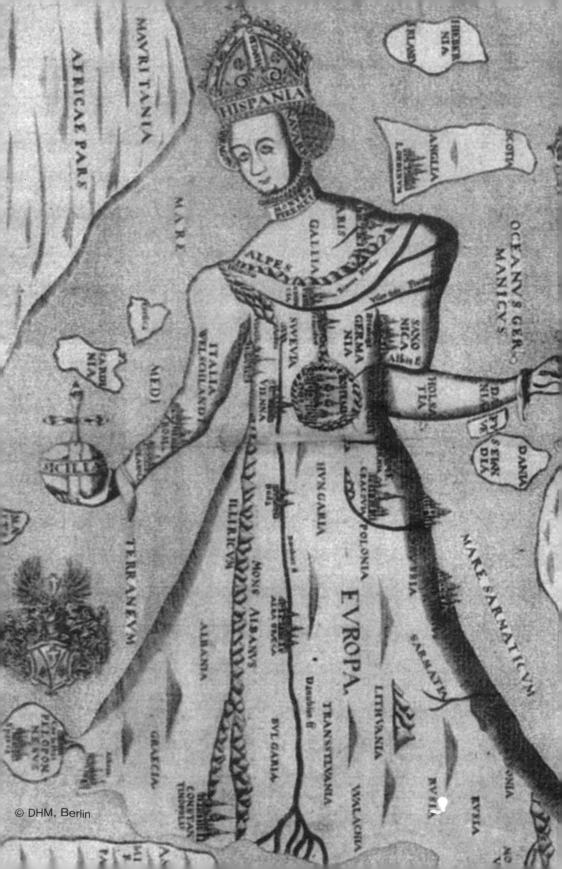

HIBERNIA

ANGLIA SCOTIA

AFRICAE PARS

MAVRITANIA

MARE

OCEANVS GERMANICVS

HISPANIA

GALLIA

ALPES

ITALIA WELSCHLANDT

SICILIA

MEDI

SARDINIA

SVEVIA

GERMANIA

SAXONICA

HOLLANDIA

DANIA

VIENNA

HVNGARIA

POLONIA

MARE SARMATICVM

ILLIRICVM

MONS ALBANVS

EVROPA

SARMATIA

TERRANEVM

ALBANIA

BVLGARIA

LITHVANIA

TRANSILVANIA

WALACHIA

RVSIA

RVBIA

GRAECIA

CONSTANTINOPOLIS

Writing Europe

What is European about the Literatures of Europe?
Essays from 33 European Countries

Edited by

Ursula Keller and Ilma Rakusa

C E U PRESS

Central European University Press
Budapest • New York

First published in German as *Europa schreibt.*
Was ist das Europäische an den Literaturen Europas?
by edition Körber-Stiftung www.edition-koerber-stiftung.de in 2003

Published with the support of Pasts, Inc. Center for Historical Studies

C E U **Pasts, Inc.®**
CENTER FOR HISTORICAL STUDIES
English edition published in 2004 by

Central European University Press

An imprint of the
Central European University Share Company
Nádor utca 11, H-1051 Budapest, Hungary
Tel: +36-1-327-3138 or 327-3000
Fax: +36-1-327-3183
E-mail: ceupress@ceu.hu
Website: www.ceupress.com

400 West 59th Street, New York NY 10019, USA
Tel: +1-212-547-6932
Fax: +1-212-548-4607
E-mail: mgreenwald@sorosny.org

Cover design: Groothuis, Lohfert, Consorten (www.glcons.de)

ISBN 963 9241 89 X Cloth
ISBN 963 9241 90 3 Paperback

Library of Congress Cataloging-in-Publication Data

Europa schreibt. English
  Writing Europe : what is European about the literatures of Europe? : essays from 33 European countries / edited by Ursula Keller and Ilma Rakusa.
    p. cm.
  Includes bibliographical references.
  ISBN 963924189X (hardbound) – ISBN 9639241903 (pbk.)
  1. European literature–History and criticism. I. Keller, Ursula, 1940- II. Rakusa, Ilma. III. Title.

  PN501.E8413 2004
  809'.894–dc22

                                    2004007147

Printed in Hungary by
Akaprint Nyomda

Table of Contents

Ursula Keller

The essays of authors from the eastern part of the continent sharpen our awareness of the harm the new Europe will do to itself if it ignores the great literary wealth on its doorstep.
© Michael Zapf

Ursula Keller

Germany

Born in Łódź, Poland in 1940, Ursula Keller studied German language and literature, Romance languages and literature, and philosophy in Göttingen, Tübingen, Heidelberg, Aix-en-Provence (France), and Frankfurt. After various teaching assignments and research projects at the University of Tübingen, she completed her PhD in 1980 with Walter Jens. From 1980 until 1991 she worked as a freelance television journalist (literary portraits and film essays) and as a theatre script editor and co-producer (TAT, Schauspielhaus). Since 1992 she has been program manager of the *Literaturhaus Hamburg*.

Writing Europe

*Fündiger, was das Gemeinsame im Verschiedenen
angeht, sind die Autoren, die es in einem gemeinsamen
europäischen Raum der Erfahrung, der Erinnerung, der
Lektüren und Erzählungen aufsuchen, in jenem
transnationalen kulturellen Echoraum, in dem sich die
vielen verschiedenen Stimmen Europas am ehesten
berühren, überschneiden, verknüpfen und vernetzen.*

Europe and Literary Authors

There were times when the idea of a united Europe was a profound
and emphatic concern of the great European writers, giving rise to
an abundance of meaningful essays on Europe. Novalis, the
Schlegel brothers, Victor Hugo, Heinrich Heine, Rudolf Borchardt,
Hermann Hesse, André Gide, Ortega y Gasset, Hugo von Hof-
mannsthal, Thomas Heinrich and Klaus Mann, Stefan Zweig, Hermann Broch, and Alfred Döblin were all writers that not only
pinned their political and cultural hopes on Europe, but also
worked in various ways toward the establishment of a broader
European feeling of community that would reflect pride in the
variety and diversity of its culture.

And yet since Europe stopped being the playground and battle-
field of megalomaniac power fantasies or the subject of high-flown
ideals and hopes and dreams, since its descent from the utopian
heights to the depths of pragmatic realpolitik, the European idea
seems to have lost much of its emotional appeal and intellectual
power. Moreover, for some time now, the Europe under construction in Brussels appears to have purposely avoided calling upon
intellectuals or ordinary citizens to reflect upon or identify and
engage with the European project. It has, at best, attracted mere
angry polemics. In his essay *Brüssel oder Europa—eins von beiden*
(Brussels or Europe—one of the two), Hans Magnus Enzensberger
accuses the European architects in Brussels and their institutions

not only of creating decision-making processes lacking in both transparency and in democratic legitimacy, but also of promoting a centralism that will quash Europe's great diversity of social forms, cultures, traditions, positions, and talents. *In order for Europe to survive as an economic power, everything that distinguishes our part of the world from others must be eliminated as quickly and as thoroughly as possible. A competitive Europe must become quicker, larger, and more efficient; it must be more lucid and homogeneous – a kind of synthetic superpower.*

The fact that in the early part of the year it was not overgeneralization by Brussels, but America's excessive aggression that drove the citizens of Europe onto the streets is not perhaps adequate proof of the formation of a new European public opinion. It does, however, demonstrate the need for Europe to reflect upon itself and the manner in which such public opinion might form. There can be no better time than now to draw Europe's intellectuals and writers into a discussion about what Europe really means, and about what the continent could and must become if it wishes to be more than merely a pressure group for economic expansion with limited political responsibility. Even without their differences with America, Europeans currently have many good reasons to consider the development of a Europe that is rather different from the Euroland envisaged by Brussels. For this to happen, Europe needs – perhaps more than it realizes – the self-understanding of writers.

Since Europe's inception, it is literature, the most self-reflective of the arts, that has played a decisive role in the development of European culture and self-reflection. In the myths, pictures, and stories through which it has told of itself and tried to comprehend itself, Europe has consistently reaffirmed the peculiarity of its culture and its special way of viewing and interpreting the world. At present, however, the continent's self-image appears more blurred than ever. The Europe in which present-day Europeans might recognize themselves has yet to find its contours.

Europe's *"Best Self"*
It is this Europe, so unaware of itself, that the writer and former president Václav Havel takes to task when he writes: *The only*

meaningful objective for Europe in the next century is to be its "best self," that is, to revitalize its best intellectual traditions and thereby contribute creatively to a new form of global community of living.

Perhaps Europe will find it easier to be its *best self* because— more than any other continents and cultures—it has had ample opportunity to become acquainted with its "worst self." In the course of its history, so full of both promise and devastation, in the course of its dramatic success story, which has outdone all other continents and cultures in terms of the conflict between the most brilliant intellectual, cultural, and social achievements on the one hand and the darkest excesses of destruction and self-depredation on the other, Europe has come to know itself. And in doing so it has exorcised all previous feelings of superiority as well as any naive notions of innocence à l'américaine.

And thus the soft image of the future Europe that appears on the horizon in the essays composed for the symposium and in the discussions of the invited authors is a long way from that of a proliferating superpower. It is a more considerate Europe, a Europe that recollects, reflects, doubts, and hesitates; a Europe that allows itself the luxury of asking questions before it acts and that refuses, even in the field of politics, to equate an appreciation of complexity with time-wasting or indecision.

As we know, there is, in today's world, no shortage of complex and obscure situations in which such European qualities could prove their political worth. To perceive such qualities as strengths and to apply them responsibly in a global context—this is what could enable Europe's *best self* to contribute to the new form of global community envisaged by Havel. At present, there is no other actor in sight that would be suitable for this role.

The essays of *Writing Europe* offer a first impression of the manner in which European literary authors—who are, after all, experts in matters of complexity as well as scholars of worldly obscurity—could contribute to the purposeful development and application of such qualities. And they may reveal something else too; namely, the extent to which writers—who are also experts in matters of difference—could assist a unifying Europe in recognizing its real wealth, the incredible value of the variety and diversity of its cultures and languages, and of its ways of living and thinking. What could better resist the destructive force of a global mass culture that dispenses with difference than the natural cultural wealth and historical diversity of this patchwork continent?

What is shared in diversity

The existence of so much difference in such a small area is an ongoing concern of the Eurocrats. But then Brussels still has to discover that such diversity also constitutes a considerable potential. But before it can make such a discovery, Brussels must first develop an awareness of the vital importance of culture for the multicultural and open European identity of the future. This requires it to view the many voices of European culture as sources of energy. It is this very energy that could make Europe's multiple voices audible to each other, revealing their common tone, if only one could make the contours of an image visible in which Europeans, with their need for difference, might recognize themselves. For only then would they stop saying: *"We don't feel like Europeans even if we are Europeans"* or *"It's only in America that you realize you're a European."*

It is this balance between difference and similarity, a balance we still have to locate, that many of the essays address. The tension between the two is not to be dispelled by slogans such as "unity in diversity." It is this tension that makes the European project an open process, for it is within the still unresolved and tense relationship between local, regional, national, and European allegiances and interests that all issues of European identity must be considered, unless we argue them existentially. Europe's future character will depend upon the success of how we cope with difference.

A single identity, no identity, or multiple identities?

This is currently the big question facing Europe. Europe has been so taken up with its search for a future political form that it has completely forgotten to examine, a little more carefully, what is often repeated about European identity and its suitability for

Europe. What does identity mean for a continent that comprises, above all, difference and contrast and whose very potential lies in the diversity of language, lifestyle, and experience? It comes as no surprise, therefore, that the writers—whose living is based on the art of making distinctions—tend to give somewhat varying and skeptical assessments of whether Europe has one identity or many identities, whether it lacks an identity, or whether it really needs an identity at all.

Adolf Muschg, drawing on his Swiss experience, lodges a plea for an open, flexible, and vague identity—if any at all. He hopes that *the renewable collective energy of Europe will not be absorbed by a single and monotone identity, and promises to stubbornly refuse, if necessary,* any unprincipled social metabolism that *time and again does away with identity only to re-establish it in some new form.*

This organic and process-oriented identity strategy is supported by the Slovenian poet and essayist Aleš Debeljak in his conception of *concentric circles of identity.* These *emanate from most local and fecund surroundings, from the neighborhood to a region, rippling outward in an ever more abstract manner to national, state, and European identities.* They end perhaps and with a bit of luck in *our common humanity.*

Such postmodern ideas of concurrent or adjacent identities leave the Irish narrative writer Colm Tóibín cold. For him there is simply no European identity—or at least nothing that *might be felt with the same emotional strength* as the two other essential identities: the one *bound up with memory, family, community, and personal experience,* and the other centering *on a nation, a state, and an imagined community.* For him Europe is nothing more than *a name for a set of interests, organized into the European Union,* whose liberalizing and secularizing power Tóibín, the Irishman, has nevertheless learned to value. Meanwhile the novels of the Spanish narrative writer Eugenio Fuentes are more concerned with conflicts arising at the *transition from regional to continental. If, as a writer, I try to grasp what Europe means for the people who walk its streets, it is my duty to warn that the concept holds both promises and threats.* Whether we shall succeed in realizing what is shared and continental without damaging what is peculiar and regional is still an unanswered European question.

In the view of the Estonian Emil Tode a socially binding identity *cannot be founded on purely abstract ideas — it requires real people and meaningful symbols... In my view the attempt to create a common cultural identity in Europe ("European literature," "European music, "European film") aims at constructing a counterweight to this dominant power, constituting a nostalgic reminiscence of one's own lost supremacy ... It would be best if Europe stopped being so self-analytical because Europe fails to find itself — there is nowhere that is not Europe.*

While Tode sees Europe everywhere, the Italian Mario Fortunato, who resides in London, sees it nowhere anymore. For him Europe disappeared some time ago in the fog of *planetary homogenization* that blurs all contours. *Yet again: no homeland. Not in the Fatherland, not in Europe, nor Elsewhere either.* There is nowhere else, nowhere: *everything the same, everything homogenized and shrunk.* This is how he summarizes his thorough disillusionment.

Europe of Books

When it comes to discovering things we all share in spite of our differences, the most successful authors are those who search in the common European space of experience, memory, reading, and narrative, in that transnational cultural echo-chamber in which Europe's many different voices come together, intersect, combine, and form a network.

With great empathy, the French narrative writer Jean Rouaud describes, in his homage to Ernst Wiechert, how two related temperaments and pitches encounter each other in this echo chamber, recognize themselves in each other, and come to the realization that *we belonged to the same geographical and mental region —* German–French resonance in a place where one might not expect it.

As a child my first European guests were dead people: Madame Bovary, Robinson Crusoe, Isadora Duncan, and Molière, writes the Turkish-European Emine Sevgi Özdamar. *I was in Europe, among*

my dead friends. And they did not leave me alone. Prince von Hom-
burg, Woyzeck, Hamlet ... Brecht, Kafka — all reside in Europe's sky,
next to the moon, and touch the lives of people even if they are far
away. The dead have created the European sky.

Books you read in childhood form your image of the world; they
are a writer's third parent, writes the Serbian author Dragan Velikić.
My tower, which I have inhabited since reading through all of Karl
May's novels, is built from Cervantes' humor, Italo Svevo's tensions,
James Joyce's circular routes, Danilo Kiš' Pannonian remem-
brances, from Herman Broch's sleepwalking.

And just like his tower, so also the towers of many of the authors
in both east and west are inhabited by the same pillar saints of
European literature. Cropping up time and again, Dante, Shakespeare, Goethe, Kafka, Musil, Dostoevsky, Flaubert, Nabokov,
Proust, Joyce, Woolf ... — the Europe of books is astonishingly homogenous; and astonishingly "eurocentric": Neither Americans,
nor Asians, nor Africans appear to have access to the innermost
sanctuary of the literary pantheon of European writers. It matters
little whether they are reading in the east or in the west or how
they feel about Europe, as European authors they are embedded in
a cultural context that shapes and contributes to their texts and that
they, as writers, continue to mould through their texts.

Europe As an Intellectual Space

It appears that this cultural context, this Europe considered as a
mental space is for many of the authors — in contrast to politicians — unconnected to geographical boundaries. And this is true
even if they consider and evaluate Europe's detachment from the
geographical in very different terms. For Adolf Muschg, Europe
tends to be an *intellectual position*, while Andrei Bitov thinks that
one can be a European anywhere. For Emil Tode *there is nowhere*
that is not Europe while for the Cypriot narrative writer Panos
Ioannides *the terms "Europe" and "European" not only define the*
specific geographical area and its history, but something bigger and
wider: they define man himself. Still, regardless of whether they
consider it placeless or ubiquitous, mobile or universal, none of the
authors really wishes to imagine a Europe closed in by, or locked

behind, its geographical borders. Regardless of whether they refer to this cultural context as *collective memory*, as a *European narrative*, or a *network*, *web*, or *fabric* that connects over time and space, and whether they perceive it as an invisible *watermark* in their writing or as a *Palimpsest* on which they continuously register their thoughts, what is always present is the idea of a common intellectual space permeated by the notions that Europe has thought and stories that Europe has told (to itself).

I imagine Europe as a living thing cloaked in an aura, an invisible mental substance woven out of every thought, memory, notion, illusion, dream, anxiety, obsession, and trauma, writes the Czech author Daniela Hodrová. For her, stories — *individual and collective, ancient and contemporary* — are the fabric of *the narrative web of literary Europe.*

Writing Europe and reformulating Europe — for the Slovak poet Ivan Štrpka, this would better serve the European project than would any definition of a limited space. *Today I wouldn't describe Europe as a continent, more as a form-creating context. It is an open context in the midst of other contexts. It is writing itself. It is as open as the sea and it continues to open itself, bridgeable, overlayered with contexts ... We are writing ourselves. We are writing Europe. On a clean page? Or on a new palimpsest?*

Of the many possible Europes, Mircea Cărtărescu claims just one for himself: *my Europe. It is not hard to see that my Europe has taken on the shape of my own mind and that, indeed, my way of thinking has defined its structure. The surface of my brain, with its motor and sensory areas and zones for language and understanding, is ridged and deeply grooved, but nowhere has it stone walls or iron curtains. It knows no borders.*

The brain of the Belgian Jean-Philippe Toussaint cannot manage completely without borders: *I am, then, as much in my life as in my books, a pluralist and nomadic European, taking playful delight in the variety of languages and cultures proper to Europe, at home everywhere on the continent — or nowhere, which amounts to the same thing — as much in Brussels as in Paris, in London as in Venice, in Madrid as in Berlin.* One could hardly say it in a more core European way. For him, even today, *everywhere in Europe* clearly still does not mean Budapest, Bucharest, Prague, Warsaw, Sofia, or Vilnius. The scope of the plural nomads and their intellectual curiosity appears not to reach so far east even now. Even today West Europeans are still far more interested in cultural developments in America than in the literary exploits of their European neighbors. The continuing unequal distribution, on the literary map of Europe, of the scarce resource attention, and the extent to which mutual perceptions are still distorted by ignorance, prejudice, misplaced expectations, and clichés are matters dealt with in many of the essays. It is a European *desideratum*.

Another recurring theme is the tension between local, regional, national, and European loyalties as well as the radical singularity and exclusive identity of the writer. Before the authors even begin, in their essays, to consider traces of the European in their writing, they describe themselves as inhabitants of a universe of words, whose sole inhabitants they are. But they do so without overlooking the extent to which this concept alone — the radical autonomy of the writer— identifies them as disciples of the European spirit.

Is the Autonomous Author European?

For the Danish narrative writer and European *escapist* Jens Christian Grøndahl, any form of belonging is suspect. For him it is the radical singularity of writing that permits the *whimsical claim to such a thing as universal truth*. It is his way of writing: *setting plots aside in favor of introspection, memory, observation, and reflection, articulating the adventures of the mind rather than those unwinding out there in Reality.*

A novel is not about reality, but about existence, writes Milan Kundera, and the Norwegian author Geir Pollen sees in this position—in this manner of asking existential questions, of groping one's way forward, of leaving open rather than closing off, *always aware that life is never seized* and that *one writes to think through what one doesn't understand*, rather than merely to recount events—*the European signature in my novels.*

For the Hungarian author Péter Nádas, Europe has been, for as long as we can remember, *an addle-brained monster slumbering in her beastliness,* and writing is a lonely spiritual exercise necessary if one is to each day lift oneself *out the primary matter of one's simple-mindedness.* The written word is for him the bulwark, always under threat and always requiring reinforcement, against our sinking back into chaos and modern illiteracy.

European civilization was built with the participation of the literary hero. First of all, the knight, says the Russian narrative writer Andrei Bitov, and tests some of these heroes for their special qualifications as Europeans. In doing so he reveals, in respect to both the heroes and their inventors, the unmistakably European ability to find one's own measure, a human measure. *We can't invent anything different. Our own dimensions are our mentality ... In this respect the experience of European civilization is very relevant ... In order to retain our human countenance ... Let us think about people!*

For the Icelander Guðbergur Bergsson, the autonomous author, who repeatedly creates and destroys his or her own literary universe and who repeatedly reinvents and reformulates himself or herself, is following a dynamic of destruction and renewal that is specific to European civilization, in the course of which *the towers of Europe are constantly collapsing while their foundations remain intact.*

To the German poet, essayist, and self-declared European Durs Grünbein, in this untiring desire for renewal, understanding, and form, in this *so promising intimation of a mixture of an intellectual adventurousness and an almost erotic predilection for personal liberty... there seems to lie a pan-European attitude. You could also call it existential curiosity or a desire to think the unthinkable.*

Europe A and Europe B?

The fact that the broad scope of European attention was focused for so many years on the impenetrable wall dividing the continent, and then turned almost exclusively to the West (whence it will not budge), resurfaces in many of the essays as a blind spot in our self-perception and an open wound in the cultural body of Europe. Whether or not the authors from the eastern part of the continent perceive the West's absence of glance as disinterest, cultural hegemony, arrogance, or ignorance, their essays nevertheless sharpen our awareness of the harm the new Europe will do to itself if it ignores the great literary wealth on its doorstep. Aesthetically far too aware, contemporary and European to allow themselves to be demoted to the rank of witnesses of events in the east for Western consumption or of mere chroniclers of Balkan chaos, they insist upon their right to be perceived and acknowledged at the height of their literary competence.

In *Europe B*, the Serbian novelist Dragan Velikić's essay *Europe imagines the outskirts gazing at it with a certain look in their eyes.* This narcissistic view awaits the confirmation of its expectations, that is, *a regular supply of stereotypes rather than authentic art pieces*—images in which the Balkans are offered up to the civilized West as a *place of pure insanity ... as an almost mythical place, a wild place where all is allowed.* Graffiti from the darkroom of the continent, enjoyed with a shiver and a shudder. It is this internal European border that is identified by the author and politician from Finland, Jörn Donner. Writing in Swedish, he approaches *Europe from the fringe. The big difference between the European center and its periphery is hard to comprehend for those living in the center, which includes a fairly big area.* He also sees the Europe of languages transversed by such hierarchies. *European languages are often said to enjoy equal rights. This is not true. Especially in the field of literature, we can see a one-way street leading from bigger to smaller languages.*

Looking from another edge, the Albanian author Fatos Lubonja believes *the nature of creativity* will be jeopardized by *the reluctance of Europe to accept writers from small countries ... as European writers*, and if it continues to accept them on the literary market only as local witnesses or reporters from remote regions.

The novelist, essayist, and poet Mircea Cărtărescu has had quite enough of being passed around in the West as a *"duty-Romanian," an East European author* with responsibilities dictated by the West. *Remain in your designated ghetto... Write about your Securitate, and that dictator of yours, Ceaușescu, and his People's Palace. Put in something about the feral dogs, the street urchins, and the Gypsies ... As for creating the avant-garde, supporting significant innovations, and generally enjoying normal culture—better leave that to us as well.* The literary cosmopolitan from Croatia, marked with the label "Made in the Balkans," Dubravka Ugrešić *had overlooked the established codes between the cultural center and the periphery. I was expected to confirm stereotypes about the periphery, not destroy them. As far as my literary mastery was concerned, I could have chucked it in the bin since it appeared simply to irritate my foreign literary surroundings.*

Twinkling with irony, her essay is at the same time a radical renunciation of all forms of national, regional, or ethnic attributes and identities, including the European. In a world that has become borderless, mobile, transnational, and global, they simply make no sense. For her, the highest point of the mental unification of Europe is the *Eurovision Song Contest*, while the embodiment of things European is *Joydeep Roy Bhattacharya, an Indian living in America,* who writes novels that take place in Budapest and Dresden.

Europe—Promise and Disappointment

Not all the authors are able to depart so happily from the great promises Europe once held for them. Feelings of belonging to the European cultural space became, for East European authors during the decades of their banishment behind the wall, a matter of spiritual survival. Their stubbornly preserved inner Europe was an emphatically loaded place of longing, a refuge saturated with culture, an intellectual home, and a place of escape. And unlike their disenchanted and disillusioned colleagues in the West, and despite all disappointments, they still take Europe's promises seriously. Everything that they continue to connect with and expect from Europe is, in form and in substance, far more emphatic, even when it is expressed in ironic terms. Even disillusionment has worked to different effect on the two sides of the wall.

This Europe, which was not *one continent, but a state of mind and of words*, permitted the Bulgarian poet Mirela Ivanova a life *in two parallel worlds*, the dusty world of everyday communism and the illuminated world of free European culture. The names of the great poets *luminous like altar candles in ubiquitous darkness.* And yet despite all the disappointment that *the conceited indifference of*

Europe brought with it to our daily lives, this Europe is still a good place for *the parallel existence of two worlds.*

The Latvian playwright Māra Zālīte is tougher on Europe. In her view, the continent has stunningly failed to live up to its potential and lags far behind its great promise: *Spirituality, humanism, civilization, democracy—the splendid garb of Europe. Lack of air experienced in a Communist reality makes one take deep breaths of this idealized Europe. Distilled, extracted, clean.* The real Europe, however, *there is no time to think things through ... Globalization, cultural standardization, and cultural imperialism. A transformation of the world—not included in it, the transformation of awareness, soul, and morality—the Faustian discourse.* She sees in Faust the tragic European hero of rash thinking and overhasty action.

The Greek author Themelis also notes the intellectual drying up of the West. *I have the feeling that those values and principles that formed the ideological backbone and the cultural foundations of postwar Europe, and which were distilled in European thought over the course of centuries, are becoming marginalized. I am convinced that citizens are increasingly being presented with oversimplified dilemmas while their problems are becoming increasingly complex.*

We should therefore consider long and hard whether we really wish to raise, for the sake of simultaneity, the European "romantics" from the East to the level of Western disenchantment and disillusionment and the "velociferic" acceleration and virtualization of reality. When it comes to literature, this kind of cleansing of "unsimultaneousness" would not only be a loss for cultural Europe, for it is from the great East European literature of the present, which owes its aesthetic qualities and innovations as well as its intellectual complexity and depth not least to a far more radical confrontation with social reality, that "old" Europe—with its reality-fatigue—could obtain important impulses for the construction of a new Europe. Moreover such impulses will never be found in the smooth and polished American best sellers currently admired by so many. The full extent of the impressive and unknown work still awaiting exploration was one of the most encouraging discoveries on this pan-European journey through literary Europe.

Europe's "Weak" Strengths

The myth of the bull's abduction of the virgin Europa, *the account of the founding of our territorial identity, involves not only an act of violence, but a unique historical maturation, generosity, self-determination, and tolerance* writes Durs Grünbein, who sees in this ambivalence and inner conflict a central figure of European civilization. *The trauma of the story and its extraordinary promise have both contributed to its historical destiny.*

The peculiarities of European culture and European thinking cannot be separated from the underlying tension between the un-paralleled success story and the havoc of disaster. It is this tension that has given rise to many of Europe's "weak" strengths, which may become urgently needed during the construction of a new, alternative Europe and in the global context.

Adolf Muschg sees the Europe of today in the *duty "to hold on to much—as on the shoulders a burden of failure" (Hölderlin) ... . In essence, the Europe I am speaking of is a common attitude, the fusion of national memories whose components are no longer dis-tinguishable. A civilization of memory. I honor vision, but it can only emerge from retrospective vision. To keep alive and sanctified in memory the horror and atrocities of Europe and to use this mem-ory as a source of equilibrium is a difficult task; but history de-mands that Europe not shirk this responsibility.*

For the Austrian Jew Robert Schindel, Auschwitz is not only the *zero point* of European history and *the place of its rebirth,* as it is for Muschg, but it also requires us to take a final look in the abyss of our own making, in the *"European Archipelago"* indelibly in-scribed onto the map of Europe, *a finely meshed spider's web hold-ing thousands of flies, a city of death serving so many places ... The United Europe of Slaves, of the Aggrieved, of the Dead ... Hardly a nation was missing from the list of inmates. They fed from the same tin basins in harmonious unison, though the harmony was broken when they were shouted at ... the Italians, the Poles, the Germans, the Greek, the Czechs, the Slovaks, the French, and the Dutch ... I emerged from under all that rubble.*

It is from under other no less weighty rubble that Lídia Jorge sees Portugal emerge after the loss of its colonies. Amputated, traumatized, without orientation, and overwhelmed by feelings of guilt, it provoked its writers to a radical and sometimes obsessive confrontation with the bloody past. Acting as proxy, so to speak, literature placed itself "on the couch" and began to tell the shocked country about its mental condition. For Europe, *the most important thing that Portuguese literature has to offer is what it says about its relationship to the Other, those that are different.* In its multicultural future, it will need the painful experiences — now stored in literature — of the *boundary of difference*, as well as the bitter realization of the imperative need for dialogue.

Alongside a Europe that has learned to remember and to enter into a dialogue with difference, the essays refer repeatedly to a Europe whose history, so rich in ambivalence, has taught it to hesitate, to doubt, and to question, a Europe with the power to ask questions and raise doubts about itself. It is a Europe that insists upon its moral uneasiness and that prefers to reflect rather than be carried along by an aimless dynamic and an uncontrolled acceleration. A Europe that takes *the time to think.*

Being European, says Mircea Cărtărescu, *is not tantamount to being good — or better than the rest; but to being complex, a creature torn by internal conflicts, one who has been able to recognize his inner contradictions and attempted to find a balance between them.*

Nike is most beautiful at the moment/when she hesitates, cites the Polish author Stefan Chwin the poet Zbigniew Herbert. And he does not want this sentence to be understood merely in an aesthetic sense. *I would like to make it clear: the real Europe is for me the Europe that hesitates. And that, despite hesitations, can act effectively. The Europe that can, therefore, move through that difficult space between a consciousness of the world's lack of transparency, which (we sometimes think) weakens us, and the necessity of unambiguous decisions, between doubt that is full of scruples and hard certainty that one is right, between critical self-irony and fervor. It is a moral space that many simply call the space of the European conscience.*

The space in which such traits of European thinking could develop are seen, in two of the essays, as either structured by the European conception of time or illuminated by the special light that shines over Europe.

For the Bosnian novelist Dževad Karahasan, *the unbreakable connection of culture with time is nowhere so obvious as in Europe ... If there exists anything on the basis of which Europe exists as a kind of cultural unity, then it is time—a shared assumption about time ... For all its differences, Europe was always some kind of cultural whole because it was always integrated around an image of time.* In the meantime, however, Europe's fateful history has seen to it that the heart of the continent no longer beats to the same rhythm. It has not only allowed our senses of time to drift wide apart in a *Europe of different speeds*; it has also transformed the wall between East and West into a time wall, before and behind which Europeans live in different eras. Much will depend on how the uniting Europe copes with this discrepant heartbeat. In respect to this crucial European difference in matters of speed, once again the East would be well advised to steer clear of the fatal and no longer controllable turbulence set in motion by the West, a turbulence that experts in time have learned to fear as *raging standstill* and that within the Western time aggregate may be considered irreversible. Might not, in this area too, real help be available in the East? Instead of vain philosophical appeals for a life-preserving rediscovery of slowness, we might consider a return to a lived-out slowness stemming from economic backwardness that has protected not only town and landscapes, but also ways of living and thinking from the planning of capitalistic high-speed phantasms. Before "real time" reaches the East, a Europe that is reinventing itself should reflect upon the attractive aspects and creative potential of a reduction in velocity and perhaps move towards a compromise of its various speeds rather than place the East under pan-European time pressure through the subsidized import of the West's frantic pace.

Just as Karahasan makes his Europe legible through various conceptions of time, so the Swedish narrative writer and essayist Richard Swartz discerns it in the specific qualities of European light: *Europe's light is distinct from light elsewhere in the world ... Our European light often reaches us in roundabout ways. At times* we come across it just by chance. Then it reaches us as a reflection or an afterglow... without this indirect light there probably would be no Europe as we know it. From perfectly natural reasons a light such this is not particularly warming; for us it seems to evoke thoughts and feelings rather than to warm our bodies.

A plea for a bit of freedom in the European multilingual home is made by the Dutch author Hans Maarten van den Brink, who sees his Europe as *a Europe of translators ... My Europe is a house where no one is completely at home and where everyone speaks a language he hasn't quite mastered. It is a salon where people converse in French, a trading floor where English sentences ring out, a coffee house where lines of German poetry are—always incorrectly— quoted, and a museum where sick and dead languages are lovingly nursed and studied, but without their being imposed on anyone. It is a hotel that earns the Dutch a pretty penny. It sees itself in perspective, but not for want of care or love. It does not retreat, it expands.*

And the Lithuanian poet Tomas Venclova, who lives in America, also constructs his future European home on an altered concept of identity. *Part of the beauty and diversity of the world lies in its borders—to the extent that they don't become insurmountable. The cult of the national state will disappear, but the sense of Heimat and love of a certain region will, I think, always remain. Every region of this kind is a point of intersection of several cultures, and our identity will be precisely of such nature: mosaic-like, made up of segments ... We will not so much inherit as create it ourselves. Although one will always have one's principal language, multilingualism will become the norm. It's precisely writers, I think, who will become the pioneers of this future world.*

L'Europe Existe, en Miniature

However diverse the thirty-three European voices that assembled here may have been—in terms of their perspectives and positions, their experiences, expectations, hopes and assessments—the multi-perspective image of Europe that they draw in their essays demonstrates one thing: a centralized, compact identical, exclusive, disassociating, and fortified Europe will not be acceptable to European writers. Perhaps, however, their very different ideas of Europe as a *mosaic, network, fabric, narrative,* and open, porous, and self-transforming *context* holds more potential for a cultural Europeanization of horizons than does anything so far envisaged by political Europe. Perhaps these ideas of a Europe of difference, experienced by people as an exchange and a growing network, conceal more that could be used in the construction of an open, dynamic, flexible, and dialogically cultural identity than does an identity debate based on abstract general principles and standardized political and economic rules. Such a constantly growing network of cultures would significantly strengthen Europeans' interest in each other, providing them with real opportunities for mutual discovery. Europeans will become able to see what is shared rather than what divides; to find a common language to express their different experiences; and finally to discover a feeling of community that is proud of the diversity that sustains it.

As if we had been partaking in a European experiment, for the course of a week we could experience some of all of this at the *Literaturhaus.* The writers and their various languages, experiences, thoughts, and discourses touched each other, intersected, jolted, and flowed together in a multivocal discussion that spanned many borders. The discussion became permeated by underlying and unexpected cross connections even between the most distant positions; an echo chamber of European resonance was formed. Alongside the multilingual moderators and translators, the writers joined together in a discussion on a common theme serving to highlight their differences of perspective. They formed, for a moment, something like a Europe in miniature. While outside the larger Europe began to divide into the *new* and the *old*, inside "writing Europe" gave us a brief glimpse of how things might look if the European project were to succeed.

— *Translated by Andrew Gane*

Ilma Rakusa

Yes, the contrasts and the arguments.
Europe is a promise. Europe is a threat.
Europe is a poem. Europe is a conglomerate
of interests.
© Susanne Schleyer

Ilma Rakusa

Switzerland

Born in Rimavská Sobota (Slovakia) in 1946, the daughter
of a mixed Hungarian–Slovenian parentage, Ilma Rakusa
is an author, writer, literary scholar, and translator of many
works from Russian, French, Hungarian, and Serbo-
Croatian (including works by Marina Tsvetayeva,
Marguerite Duras, Imre Kertész, and Danilo Kiš). She has
received many awards for her work, including the Petrarca
Prize for Translation in 1991, the Leipzig Book Prize for
European Understanding in 1998, and the Adelbert von
Chamisso Prize in 2003. Ilma Rakusa lives in Zürich,
where she has been a university lecturer since 1977.

Further Reading:
Steppe. Translated by Solveig Emerson. Burning Deck,
1997.

Impressions and Conversations during the Intervals

*Nach einem langen Tag und Gesprächen in sechs
Sprachen träume ich von einem Gletscher. Ich sehe ihn
von oben, aus Helikopter-Perspektive: eine
weiss-braune Zunge, gescheckt, zerklüftet – und
schrecklich geschrumpft. Am Morgen weiß ich, ich
habe von der Sprache geträumt, Pars pro toto.*

The copperplate engraving projected on the wall and created by Johannes Putsch in 1537, portrays Europe as a noble virgin with Hispanic head jewelry and precious robes on which the names and symbols of European countries form an odd pattern. While the speakers get worked up, the virgin looks silently around. Only Andrei Bitov cannot bear her grave silence. Turning to the lady, he remarks dryly: *Russia is under her skirt.* Laughter. In fact, *Rusia* is emblazoned on the left corner of the skirt, surrounded by *Sarmatia, Lithuania,* and *Walachia.*

All the conversations get caught up in history before moving forward to the present and the future. And the East Europeans seem to bear a particular burden in this respect. Formerly isolated by the Iron Curtain, they now fear being relegated to Europe's second division. The complexes, the anxieties, and the resentments run deep.

The idea of Europe is emphatically idealized — *Europe is a state of the intellect* (Mirela Ivanova), *Europe is a poem* (Ivan Štrpka) — and commented upon with skepticism. The only chance for people on the periphery is to serve the stereotypes used by the West to think about the periphery. This is the view of Dragan Velikić from Belgrade.

We sit in the café and discuss the exodus of Serbia's young people, the European railway network, and the legendary hotels that once carried or still carry the name *Europa*: in Pula, in Sarajevo, in

St. Petersburg. Could it be that the invocation of Europe starts from the edges?

And then the sudden thought that we, at this *Writing Europe* symposium, also form a Hotel Europa: a motley and multilingual community of writers, who insist upon their individual visions and consciously accept their social marginality. The poetic play of ideas does not seek political conversion. As its freedom stems from the circumstance that it must not obey ideology or pragmatic objectives. This makes us cheerful, but also a little pensive. Péter Nádas shakes his head in incomprehension: A writer does not have to think about the effect of his words. He should concentrate on writing—a long and difficult process. Everything else is out of his hands.

At a late hour the question flits across the room whether poetic and political thinking can ever be compatible. Andrei Bitov whispers softly *no*. If literature does influence social developments, then it does so only indirectly. *It has its own speed, and its own temperature.* And already he starts on the next story, a real storyteller.

All are telling stories in a confusion of tongues. Tomas Venclova, who speaks Russian, Polish, Lithuanian or English according to the turn of his head, enthuses about his home city Vilnius, about which he has just written a successful guide. In several days time, however, he is setting off on a three-week journey to India. The introverted poet, an American citizen since 1985, turns out to be a passionate globetrotter, traveling alone to new shores. Most of the writers present are of a cosmopolitan bent. Richard Swartz—with homes in Stockholm, Vienna and the Istrian hamlet of Sovinjak— dreams of a sunlit *Stockholm on the Mediterranean.* Again, a tempting European utopia. Meanwhile a striking number of paths cross in Berlin. DAAD's apartment for scholarship-holders at Storkwinkel 12 once served as home for Mircea Cărtărescu as well as Jean-Philippe Toussaint and Dragan Velikić. On discovering this piece of shared past, the Serbian and the Belgian embrace each other in laughter. The friendship is sealed in broken English.

The symposium's friendship potential is overwhelming. So much positive interest in one's neighbor can only be a good European omen. Books circulate, words fly, addresses are exchanged and glasses raised; and soon there are debates, admissions, moving reunions. Andrei Bitov attaches to Dubravka Ugrešić's lapel a little silver angel from Odessa. Next day Bitov has a miniature Finnish wooden rabbit on his lapel. I myself am carrying Ljubljana's emblem in my bag: a tiny china dragon, given to me as a gift by Aleš Debeljak. We cough and sneeze together in rhythm. It must be the *Europe-virus*. But there is no question of ending our interesting conversations prematurely. What are the concerns of Slovenian intellectuals? Are there any signs of a cultural rapprochement within the former Yugoslavia? How does one explain the unanimous solidarity of eastern (central) Europe with the United States? Debeljak responds with verve; he thinks Eastern Europe's special position is understandable but nevertheless irresponsible; as regards Yugoslavia, he is taking part in several magazine projects promoting cultural exchange among the successor states.

After a long day and discussions in six languages, I dream of a glacier. I see it from above, as if from a helicopter: a white and brown tongue, blotchy, rugged — and alarmingly shriveled. In the morning I know I have been dreaming of language, pars pro toto. What is under threat? Diversity? And then, all of sudden, I am struck by something Hans Maarten van den Brink has said: Languages do not have *a historical right to exist forever.* A most disturbing sentence that has somehow forced its way into my subconscious.

Van den Brink's Europe, *where no one is completely at home and where everyone speaks a language he hasn't quite mastered,* differs dramatically from a Europe of native tongues as postulated by Aleš Debeljak. An East–West divide or one between *translators* and *poets?*

Yes, the contrasts and the arguments. Europe is a promise. Europe is a threat. Europe is a poem. Europe is conglomerate of interests. Or without any mercy: *Europe is a word we should set about undermining further as time goes on* (Colm Tóibín). The criticism comes from Ireland: England has simply stayed away.

Irreconcilable positions are presented on the rostrum in a civilized manner. At the restaurant table it is America that causes the greatest stir. A *common European identity* is little to be felt, but this does not diminish our fellow feeling. People who approach phenomena by writing about them share a basic experience that gives rise to an almost familial sense of togetherness. Like an old acquaintance, Lídia Jorge tells me of her years in Angola during the Portuguese colonial war. The horrors of that period abruptly matured her and banished all illusions. I think of my life in a Switzerland sheltered from history, and of the connection between time, place, and fate, that love — which we also talk about — so completely overlooks. Perhaps it would be better to anchor the European idea to anthropology. Back to the roots.

One should not understate the human, the all too human, which includes illness. On the day of his planned appearance, the Bosnian author Miljenko Jergović sends the following fax: *I was thinking about the future of a united Europe, about European borders, and about whether or not my part of the Balkans is still in Europe — and, in the midst of these thoughts I came down with chickenpox. A political metaphor reported back in its original sense. And this said that the transition countries were suffering from the children's illnesses of democracy.*

No contemptuous (English) cancellation, but a clever if regrettable coincidence. Bosnia is absent. Belarus and Ukraine are absent too. And a young woman tells me shyly of her homeland Moldava, where there are wonderful writers living in a desolate isolation. For her, Europe is a magical vocabulary, a symbol of freedom and culture.

The continent is still torn in two.

Is a Europe without cracks thinkable? Europe's past has so many fault lines that a pragmatic European construction seems illusory. So culture, with its differentiation and patience, should offer a helping hand. And this will need time, like any complex process.

In the course of the week, we observe in miniature how opinions are formed and positions revised, how an exchange functions as giving and taking, listening and reacting. Both the "aha" phenomenon as well as shock are part of all this, alongside honesty and a willingness to argue. Europe as *work in progress* presupposes a frank flexibility on the part of individuals. This is what is demonstrated and practiced at the *Literaturhaus Hamburg.*

A late evening round. Robert Schindel rummages in his jacket bag and pulls out several creased bits of paper. It is only now, he confesses, that he has acquired his parents' family tree. He had no idea of who his grandparents were and where they lived. A Jewish institution in Vienna has done the research, and he can no longer sleep because he keeps trying to imagine all the people. The grandmother from Galicia and his grandfather, director of a Prague brewery, as well as all the other relatives that finally, and without exception, fell victim to the Holocaust. Names, dates, careers, they are all there in black and white, yet unfathomable.

Central European Jewry went down in the *United Europe of the slaves, and the victims, and the killed.* The trauma might become a unifying factor if it contains a *Never again.* European action cannot do without the European culture of memory.

Over a glass of red wine, Robert Schindel converses with Stefan Chwin, who is counting on the history lesson and its consequences: on Europe's moral uneasiness, its hesitation, its conflict awareness, its ability to differentiate, and its questioning. Characteristics that must stand up to the pressure of America's black-and-white thinking and dictates to action in order to be perceived as an opportunity rather than as a sign of weakness.

In the heated discussion, Europe's diversity and contradiction sparkle under the protection of the beautiful and strict Virgo. It is better to imagine Europe in the form of a woman than as a Brussels bureaucracy. A vision needs sensuality and cannot be formed out of paragraphs. Mircea Cărtărescu envisions a Europe molded *by Dante's stars, John Donne's compass, Cervantes' lance, Kafka's beetle, Proust's madelaine and Günter Grass' flounder.* A Europe of the Hellenes and barbarians, the smiling Mona Lisa and the mustached Gioconda by Marcel Duchamp. Europe is not an archive, but a palimpsest: described in multi-layers, with the old lines shining through from under every new text. In other words: Europe can only ever be plural.

Sometimes the writers seem like monadic embodiments of thirty-three different Europes. Different colors and contours mark their inner maps; none are the same. But paths are paths, rivers are rivers, and mountains are mountains. And the discussion is already underway. And at the rostrum table or in the white-table-clothed restaurant, horizons appear that are alien to none.

We learned much about ourselves in Hamburg. Because we did not shun friction and argument. There was no feigning consensus, no official objectives—nothing like that at all. The European vocabulary filled up with stories and fortunes, full of life and malleable to the point of fantasy.

If it were up to the poets and writers, Europe would pass its current test of endurance with ease.

— *Translated by Andrew Gane*

Guðbergur Bergsson

A novelist has no real homeland except in
the universe of his works. He makes this
world, land, or continent though writing,
and in accordance to this, he makes
this language the language of his works.
Truly he has no other mother tongue
except that contained in his stories.
© Maxim Segienko/PHOTOMAX

Guðbergur Bergsson
Island

Born in Grindavik, a fishing village in southern Iceland, in 1932, Guðbergur Bergsson qualified as a teacher and then spent many years in Spain, studying Spanish, literature, and art history in Barcelona. Since his writing debut in 1961 with *Músin sem laedist* (*The Creeping Mouse*), he has published many novels, poetry volumes, short stories, and a children's book. Guðbergur Bergsson is considered one of Iceland's most innovative authors. He was awarded the Icelandic Literature Prize both for his novel *Svanurinn* (*The Swan*), published in 1991, and for his autobiographical novel *Fadir og módir og dulmagn bernskunnar* (*Father and Mother and the Mystery of Childhood*). He lives and works in Reykjavik.

Further Reading:
Swan. Novel. Translated by Bernard Scudder. Mare's Nest, 1991.

Europe Untitled

*Sögumaður á hvergi heima nema í eigin verkum, þeim
heimi, landi eða álfu sem hann býr til sjálfur. Tunga hans
er líka tungutak verka hans. Í raun og veru á hann ekki
annað móðurmál en sagna sinna.*

I have the impression that no writer at work is in any way conscious to which nationality he belongs, and that if such an idea
would occur to him, he would most likely react against it, he would
be against any kind of nationality, and intentionally against any
kind of nationalism.

The author is possibly still less concerned about which continent his works are originated in, or if his own nature springs from
another possible world than in his own soul, trying to turn that one
into a kind of islands. Groups of islands created by an author, are
the stories he tells and gradually, in the process of creation, he
turns them into his only fatherlands as they erupt from the sea of
his ideas. That is to say, a novelist has no real homeland except in
the universe of his works. He makes this world, land or continent
through writing, and in accordance to this, he makes this language
the language of his works. Truly he has no other mother tongue
except contained in his stories.

Different things happen when a writer wants to gain fame and
popularity, not writing in his own terms, but lending himself to a
social movement or ideology. If he prefers to stand on such limited
ground, he most likely will become a link in a movement or ideology and begin to write for those who expects from him nothing but
a simple statement of their opinions and to demonstrate in writing
that their approach to life is the correct one. In this case, his fans—
the followers of the correct ideology—joyfully await the publication

of works from "their author" which are based on arguments that would neither pass the limit of correct expression nor betray a decent parishioner with unusual contexts. At this point he will fully dedicate himself to the art of bringing newer surprises.

The artist at work should not be in any other place than in the process of creation, that uncertain state of mind. But still, it is from the uncertainty that works spring forth with defined arguments and well formed global vision. But although an author would admit to some degree of didacticism regarding aesthetics in his art, he seeks, above all, to discover his personal way of thinking; which does not always shield him from the outside world.

In general, with regard to the European novel, even though the writer is highly original, one can tell from which nation his works have grown and if they are exclusively European, or in any way a fruit from other corner of the world. In spite of diversity, European writing has strong national characteristics, the taste of the path, even the specific region that molded the artist as he was becoming a human being, both in a spiritual and physical sense. Still, he might have educated on his own, because the artist early becomes conscious of hit individuality. Despite that, his foundations are based on his birthplace and fatherland mixed with a desire to escape to broader horizons. European art longs for the faraway. But in spite of that desire, no author can escape his homeland. It follows him as his double. It makes no difference how an author tries to escape the unpleasantly narrow life of his fatherland, in his attempt to become cosmopolitan he will eventually fail, except if he has gone astray, to that place where freedom become shear chaos.

No matter what a theme a free writer uses, he will treat it in terms of himself. A biography is everything that happens with regard to the flesh and inner life. Thoughts, outlook, opinions are as important parts of life as having had an accident, forgetting to get the gas, loosing a leg in war, singing about sexual potency, or appearing on television. That person who writes a story is, at once, the reader and the author, later, when he looks over his work, he usually becomes his own critic as well. It is not until the book is being published that he becomes the author.

To realize this and to express it without hesitations is to be
a European writer. Generally speaking, European writers tend
to practice the interaction of the self-observation and social
analysis in their works. In other regards, authors do not have the
feeling that they are something special, though they possibly
conceal a desire to become something. No book is anonymous
any more.

A novice not only writes a novel, he composes he himself and
changes from an undefined mist into defined material. It is impossible to know how he will appear in the end. But it is certain that if
he goes on writing, he will have to wipe out a great part of himself
and then rebuild himself with the next work. The art of writing is
the art of erasing one self in order to form one self again. It is
similar to the art of remembering and to forgetting. Above all it is
the art of remembering by means of forgetting.

How often has the European culture have had to use this artifice
in order to save itself from destruction by the means of the art of
simply forgetting or forgetting-remembering?

Even if his sense of nationalism is not strong, it is rather easy to
see in the writing of an author, the style, the general atmosphere,
and plot—if the novel has any value—he is not only of his own
nation, but a still superior nationality, though only in his art. In
this way, Goethe could have only been German, Cervantes Spanish
and Dante Italian. Nobody would think them being Danish. On the
other hand, H. C. Andersen could only be a Dane. These authors,
each in his way, have found readers in most nations although it
might have taken a long time to reach them. The reason is that the
mentality of the European ruling classes is open and closed, liberal
and full of prejudices. The same laws seem to apply to literature as
in politics; thus the towers of Europe are constantly collapsing but
their foundations remain intact. For a similar reason American
literature, local or provincial, has been dominant, not because of its
quality, but because of American domination in general. But now
the whole empire seems to have taken so many steps towards its
decline that many people have dared to become tired of it. As a
result, the European culture might begin to once again become
similar to the independent author. He does not write to express

faith, but in the spirit of autobiography. Once again one could even expect anything, a real surprise even, from the European culture, because it knows from bad experience that its message cannot be blind nationalism and praise of a leader.

To begin with, European culture should admit that it took a long time to see the humiliation of writers and literature in light of the following truth:

Most of the so-called "great writers" humiliated European culture and the arts in general during a better part of the last century. And this could explain why so few people now take writers seriously any more and why buyers, rather than readers, just gulp down fluff, as if a novel were something like an American hamburger in a fast food restaurant in which it is announced:

We are closing down. Everything has been sold!

This is now the general situation with regard to European literature. Authors have to face facts—it is only up to them and in their hands to save themselves from difficulties and regain their former dignity, most of which has been lost.

Andrei Bitov

But I am from Petersburg, Russia's most
European city, that unwashed "window
on Europe." I have never understood: was this
so that they could look in from the West,
or we could look out from the East?
© Maxim Segienko/PHOTOMAX

Andrei Bitov

Russia

Born in Leningrad in 1937, Andrei Bitov studied geology
and lives as a writer in Moscow and St. Petersburg. Since
1959 he has published short stories, essays, novels, and
travelogues. In 1990 he was awarded the Pushkin Prize
by the FVS Foundation of Hamburg. He is president of the
Russian Pen Club.

Further Reading:
Life in Windy Weather: Short Stories. Edited by Priscilla
Meyer. Ardis Publishers, 1986.
Ten Short Stories. Moscow: Raduga Publishers, 1991.
The Monkey Link: A Pilgrimage Novel. Translated by
Susan Brownsberger. Farrar Straus & Giroux, 1995.
Pushkin House. Translated Susan Brownsberger. Dalkey
Archive Pr, 1998.
A Captive of the Caucasus. HarperCollins, 1999.

The Literary Hero as Hero
A Discourse in the Genre
of the Intellectual Primitive

Я же из Петербурга, самого европейского города России, самого немытого "окна в Европу". Так и не понял: это, чтобы заглядывать в него с Запада или выглядываться в него с Востока?

This genre, as I define it, is governed by the ambitions of the visual arts, not the intellect: the idea comes *to* the mind, not *from* it. We don't set it forth, we send it forth. With a benevolent gaze.

The starting position is this: European civilization was built with the participation of the literary hero. First of all, the knight.

Tristan (who is nothing without Isolde). Hamlet (let's not forget that he's a fat, clumsy D student). Don Quixote (keep in mind that he's a parody, and that the future — Sancho Panza — is already relentlessly present). D'Artagnan (credited with inventing the Hollywood hero). Sherlock Holmes (a post-knight, as in post-literature).

> Gargantua, Robinson, Gulliver
> — for scale in space and time.
> Ariel. Homunculus, Frankenstein, Dracula, Golem —
> antecedents of the Transformers.
> Let us think about people!
> We will find nothing human but Winnie the Pooh.
> > Read only children's books,
> > Keep only children's thoughts,
> > Cast grown-up cares away,
> > From sorrow's depths arise.
> But ...

(Mandelstam, 1908)

Chapter Two. A SCYTHIAN'S DREAM

I am sixty-five, and I suffer from graphophobia. For the last two years I have been dreaming unwritten texts. Rather ghastly ones. Not even worth writing. I wouldn't think of writing them. They are exactly the ones I didn't used to write.

Nowadays I write when I'm up against a commission, a deadline. I picture this line, literally, as the line of death. It was displayed to me on the operating table in 1994, and since then I wait for my deadline to take me by force, make me "relax and enjoy it." The same with this text. I saw at once what I could write, and how, and again this was enough to render me quite unable to sit down at my desk.

Yesterday, at last, I somehow sat myself down and somehow forced it. There was no special enjoyment in it. And I keep having a dream. I wake up deeply ashamed and realize that I have just received a commentary on yesterday's text ...

I am in Denmark, settling in at some sort of hotel with my wife. All this is soporific enough—shabby, but of course clean. The desk clerk, or someone, is talking like a didactic tour-guide: "And Denmark isn't a small country, by any means! We have capital and profits ... It's all that damned prince! And why must you Russians call us Dutchies? We're not Dutch! Seven hundred years we've been conquering and being conquered! We are Danes!" He's obviously making this speech for my wife, it's her first time in Denmark, her eyes are round. Weighing heavily on the dream is my Soviet past—the dorm. But clean. Two soldierly cots: one of them made up for us, the other with linens on the pillow. The one, however, will be too narrow for two people. We look out the window: it's the real Denmark out there. My wife is enchanted. I'm exploring, opening doors, that's the bath, that's the closet ... I open one more—and shouldn't have: it's a different life in there, altogether Danish, their own. They're sitting around a table drinking tea, staring at me in bewilderment. I'm violating their privacy. "Sorry," I mumble, in English, "sorry." I withdraw. Now another novelty: a roommate for us. Enter the well-known Petersburg writer and historian G. Slightly self-important, with the independent air of the Russian traveler who has already been abroad, though not necessarily to Denmark.

Can more or less express himself in English or German. Very businesslike, organized, which immediately betrays his inferiority complex as a non-European. He immediately sets about making the bed. Here I realize that something's wrong. However shabby the hotel, it cannot be a Soviet dorm. They cannot install a couple in the same room with a neighbor, and the guest is not supposed to make the bed himself. "Stop, wait a minute," I say to G., unconsciously demonstrating to him, or to my wife, that I know a bit more about Europe than he does. "There's been some mistake. We should at least call the chambermaid." The chambermaid appears instantly, takes the sheet from G.'s hands, and with many apologies leads him to the next room. "There, you see!" I tell my wife smugly, and at this point two smart-looking nutcrackers march out of the closet wearing old-time uniforms. "Whereas you say ... And now you're so touched you're going to cry!"

I wake up and realize that somehow I treated Europe boorishly in yesterday's text. But, owing to my Russian mentality, I don't understand how. How could I hurt them, when they're so civilized? When I'm so insulted and injured? It's December 13, black Friday ... Who do I think I am, Dostoevsky? But I *am* from Petersburg, Russia's most European city, that unwashed "window on Europe." I have never understood: was this so that they could look in from the West, or we could look out from the East? I decided to read over what I had written yesterday, to have caused such a dream ...

Chapter One. ANACHARSIS (Yesterday's text)

It's not right to think of the New Testament as an artistic work, but where could we find one earlier or more postmodern ... the way it tells and retells, four times in a row, the same story of a man's betrayal? Despite all, European civilization is primarily Christian.

Then Christ, despite all, is primary. The Superstar.

Geography is even more primary. The Mediterranean. Its indented coastline. Peninsulas and islands. Mountains, seas, and rivers. Europe has more of all these per unit of geographic area than any place else. Toward the East, Europe bulges and erodes, transitioning to my homeland, which transitions to Asia.

At one time I couldn't be bothered to press the button of a camera. I traveled halfway round the world and hardly took one roll of film. When I developed it, I discovered it was all the same scene: hills. Low, smooth, green hills — man's favorite landscape, as ethnology has made clear. The shepherd's ideal. These were the hills of three countries: Italy, Israel, and Russia. So the sheep-herding civilization was quietly encamped at the foundation of the pre-Christian. Shepherds were the first to consider the stars, the first to see the Star (of Bethlehem).

Then the history of European civilization is easily described: the shepherd climbed a hill from which he had a good view of his flock, grazing on slopes covered with good grass. The shepherd grew strong and became a feudal lord; on top of the hill he built a castle, from whose tower he scanned frontiers that he could defend against his neighbors. The higher the hill, the wider the boundaries — thus were the first principalities formed. The principalities coalesced and formed states. When rivers, mountains, and bays outlined the frontiers of languages and dialects, Europe had been mapped. The feudal lord came down from his hill: the castle was replaced by a monastery. When it grew rich through indulgences, the monastery yielded up its body to the university. Castle-monastery–university: Europe had come into being.

There you have the West, as seen from Scythia.

"And the province started writing!" — as we Russians say when everything has been set in motion.

I wish I knew where that saying came from (before Gogol used it). History has forgotten, but the language has held on to it.

"Writing Europe" sounds derisive in Russian, because it exchanges winks with Soviet slang: "the office is writing." Everyone knows what kind of office. Europe has nothing to do with it.

Yes, we are Scythians! Yes, we're Asiatics,
With slanted, greedy eyes!

wrote Alexander Blok in 1918, ostensibly welcoming the revolution.

Russian literature is a very greedy literature. To the point of devouring its own children. Also, however, a generous literature ... it will never satisfy its ambitions, for it gives everything away free, right and left, trying to persuade the West who we are and failing to communicate this to us ourselves.

That same Blok, before the revolution, on returning from Italy, wrote: "Whatever a man does in Russia, he is above all pathetic. It's pathetic when a man eats with gusto. Pathetic when a customs clerk who has never been abroad asks you what the weather's like over there ..." So wrote Blok, only to perish at forty in 1921, the same year as another poet (Nikolai Gumilyov, Anna Akhmatova's husband), without living to see the day he received his foreign passport.

Who were the Scythians? It's a killer question. Tribes of some sort, who lived at some time. But Scythian gold has lasted better than Bolshevik gold.

One Scythian, at least, existed as long ago as the sixth century B.C.E. His name was Anacharsis. He was of noble birth, but fled to Greece. Dusty and ragged, he presented himself at Solon's palace. "Why have you come?" "To find friends." "One looks for friends at home." "But *you* are at home!" Humbled by this boorish logic, the king let him in. To the question whether the Scythians had flutes Anacharsis replied: "We don't even have grapes." Though accustomed to his boundless native steppes, he was afraid of the sea and invented the anchor. Having thus become one of the "seven wise men," he returned to his homeland, to be murdered by his own brother, who feared for the fate of the throne.

So, if we are indeed from the vanished Scythians, to what extent are we Asiatics? That, as they say, is an interesting question. Another killer. Our historians take pride in the fact that we halted the Tatar-Mongol invasion, thereby saving Europe, though we lagged behind her by three hundred years. (We would save her again, more than once—first from Napoleon, then from Hitler, each time reducing that lag by a hundred years.)

To perceive ourselves as a kind of pillow for Europe to rest on may be an honor, but it is also distasteful. Whatever the case, in liberating herself from the Tatars, Russia moved Eastward at a speed suggesting that we meant to eliminate Asia as a geographical concept and annex it to Europe. We came to our senses only in California: it turned out we had fled Europe.

Russia all but drowned in her space in the East, and she has sought friends in Europe ever since. She does this in a peculiar way, albeit no less sincerely than Anacharsis the Scythian. Europe is small, and Peter is Great. He stands, like Gulliver, with one tall boot planted in Hamburg, the other in Amsterdam, and tries to solve the problem of how to magnify all this—so small!—to Russian proportions. If claustrophobia is the fear of a closed space, what is the fear of boundless space? People claim that Peter was the one who called Russia not a kingdom but "a sixth of the world." Curiously, the too-high ceilings of European palaces weighed heavily upon Peter the Great, and the hospitable Europeans hung special canopies for him in his bedchamber: this relaxed him, reminded him of his childhood, the Kremlin apartments, and he could hit the ceiling when he spat.

When we think about whether Russia is Europe or Asia, Russian literature stands out as a special case. It is certainly NOT Asiatic. But is it European?

Because Russian literature took less than a century to gallop the path from Pushkin and Gogol to Chekhov and Blok and show the world Dostoevsky and Tolstoy, it kept its innocence, confusing genius with ambition, license with liberty, talent with profession, and valuing the nature of the word over genre, emotion over character, idea over plot, the pattern rather than the product. At the end of that hundred years the revolution took place and plunged our literature back into the position of being young.

Hence the nature of our avant-garde, which became almost our only twentieth-century achievement to win worldwide recognition.

But the same thing had also happened in *my* past century—the nineteenth. After all, it followed the eighteenth!

Every post-epoch tries to give rise to a new style. Therefore it begins with parody, or in other words, an avant-garde. Very little time need pass before the avant-garde assumes an air of tradition. Russian literature took shape suddenly—in the twenties of the nineteenth century, our "golden," Pushkinian age—as a post-European literature. Because of its neophytism and dilettantism, it harbors practically all the features of the postmodern that contemporary theoreticians try so hard to distinguish. A parody is even easier to parody than the original. Thus in 1995, experiencing the problem of "if I can only live to see the year 2000" and finding myself a quasi-professor in New York, I had no trouble giving lectures like "Russia: Homeland of Postmodernism," and "Pushkin: The First Postmodernist." The audience heard me without a smile. The only smile was the professor's. That was when I developed this view of Europe as seen from America—which proved to be merely a view of myself, or more precisely, of Russia.

And Gulliver proved to be a leading character.

Thank goodness that's a children's book. As is *Robinson Crusoe*.

For Russia, Robinson is one of the family. But of course! He survived under inhuman conditions. This we understand, this we're familiar with. The image of incarceration ...

In 1985, when the ban on me was lifted, I wrote my first commissioned article, a foreword to *The House of the Dead*, for Germans (who at that time were still "with us"): "When an artist like Dostoevsky thinks about Dante (the scene in the bath) or about Cervantes (Prince Myshkin), he is thinking about scale, not form. Dostoevsky chose the scale. But hardly anyone, not even he himself, realized that his book was taking its form not from *The Divine Comedy*, but from a novel by Defoe."

An island is a jail. Both, in the human sense, are uninhabited. Dostoevsky, along with Defoe, was the first to describe that kind of isolation. Exactly another hundred years would pass and Solzhenitsyn would discover the archipelago. Imagine an archipelago of uninhabited islands, with a Robinson on each ... Where will we find that many Fridays?

No Russian has read Robinson to the end—that's *boring*. Robinson *returns* to the island, claims it and develops it. After plundering it well and getting rich he comes back, builds a fireplace, and around it a house, sprawls by the fire, and only then begins to tell his children about his marvelous adventures.

The more space, the less freedom. This is why people invented prison.

Gulliver is a different matter. True, he's another one who isn't especially read to his prophetic chapters, the Laputans, Houynhnms, and Japan; people limit themselves to the *story*.

And really, it's far more important that he visited Brobdingnag and Lilliput.

By measuring himself against them, he finally found his own size, his human size. Which is to say, he became a *European*.

I know that Robinson is an Englishman, but I get it wrong every time, thinking he's a Dutchman, from the biggest small country and the smallest big one.

We can't invent anything different. Our own dimensions *are* our mentality.

Look at the huge countries ...

They don't know their own size. Some have never once been to Brobdingnag, others never to Lilliput. Nor have their literatures had heroes commensurate with European ones. The Russians, though, were the first to invent the characterless modernistic man (Onegin, Pechorin, Oblomov, and so on), and on the other hand the "little man" as hero (in Pushkin and Gogol, up to Dostoevsky), whereas the Americans hatched Hollywood mutants of Robin Hood and d'Artagnan.

Nowadays, without leaving the prison camp of Socialist Realism, Russians are using American methods (lagging behind as always) to breed mutants of bandits and KGBeasties. Russian literature is finally becoming professional, or rather, ceasing to be the literature that we are accustomed — and have accustomed the world — to admire.

But, as before, it has no hero. Except for the writer himself, who tries to remain a human being so that he can mirror the experience of being human. All he can preserve is proportion and scale. To keep from losing a human face. In this respect the experience of European civilization is very relevant. Although Europe has indeed lost its coins, to my childish numismatic disappointment. Oh well, all the more of them will stay in collections.

Like children, we rejoice in the New Year, hoping to receive the gift of liberation from the old year. Nevertheless, strangely enough, the historically established division into centuries, which is quite arbitrary from the standpoint of logic, has turned out to be *history*. The young century comes after the old. You and I are in a newborn century. Nothing has changed — we have more problems than ever. Yet there has been an epochal change in the way we write about them. I assert this as a Russian writer of the second half of the last century. The new epoch will become visible only to our descendants, after this century passes (God grant that it may!). And so, no one yet knows what we are writing today. A good reason to gather at symposia.

— *Translated by Susan Brownsberger*

Hans Maarten van den Brink

My Europe is a Europe of translators. My Europe
is a house where no one is completely at home
and where everyone speaks a language he hasn't
quite mastered.
© Maxim Segienko/PHOTOMAX

Hans Maarten van den Brink

The Netherlands

Born in Oegstgeest in 1956, the writer and journalist Hans
Maarten van den Brink studied Dutch at the University of
Leiden. He worked as editor, editor in chief, and
correspondent in Washington and Madrid for the leading
newspaper *NRC-Handelsblad*, before becoming editor in
chief at the Dutch television station *VPRO*. He is vice-
president of the Dutch Literature Foundation, editor of *De
Gids,* the oldest literary magazine in the Netherlands, and
writes a weekly cultural column for the magazine *Vrij
Nederland*. His first novel *De Vooruitgang* was published
in 1995. He has also published works on the culture of
the Netherlands Antilles, on the United States, and on the
Spanish tradition of bullfighting. In 1998 he achieved
international renown with his novella *On the Water*. In
1999 he published the novel *Hart van glas*. Hans Maarten
van den Brink lives in Amsterdam.

Further Reading:
On the Water. Translated by Paul Vincent. Faber and
Faber, 2001.

Language and Terror
Seven Remarks on the Languages of Europe

Mijn Europa is een Europa van vertalers. Mijn Europa is een huis waarin niemand helemaal thuis is en waarin iedereen spreekt in een taal die hij niet helemaal beheerst.

1

I do not love my language, Dutch. Not unreservedly. It is a capricious instrument. Sometimes I think I know precisely what I want to say, and the revelation of the meaning if life, or at least a magnificent novel, seems within my grasp. But when I try to put what I mean into words, I fumble. And it's gone. Language refuses to do what I ask of it, the tone is wrong, the cohesion is missing, not one word means exactly what I expected. At such moments I sometimes dream of having another language at my disposal, a real one. French, for instance, or German. If need be, Serbian or Danish. After all universal communication is effortlessly achieved in them.

Could I still cast Dutch aside and start afresh with better tools, as Conrad and Nabokov once did? But that's the point: in a way I cannot rationalize, at least not in my own language; I am convinced that this would not be a solution to my problem. And the writers I mentioned were probably not in the least dissatisfied with Polish or Russian, but were simply determined not to be held back by the chance circumstance of being born in Krakow or Saint Petersburg. They just happened to be extremely talented.

However, the fact that they were able to leave their own language area and achieve mastery of English does say something about the nature of language. You are not imprisoned by language, although it may occasionally seem so. Unfortunately, however, neither is language ever a safe haven. You may learn several lan-

guages, but in no language will you coincide completely with yourself. Language confronts you with the harsh truth that you are not
someone who is all of a piece. If you were, you would probably no
longer need a language. So distrust those who glorify their mother
tongue unambiguously. They understand nothing about language
and very little about themselves.

2

Because language is not a home, it has nothing to do with territory.
In the house in which I grew up, German and Dutch were spoken;
these days Italian is often added, as well as the occasional bit of
French. Just as in Europe at large we speak English at the table
because everyone can more or less make himself understood in it.
If we sometimes fail to understand each other it is not due to our
insufficient command of English or the barriers between the various languages. If only that were so, because then arguments could
simply be settled with the aid of a language course. It is not a specific language, but language itself, in all its inadequacy and imper-
fection, that trips us up.

Only my aged mother, now a grandmother, is still occasionally
inclined to mutter to herself that you can really only express what
you feel in your own language. Evidently she still has German
feelings, though she has been away from Germany for most of her
life. "That's really sad!" I say. "So you never really understood your
father?" Her father came from Poland, but never taught her Polish.

"But of course I understood him," she says. "He was my father,
wasn't he!"

"And what about your children," I continue to probe, "who prefer English to the language they grew up with?" My two brothers
left their country almost twenty years ago and no longer ever
speak, write, or think Dutch.

"I can understand my children perfectly well!" she says indig-
nantly. "My own flesh and blood!" Then she switches on the television to watch the news. She is anxious to know what is going on
in her country. It is German television. Her home has been in Holland since time immemorial.

3

Anyone who has taken holiday in the more picturesque areas of Europe, and sometimes the less picturesque ones too, will have passed the occasional place-name sign that has been rendered illegible and on which a corrected version of the original designation has been written. At such a moment one is confronted with the struggle for emancipation of a language used by a minority in the country, or even region, concerned. It is often a minor language that is involved, like Basque or Welsh, or a language that is so vaguely defined that it is scarcely acknowledged as such, like Groningen or the Aragonese dialect. It strikes one at first sight that minor languages do not go in for small print. They write not with the pen, but with the paintbrush or the spray can. Subtlety does not seem to be a characteristic of minor languages.

For a long time I regarded it as an innocent joke, this crossing out and whitewashing over of place names. A more or less folkloristic activity, evincing love for one's own culture, on the one hand, and a playful streak on the other. The few times that we lost our way were just part of the experience. Since I have become familiar with the reality of language struggle, I feel differently about it. Making a name illegible is an act of aggression that is no laughing matter. It is an act befitting a minor civil war, which almost always follows the same pattern.

It does not begin when a totalitarian power suppresses the language of a minority and imposes a uniform, state language. Only when such a power starts to become tolerant, when the oppression is no longer as intense, and the first democratic reforms have made their appearance, do the heroes of the language struggle awake. First, the formerly oppressed population demands the right to speak its own language in public, to print its own books and newspapers. Then there follows the request for equality in public life. At school, in court, and in the town council a second means of expression is permitted alongside the national language. Once that stage has been reached, place-name signs in two languages appear at the boundaries of villages and towns, regions or provinces, and we find that the same location must have two names: San Sebastián and Donostia, Kishinov and Chisinau. Not because the locals had been losing their way—that is only starting to happen now—but to anchor the newly acquired rights in geography.

I have misgivings about speaking several languages at one table. It is not good for the cohesion of the gathering and not good for conversation. The activists for the rights of minority languages know that too—and that is why the emancipation process never ends in multilingualism, in the equal status of different forms of expression in the same society. Once the second language is consolidated, lawyers and teachers start maintaining that they simply cannot understand the first language, and in any case have the right not to listen to it. The youngest activists again set out at night armed with brushes and spray cans, this time to cross out the Spanish, German, English, or Russian on the bilingual signs and signposts. The terrorists do not do this in the name of standardization—that is a loaded argument. This is when the historical card is usually played. The major language is the language of oppression—nothing can change that. For that matter the minor language has more "historical rights," and these must be restored. In this way of thinking about history the last fifty, hundred, or even thousand years are, for the sake of convenience, declared invalid. But neither is there room for the notion that language acquisition begins only after the birth of each individual, and hence from a historical point-zero. Nor for the idea that mastering a second, third, or fourth language represents the opening of multiple avenues of self-realization. Everything is sacrificed to the imagined rights of the historical language.

But was what was described above as "language struggle" really about language? Are there not always quite different reasons, social and economic ones for example, for taking up the struggle? Is not language simply being used to make one's neighbor, fellow townsman, or fellow villager an alien whom must be driven out? Languages have nothing to do with land and nothing to do with flesh and blood. Nor do they have a historical right to exist forever. Whoever thinks that is thinking unhistorically.

4

In December 2002 many European papers carried a report about an area of Ireland, to the west of Galway, where nationalist politicians wanted to restrict the sale of land for house construction to those with a command of the original language of the country, Gaelic. The politicians supporting this measure fear that Gaelic, in which only about ten percent of Irish people are fluent, will otherwise die out. But why would that be so awful? More awful than last year's snow that has melted away?

For years the Irish government has been allocating large sums of money to keep the ailing tongue alive. Radio and television programs in Gaelic are subsidized, as are books and magazines. Government departments relocate to areas where this language is spoken a little more commonly than elsewhere. At school Gaelic lessons are compulsory. In this, Ireland is doing the same thing as many other democratic countries confronted with minority languages have done. In my country, the Netherlands, it is Frisian that continues to exist thanks only to subsidies. You can study the subject, voluntarily, as part of your graduation exams at high school, though there is virtually no interest among Frisians. You can demand that all government documents be translated into Frisian, if necessary for your sole use. And there are not only writers, but also translators, whose task it is to perpetuate the illusion of a Frisian literature by, for example, rendering *Also sprach Zarathustra* into Frisian at government expense. There is not a single reader who has a practical need for this because his command of Dutch or German is insufficient. It is pure gesture politics. But it will never really work, because there are no other interests bound to it.

Those Irish nationalists got it right after all: only force and violence are really effective in reviving a moribund language. Or the creation of a common enemy, which is present not only in the realm of language. In Spain the nationalist governments of Catalonia and the Basque Country oppose Madrid partly for economic reasons. In this, the language issue serves as a weapon, a way of establishing more distance. In these areas one sometimes encounters an antipathy, apparently genuine, to Spanish, a language whose popularity is growing continually in the rest of the world. Nor is there anywhere in continental Europe a popular movement against English—only a few intellectuals worry about its advance. Only when too many English people buy a second home in Italy or

France do the locals in some areas suddenly develop a passionate love for their own language. With the accompanying racism.

5

The extinction of a language is no different from that of the European hamster or the dodo. There is something tragic in both cases; however the aforementioned creatures are irreplaceable, while a language is by definition replaced. By another language. Is that a bad thing?

There is another difference that is related to the first. A language is only really dead when it no longer dies a little every day. Most of us feel alienated when we read or hear our own language as it was fifty, or even twenty, years ago. The amount of change in a human lifetime and the number of words and turns-of-phrase that have died out! Just as well, since it is proof that the language is still alive. It is a commonly held view among translators that a classic work should really be retranslated every fifty years, so the (unchanged) source-text remains accessible in the (changing) language of the translator. I have sometimes wondered why the same should not apply to the work in its original language. But chronological adjustment, what one could call vertical translation, is, in fact, wholly accepted only in the case of stage adaptations or children's versions. Goethe is seldom translated into German.

Honesty compels me to state that it is not usually the writers and poets who provide the necessary changes. They are nostalgic by temperament, tragic figures that have made a profession of the battle against the advance of time. No, the dirty work of language renewal is done in the street, by ordinary people who have other things to think about than pinning down meanings. People who unwittingly abuse their words and interpret wrongly, who swap and borrow, import and export. In this way, without realizing it, they are constantly breathing new life into the language. And try as literature may: if the street is no longer interested, its language is doomed. Language then becomes a cherished object of study, something for collectors and scholars. A museum piece. I often prefer being in a museum to being in the street. But that sums up the condition of the writer.

6

It is important that the division of roles between street and script retain a certain sense of tension. It is good for writers and poets to continue opposing dynamism with their precision and criticism, for them to continue rowing upstream, to continue correcting and amending, to continue their pathetic resistance to every form of inevitability. Suspicion is called for when the interests of poets, politics, and public turn out to coincide. It is sustainable in exceptional situations, but it can never last for long. From the period of the German occupation of the Netherlands comes the line "my word, a weapon to resist," which later became the title of a collection of resistance poetry. This line suggests a sense of helplessness: the people, here given a voice by the poet, have only language with which to stand up to the occupier. That sounds wonderful and, in this case, may have been true, but as a general statement it is horrific nonsense. Poets who place themselves at the head of a popular movement are not at all innocent; to the contrary, they are deadly dangerous. Their words are not innocent. They can do more damage than bullets or bombs. Though censorship is always wrong, there are poets whose weapon permits I would gladly confiscate.

7

My Europe is a Europe of translators. I am not shutting my eyes to what has been called the problem of untranslatability. But the problem is just as much a matter of time and class as of borders and languages. It is an interesting and fundamental, but literary, problem. From a social point of view it is irrelevant. About the politician who maintains that his words can, in fact, only be understood in his own language—and hence by his own people—I can be even more succinct: he is a scoundrel.

My Europe is a house where no one is completely at home and where everyone speaks a language he hasn't quite mastered. It is a salon where people converse in French, a trading floor where English sentences ring out, a coffee house where lines of German poetry are—always incorrectly—quoted, and a museum where sick and dead languages are lovingly nursed and studied, but without their being imposed on anyone. It is a hotel that earns the Dutch a pretty penny. It sees itself in perspective, but not for want of care or love. It does not retreat, it expands. Consequently my Europe is not confined to the physical borders of the present Union, or even to those of our continent. We also find it in South American ports, in the African bush, in housing tenements in Japan or China. In fact, we find it everywhere that people regard it as a mark of civilization not write and speak their own language under all circumstances.

— *Translated by Paul Vincent*

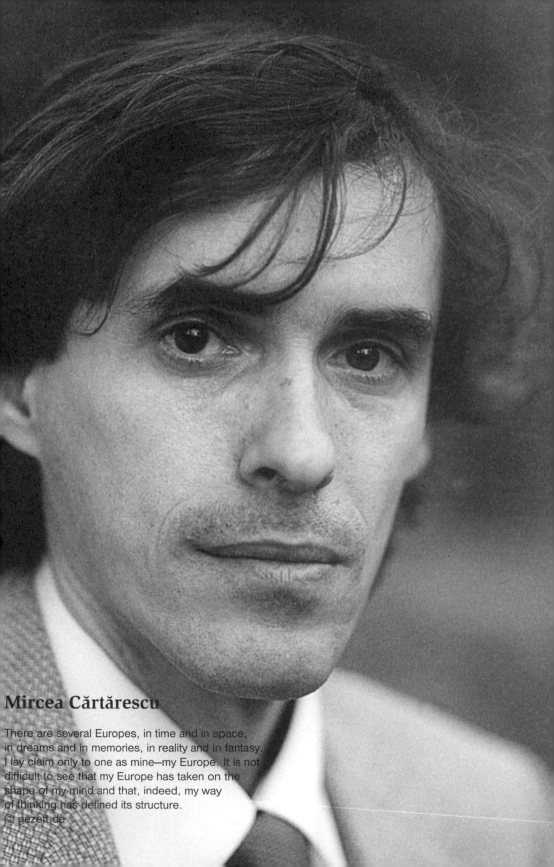

Mircea Cărtărescu

There are several Europes, in time and in space,
in dreams and in memories, in reality and in fantasy.
I lay claim only to one as mine—my Europe. It is not
difficult to see that my Europe has taken on the
shape of my mind and that, indeed, my way
of thinking has defined its structure.

Mircea Cărtărescu
Romania

Born in Bucharest in 1956, the poet and narrative writer
Mircea Cărtărescu studied languages and literature at the
University of Bucharest and published several volumes of
poetry between 1978 and 1985. From 1989 until 1991
he was employed by the Romanian Writers' Union. Since
1991 he has been an assistant then a lecturer and an
associate professor at the Department of Romanian
Literary History at the University of Bucharest. A volume of
prose *Visul* (*The Dream*, 1989), much abbreviated by the
censor, was published in full in 1993 under the title
Nostalgia. Cărtărescu's first novel *Travesti* (*Travesty*)
followed in 1994, winning several prizes in Romania.
Currently he is working on a trilogy entitled *Orbitor* the first
two volumes of which have already been published. His
works are translated in ten European languages.

Further Reading:
Poetry at Annaghmakerring. Dedalus Press, 1994.
Bebop Baby. Translated by Adam J. Sorkin. Poetry New
York, 1999.
Nostalgia. Translated by Julian Semilian. New Directions
(forthcoming).

Europe Has the Shape of My Brain

Există un mare număr de Europe în spațiu și în timp, în vise și în amintiri, în real și în imaginar. Eu îmi revendic doar una dintre ele, Europa mea, ușor de recunoscut prin faptul că are forma creierului meu.

About a hundred years ago, mighty Fortress Europe was filled with the coal smoke, ruled by mediocrities, and plagued by wars and other social conflicts. Artists were trying hard to break out of it. They had not yet realized that Europe is simply a cultural construct, or an intellectual daydream—yet another copy in a world lacking the originals, "a heap of broken images." What did Europe mean to Rimbaud? A reactionary, chauvinistic place, a shallow pond in whose unyielding mud his drunken ship would run aground. What did Gauguin think of it? A fogbound, colorless place. Mallarmé wanted to "run far away," as soon as he had read all he could find to soothe the sadness of the flesh. Even Baudelaire's "anywhere out of this world" should be translated "anywhere at all, only not in Europe." Dreadful old Europe, jaded and brutal. Where did they all escape to? Where did the colors glow more truly and life become full of richness and vigor? Why, Africa, of course. And Tahiti too. It helped to add red wine and hash. And homoeroticism. Anything to confuse the senses systematically. The important thing was to get away from what was emblematic of Europe at the time: the dull, mechanistic, and conformist rationality of its ruling classes. It was the world of the *pater familias*, properly brought up to believe in the spirit of progress and universal order, but within that world grew a soon-to-be born hobgoblin, an unimaginably terrible creature. In less than half a century it had become clear to all that Rimbaud's flight to Africa had been driven by an awful clarity of insight: "My heart, there's but a sea of blood ..."

Irresistibly, my emotional response to these great artists is to believe that they knew, somehow, what the twentieth century would bring. They expected Ypres and Verdun, foresaw Stalingrad and Normandy. In their dreams they saw it all: the slaughter as the tanks advanced across the Russian steppes, the appalling submarine chases, the flattening of whole cities and laying waste of libraries and cathedrals, of historical monuments many thousands of years old. In their own ways, some artists *knew* that the Nazi creed would lead "logically" to the Holocaust and that the Soviet version of "social harmony" would provide the foundation for the East European terror. They had, as it were, experienced it all *in nuce*. There were others, too, who knew: Kafka and Trakl, Dostoyevsky and Unamuno. They saw it all coming, understood that coldly scientific crimes would soon become accepted practice under the cover of "social engineering" and in the name of "advancing human wellbeing," crimes that entailed experimenting with the real, living bodies of individuals as well as with huge, terrorized groups of people. We have yet to overcome the consequences. Until we confront this aspect of our continent, we have no right to self-indulgently glory in its works of spiritual greatness and attempt to add to them.

As Europeans, we must take responsibility for the horrors of the past century and accept that it is our duty to remember them and to prevent their repetition. Still, I doubt that this would truly be enough to return our right to celebrate our belonging to Europe. Over the past few decades, waves of enthusiasm for political correctness and multicultural relativism have carried us gradually, but forcibly, into a postmodern world. For all its exaggerated, often utterly ludicrous features, postmodernism has meant that we now show a certain caution about laying claim to primogeniture in matters of culture. Diogenes Laertius quotes an arrogant declaration by a Greek philosopher, a leading witness in a trial: "I cannot but be grateful to fate for three things: first, that I was born to this world as a human being and not an animal; second, that I am a man and not a woman; third, that I am a Hellene and not a Barbarian." Today, discriminating in this way would signify a barbaric mindset. Could it be that we have finally distanced ourselves enough from the vision of Europe as a solitary island of high culture? That we no longer think of it as a place similar to Swift's Laputa or maybe to Goethe's "pedagogical province," where the spirit brilliantly illuminates all and where, historically, "the best has been thought and said" (to paraphrase Matthew Arnold). We are even less justified in identifying Europe with a mind-sphere—de Chardin's "noosphere" —or with fantasies about Utopia, such as Hesse's Castilia. Many of the strands in the rope binding us to our Judaeo-Hellenic traditions can be followed into other realms, some close by and others very distant. Our written characters are Phoenician, our calendar Assyrian and many of "our" inventions were first made in China. Our nightmares are stalked by the Mesopotamian monster Humbaba. We are all children of the Deluge. In our minds, Europe is a complex mental image made up from interrelated concepts, as well as a contradictory mass of sentiments, in which self-love mingles with self-hatred. Be that as it may, it is just as unreasonable and silly to believe in a cultural relativism dictating that every culture has produced heroes qualitatively as good as Homer, Shakespeare, and Cervantes, as it is to swear by these "giants of the human spirit" in a straightforward, dogged expression of Euro-centricity.

I am proud of being human because I am *also* an animal; of being a man because I am *also* a woman; of being a Hellene *precisely* because of the vital Barbarian inside me. Following the same line of thought, the pride I take in being a European is double-edged. It does not equate with being good—or, at least, with being better than the rest—but with being complex, a creature torn by internal conflicts, somehow still able to recognize his inner contradictions and attempt finding a balance between them. My whole life, including its periods of rebellion, has been influenced by the great cultural traditions of Europe. Conventional wisdom allows no differences between Europe, America, or Asia, but what speeches, what books, what ever so monumental encyclopaedias can express collective reality on this scale?

There are many Europes, no less than a confederation of multidimensional Europes distributed over time and space. To which one of these should I claim allegiance? Which of them do I detest? Some are as real as a handful of soil sprouting blades of grass, while others are virtual, ghostlike manifestations still haunting our imagination. If the world of the ancients really existed, could it be that Europe was simply a nymph, whom Zeus had carried off on the back of the boisterous Cretan bull? Surely there is no more persistent a symbol of our old continent? But then, what about the extraordinary, magic place, glowing with color as harshly as any computer game, where Arthur and Lancelot strode through teeming crowds of Arabs? Or what about reality as seen by Fragonard, with its unrestrained licentiousness, or by Napoleon, whose land of heroes had an apparently constant population of tin soldiers? Or even the flickering glimpses of a world full of coaches and men in top hats, as shown in black and white films from the turn of the century? Somebody or other has written that though our time on Earth is short, we are given transplants of false memories at the moment of birth.

I do not want to wander about, lost in the caves and bewildering passages into which—according to Martin Hocke—European thought has mysteriously strayed. I feel more connected to the Europe of today than to any other of its past manifestations, but in the greater scheme of things the present-day place has no greater degree of concrete reality than do any of the previous versions. Still, the here-and-now has guided my progress through both my conscious existence and dreaming, and must be my dominant reality.

Everything moves erratically in my Europe. For decades a perfectly idiotic wall of concrete and barbed wire divided it. Once torn down, it was obvious—maybe especially in Berlin—that the wall had kept apart two zones, defined not only in terms of geopolitics, but also of mindset. The evidence is close at hand. Even now, Europe is not united and this will not change in the foreseeable future, not even when all the nation-states in the would-be "East" have become officially integrated into that equally fantastic notion of the "West." Samuel Huntington, who saw Europe as split along the borders between opposing Christian beliefs, Protestant, Catholic, and Orthodox, only partly understood the reason for disunity. In his vision, the blocks of belief were colliding and crashing into each other like tectonic plates. This is far from the whole story. For

Goethe and Thomas Mann the great divide opened between the cold, sensible and hardheaded North and the Dionysian South.

From its base at the Ural Mountains, the entire, huge peninsula has now accepted as true three clichés or stereotypical habits of speech or even, fantasies of an almost sexual pervasiveness. I just don't get it: do we exude notions of this kind continually, like a kind of secretion, or do we make them up? Do they serve to enclose us in infantile, cozy "camps" or do they support us like the buoyant bodies of jellyfish? So, here we go: Western, Central and Eastern Europe. Civilization, neurosis and chaos. Affluence, culture and chaos. Rationality, subconscious awareness and chaos. A couple of years ago at the Frankfurt Book Fair I was chatting to a publisher, who told me that he was interested in eastern European writers. I replied at once that I did not see myself as one of them. Of course, the publisher said, as a Romanian you're really a southeastern European. What remarkable precision! What crazy subdivision of a subdivision! You should know your place and stay there was the publisher's well-meaning advice. Remain in your designated ghetto and write away on your typically southeastern European stories. Write about your *Securitate* and that dictator of yours, Ceauşescu, and his People's Palace. Put in something about the feral dogs, the street kids and the Gypsies. Proudly demonstrate what a brave dissident you were during the communist era. Leave writing about love and death to us. We will deal with happiness and agony and ecstasy. As for creating an avant-garde art, supporting significant innovations and generally enjoying normal culture—better leave that to us as well. Your only option is to give expression to what is going on in your own exotic little world. Maybe, with luck, you will find a minor publisher here that will print your work. Come on, who's worried anyway? Who's really interested? It's your choice: you can reinforce our cherished clichés or you can get lost.

I will repeat, right now, my answer to that publisher. In *no way* am I an eastern European writer. As far as I'm concerned, the tripartite Europe is *unreal*. It has no geopolitical justification, nor a cultural one, and that includes religion as well. I dream of a Europe that can take on many shapes but is not schizophrenic. I read Musil, not because I suspect him to be, deep down, a contented

Kakanian ruminant, but because I have found him to be an aristo-
crat of the European spirit. Which country André Bréton lived and
wrote in does not concern me. I have no idea where Bulgakov's
Kiev is on the map. When I wanted to find Catullus or Rabelais,
Cantemir or Virginia Woolf, I didn't go looking on a map but in the
library, where books stand next to each other on the shelves. Neither the little lambs of Romanian folklore nor the rosaries of the
Orthodox faith clutter the books I have written. My writing contains much more of Dante's stars, John Donne's compass and Cervantes' lance. I have pondered on Kafka's beetle, Proust's madelaine and Günter Grass' flounder. I see myself as competing with
writers whom I admire and love, but not with Romanians, nor with
Bulgarians, Russians, Serbs, Czechs, Poles or others from my part
of the world. True, if circumstances call for it, my material and
stage-props may well be Romanian, and my language reflects of the
psycholinguistic space to which I belong. However, my content and
its themes belong to the great European tradition, which encom-
passes both Euripides and Joyce. I recognize influences on both my
prose and my poetry, but above all on my thought—thinking being
the most important task of the artist, as George Enescu once
wrote—and these have come mainly from the great literature of the
last century, Romanian as well as international. Happily, the Romanian literary tradition is as rich and complex as any other in
Europe. Some Romanian authors have succeeded in transcending
the mental borders between East and West and possibly, in doing
so, have in some ways confirmed them. They became stars on the
cultural firmament over Europe: Tzara, Ionescu, Cioran. There are
of course many others, some no less brilliant, who were enticed
into the tempting trap of a language that is endlessly rich in expressions, and so untranslatable: Urmuz, Arghezi and Blaga remain
unknown outside Romania. Although I respect them, I do not intend to share their fate and turn into the "duty-Romanian," who
represents his country at conferences with monotonous regularity.
I have no one and nothing to represent except myself and my
books. My writing is my only motherland. I could be Portuguese or
Estonian or Swiss. I could be a woman or a Hellene or a Barbarian.
Of course the nature of what I wrote would change correspond-

ingly, but the spirit behind the words would be the same. Valéry was completely absurd when he claimed that all the poetry ever written might have emanated from a single, timeless poet or, even, from the spirit of creativity itself. While not going all the way with Valéry, I still feel that there is indeed, almost tautologically, an element of a shared European spirit in all literature of true cultural value, wherever it has been created and however extensively it has been influenced by that locality. Once this is recognized, writers as diverse as Márquez, Pynchon and Kawabata are recognizably Europeans too. Attitudes and ideologies may well be distinctive, but differences will surely fade as one searches in works of art for their elements of a great collective subconscious, of a "philosophy" in the sense of an area of knowledge, as contemplated by the ancient Greeks—searches, in other words, for fundamental premises, which may well be unspoken, but yet decisive in shaping a literary work.

For several decades now, postmodern thought has labored to expose all that is wrong with high culture—how, arrogant, elitist and self-sufficient, it locks itself away inside museums and so remains distanced from raw, real life. In a brilliant essay on art in the era of technology, Walter Benjamin has shown how the "aura" of a work of art fades in proportion to its increasing mechanical reproducibility. Both lines of thought contain truths. Back in the days of Duchamp "high" art deserved his insults—the urinal on display in a gallery, the moustache on the face of La Giaconda. Nowadays, it still deserves the attacks coming from the innumerable, almost random, varieties of new art, all seemingly more popular than the "canon."

However, entering into misalliances of this kind cannot destroy the European spirit of the ancient Judeo-Hellenic tradition. New art forms donate the fresh blood high art badly needs. Mona Lisa-with-a-moustache is meaningless unless linked to the true, immortal Giaconda, who rather than being dragged down seems to glow with even more beauty than before. The wave of "pop culture," which has been following in the wake of the widely dreaded "Americanization," will not mean the end of great art. Instead, it offers it an opportunity to surf on its crest. Although art has become "show biz"—entertainment for the moment—I will not be dissuaded from my conviction that a solid education in the arts, even in the world today, will provide an immeasurable advantage over the armies of mediocre, nameless artists, who serve a public addicted to advertising and television.

There are several Europes, in time and in space, in dreams and in memories, in reality and in fantasy. I lay claim only to one as mine—my own Europe. It is not difficult to see that my Europe has taken on the shape of my mind and that, indeed, my way of thinking has defined its structure. The surface of my brain, with its motor and sensory areas and zones for language and understanding, is a ridged and deeply grooved organ, but nowhere has it stone walls or iron curtains. It knows no borders.

—*Translated by Anna Paterson*

Stefan Chwin

The real Europe is for me the Europe that
hesitates. And that, despite hesitations,
can act effectively.
© Maxim Segienko/PHOTOMAX

Stefan Chwin

Poland

Born in Gdańsk in 1949, the literary scholar and author
Stefan Chwin became known to the public as chronicler of
German-Polish history with the publication in German of
his novel *Tod in Danzig* in 1997. In Poland the novel was
selected as Novel of the Year in 1995, while in Germany
Chwin was awarded the Andreas Gryphius Prize of the
Esslingen Artists' Guild. In January 2002, a theatre
version of his novel premiered at the Gdansk Theatre.
Stefan Chwin has published (under pseudonyms) fantasy
adventure novels embellished with his own illustrations, as
well as critical and historical studies of literature and
several volumes of essays. In 2000 a second novel *Die
Gouvernante (Esther, 1999)* appeared in Germany. The
author lives in Gdańsk, where he teaches at the university.

Further Reading:
"Hanemann." Extract. Translated by David Malcolm. *2B*
Issue 14 (1999).

The Nursery School Teacher
from Tversk Street

Prawdziwą Europą jest dla mnie Europa, która się waha.
I która mimo wahań potrafi skutecznie działać.

Any writer who thinks about what the essence of the European spirit is and what it means to be a European in today's world must face up to certain very unsettling questions.

The bite of those questions increases when we approach the really difficult issues.

As long as I've lived, and I've lived for quite a while now, I've never come across anyone who wasn't in favor of justice and truth. Everyone has always been, and still is, in favor of justice and truth. At least no one says out loud that he or she is against them.

And everyone tells me that justice is on their side, and more than that — everyone tells me: you should be with us; you should be on our side. For if you aren't on our side, you can't be counted among the just.

Some people tell me that it was just to kill the terrorists in the Moscow theatre. That if you fight for independence, it's permissible to attack the institutions of a hostile state, but surely not inoffensive folks who simply go to the theatre one evening, and then suddenly, towards the end of the first act, someone puts a gun to their heads and in a few seconds turns that nice nursery school teacher from Tversk Street, whom all the older kids love, into a political hostage. That those who are fighting for their country's independence, in reality, want to create a barbarian Islamic state between Georgia and Russia; so isn't it more just for Russia to crush the Islamic fanatics than that there should be in Europe—

yes, in Europe, because Chechnya is a European country, after all—one more of those states in which women are deprived of all their rights and corporal punishment is the order of the day? So isn't it the case that—if we have to choose—then a modernizing Russia, albeit unjust and cruel, is the lesser evil in the conflict of civilizations that they say is inevitable than the yellow crescent on the green standard?

Others try to convince me that the Chechens had no way out, that it was the Russians, themselves, who forced them to take such desperate measures by depriving a small nation of its right to independence, that a hard and harsh justice was rather on the side of the desperate fighters with the green bandanas on their heads, because in a confrontation with a great power no small nation has any chance of fighting according to the rules of war, that, mutilated, powerless, crushed under the treads of thousands of tanks, unless it lets the world know about its existence through such bloody acts, the world will forget about it, just as it has forgotten a thousand times before about small, troublesome nations, which have, without reservation, been condemned to political (and not only political) death by governments and parliaments; thus, though what happened in the Moscow theatre was cruel, terrible, and vile, was it somehow just?

And I, when I hear this, ask myself: which of these justices is more just, and which is more villainous and vile?

Some have told me that completely innocent people died unjustly in that Moscow theatre, people that had gone to the theatre to see a musical about the Russian Army, to be entertained a little by Russian soldiers dancing on stage in knee-boots, that there were innocent women there whom were cruelly threatened with death.

Others have told me that to continue to maintain, even after the experiences of the twentieth century, that in modern mass societies there exists such a thing as "completely innocent people" is to not see a fundamental change in the structure of responsibility, that in modern mass societies political responsibility is diffused, justly distributed among all, that among the audience at the Moscow musical were hundreds of men of draft age, each of whom, if he got his call-up papers, would fire on the people of Grozny without batting an eye, that the innocent women who, together with their husbands and brothers of draft age, took their seats in the audience of the Moscow theatre had voted for Putin precisely because he promised to fix the Chechens, that these ordinary, nice women said in their homes to their growing sons and daughters that "someone's finally got to fix these Chechens," just as ordinary, nice German women in the 1930s said to their children over breakfast that "someone's finally got to fix these Jews," that these nice ladies from Moscow, who would not hurt a fly, spoke in their homes about the Chechens in exactly the same way as ordinary innocent Russians spoke in their homes during the Polish Uprising of 1863 about "Polish bandits and rebels" that needed to be silenced once and for all, that this terrible blow against these innocent people, though deeply unjust and vile, was also somehow just, for it was precisely these innocent people who, when they cast their votes at the polling station, supported the razing of Grozny as part of a just "anti-terrorist operation," which enjoyed the support of a large proportion of Russians, that it was precisely that sweet nursery school teacher from Tversk Street, that smiling blond girl in the light-colored dress, whom is loved by all the older kids from the Lady Bird class, who voted for Putin so that he could finally "fix Russia and the world."

And still others say to me that it is deeply unjust and against the spirit of European culture, and even crazy, to extend responsibility to everyone. They tell me that there are people in the world who are just and pure, whom cannot be accused of any wrongdoing, that it is absurd to load responsibility for the Auschwitz concentration camp and the crimes of the Holocaust on the back of that nice, friendly German lady who, in the 1930s, while making cheese sandwiches for breakfast, said to her young son, just by way of digression: "Hans, watch out for those Jews. Jews are dangerous. Someone should fix them once and for all," and then when Hans grew up he set off for the Generalgouvernement.

For what did she have to do with his killing Jews? And would she be justly punished for it? After all, what she was really con-cerned about — as I heard recently from a young man in Nuremberg with regard to his grandmother who voted for Hitler in 1933 — was maintaining order and building motorways. Yes, all she was concerned about was order, motorways, and that there should be fewer unemployed. Not even for a fraction of a second did she think of gas chambers. The very thought would have horrified her. In any case, Hitler never said anything about any gas chambers. If he had, she'd never have voted for him. And the Jews? He just wanted to prevent them from gaining total control over commerce. He never mentioned that he wanted to kill them. So did she commit a sin for which she should go to confession when she joined the NSDAP in 1934?

And how are matters in my own Central Europe? What did that innocent gesture of voting mean in Poland, the GDR, Hungary, and Czechoslovakia in the Communist period? We, the just and the innocent, did indeed vote, because, after all — and was it not so? — we said to ourselves that we had been brutally forced to do so by a totalitarian system, that refusing to vote wouldn't even change anything, we'd only be putting our families at risk; so we voted regularly, every four years, almost all of us? And what is one supposed to think of the ordinary, decent people who, during the anti-Semitic incidents of March 1968 and the militia's suppression of the workers' protests in the Polish city of Radom in June 1976, held up the banners that had been shoved into their hands with the slogans "Send the Zionists to Zion," "Punish the Troublemakers from Radom," and "The Whole Nation is with the Party" without thinking, for even a moment, about what was written on them, because the only thing they had on their minds was that they didn't want to lose their jobs at the factory and that politics didn't concern them at all anyway? Was that gesture — that indifferent raising of the banner, that brandishing of it, that waving of it above their heads — an act that indirectly gave permission to the militia to beat the protesting workers in Radom with rubber truncheons on what they called their "health-cure paths," or was it a meaningless pantomime that the Communist system imposed on people, a pantomime that nobody (?), neither in Poland nor the rest of the world, took seriously? For, in truth, is it just to argue that someone who does not express open protest in the face of evil thus expresses indirect acceptance of it? And, indeed, scenes like these, with the participation of millions of people, took place thousands of times in the very center of Europe, wherever the Nazis, the Fascists, or the Communists took power.

And who were those who, in that December of 1970, during the workers' revolt in Gdańsk, gave the order to use the army to save people from the burning Party Committee Building, a building surrounded by a crowd of demonstrators who, according to several witnesses, were shouting "down with the red bourgeoisie!" and didn't want to let the fire engines through? Were they totalitarian criminals with the blood of Polish workers on their hands, or were they the just officials of a state that had been deprived of its sovereignty, officials who were doing what anyone would have done in their place? Or was justice on the side of those who, in their desperation, set fire to the building—to the extent that it was, indeed, ordinary desperate people who set fire to it?

In the heart of a writer living in the very center of Europe, mulling over what is most European in European culture, all these questions provoke a deep unease. So how can one mete out justice to the totalitarian evil that gave shape to half of Europe, since that evil was diffused over everyone, since it was based on the principle of the silent, indirect—and often unconscious—participation of all, with the exception of those who protested openly, that is those who ended up in gulags and prisons?

For the due processes of democratic justice—of European justice that demands hard proof of concrete individual guilt—are helpless in the face of an evil that is diffused, collective, indirect, and anonymous. And why, indeed, should it then surprise us that, after the collapse of the totalitarian systems that required millions of people to build and sustain, we usually see, standing in an almost empty court room, five former secret-police officials against whom it's difficult to prove even three criminal acts? And, in any case, gray-haired, bent, disabled, sick with cancer, tottering on unsteady legs, dropping with fatigue, they often manage to die before the trial is over. So isn't it more just to simply forget about such bygone cases and rely on the verdict of God's justice?

And the matters of conscience and truth to your own convictions? Some tell us that it is just and proper, and thus most in keeping with the spirit of European culture, to respect all religions and faiths, that we should respect a religion even if it ordains the stoning of a woman for bearing an illegitimate child and that the stones with which the woman is to be put to death be the same size, no smaller and no larger, than the hand of a grown man so that the woman may take a long time to die and completely feel her just punishment, for such is God's holy will.

Others tell us that it is just, and even necessary, and thus most in keeping with the spirit of European culture, to condemn a religion that permits such things, that it is necessary to infringe the sovereignty of a state in which such things take place, that it is necessary to overthrow the religious court that issues such terrifying verdicts, that even, if there is no other way, it is necessary to bomb the cities of such a state, scatter its army and liquidate its government, in order to liberate people from the violence of such an infamous law, as was recently done in Afghanistan.

Is it, therefore, just that authorities in Geneva, where I was told this story, immediately fired a public school teacher of Arab descent, who had written in one of the city newspapers that a Nigerian woman who had given birth to an illegitimate child should be stoned to death after she had finished breast-feeding her baby, because that was God's will and there can be no further discussion about it? Did the authorities of the Swiss city behave justly, and thus in keeping with the spirit of European culture, when they argued that a man like that should have no contact with European children? In Germany itself there are already several million Muslims, one of whom may well be elected president in twenty years, or maybe less. By this time "dying Europe" will have changed beyond recognition as a result of demographic changes and immigration from the Third World.

Some try to convince us that it is just and proper, and thus in keeping with the spirit of European culture, to suspend human rights in the battle against terrorism, and that all means are permissible in order to destroy this plague, that it is just to kidnap the citizens of foreign states suspected of terrorism and to shove them into iron cages at Guantanamo Bay without a trial and to hold them there as long as one wants, that it is just not to respect the decisions of the Hague Tribunal, because respecting them hinders effective anti-terrorist operations. And more: that it is just and acceptable, and even necessary, to send secret agents of the special services to foreign countries—to Denmark or Sweden, for example—just as the Czarist (and not just the Czarist) police did, to liquidate people suspected of terrorism as they walk down the street, that it is just and proper to shoot down airplanes with kidnapped people on board if they could be used by terrorists as flying bombs, that it's necessary to shut the mouths of those who question the validity of brutal anti-terrorist acts and call for negotiations even with the worst of fanatics, and that it's occasionally necessary to keep journalists away so that they can't inform society of what's going on.

Others, however, try to convince us that all this is deeply unjust, striking a blow against the very essence of the European system of values, and suicidal, though it appears essential and deeply just, and that if we go further down this road, after a while we won't know what we're actually protecting, so much will we have changed.

The world is genuinely mysterious—both splendid and terrible. And everything that we touch is out of focus like an image in a clouded photograph. We do not know why reality has this opaque structure, so that even the holy books on which the edifice of European culture has been raised do not give us a clear answer to the question: what does it mean to act justly in the face of concrete events?

That is why, in difficult situations, we usually choose a simplified picture of the world, because only in a black-and-white reality are we able to make decisions and mete out justice. But maybe—as Shakespeare suspected—between the deed and a deeper knowledge of the world there lies a contradiction that cannot be healed. "Yes, yes"—"no, no"—we repeat to ourselves over and over. But the reality on which we strive to keep a tight grip with our resolute words and decisions scoffs at us, even if it gives in to our will; it's a hundred times more complex than these two hard words promise it to be. Reality rarely says, "Yes, yes" — "No, no." It has many more colors and shades. Rather it is a genuine forest of things, intertwined and dark, in which the distant light that we're trying to get to shines only somewhere far ahead in the trees. But experienced people tell us that the traveler who sees and knows too much, just as the one who sees and knows too little, can miss the path and disappear.

We — just as the great old European painters — can imagine only with difficulty what the Last Judgment will look like and what verdicts will be handed down there. Certainly the just will be separated from the unjust, as in Hans Memling's famous painting with a crystal staircase on the left side and flames on the right. But we do not know how the Judge will pass judgment on the man who handed people over to the secret police to get money to save his daughter who was sick with cancer. How will He justly pass judgment on the president of a state who gives the just order to shoot down a passenger jet with children on board because it had been seized by terrorists over Washington, Hamburg, Stockholm, or Warsaw? How will He pass judgment on the Israeli policeman who, for good reason, tortures a terrorist suspect in order to drag out of him information about a planned attack, information that might save the lives of hundreds of innocent people? How will He pass judgment on the Palestinian fighter who lays bombs in the homes of innocent people, those same innocent people who peacefully cast their votes and thus deny the Palestinians the right to complete independence? How will He pass judgment on the mullahs who, certain that they are doing His holy will, condemn to stoning a woman who has dared to give birth to an illegitimate child? And how will He pass judgment on those who, with their own hands, stone that woman to death, convinced that they are doing justice because it is completely in accord with their own consciences and religious law? How, too, will He pass judgment on us if we do not try to save this woman, even if it's just by sending one letter of protest in her defense, for over the great matters of this world we have but little influence, though maybe in this one small (?) matter we have at least some? And how will He pass judgment on all those who, long ago, burnt women at the stake, convinced that they were doing this justly for the good of those women, for the good of humanity, and of the Church?

And Europe? Europe will stay Europe as long as she can ask all these questions. As long as she does not get rid of the moral unease from which these questions arise. This is her most profound heritage, even if—as the bloody history of our continent demonstrates—we ourselves, we Europeans, have many times cast this heritage aside contemptuously—"unnecessary complications" that hinder effective action, as it is sometimes said.

The most European thing about us is that we are still able to ask such questions and that we still ask them. And that European literature can still ask them. Because there were, and are, unfortunately, civilizations on earth that are not able to ask such questions, and don't even want to. What is European in us is a consciousness of the complexity of the affairs of the human world, a consciousness that protects us from a black-and-white view of things. A consciousness of the conflict between knowing and doing, ethics and politics, justice and pity, individual fate and collective responsibility, punishment and revenge, efficiency and truth. A difficult consciousness that we inherit from Shakespeare, Goethe, Thomas Mann, Mickiewicz, and the wise and ancient culture of the Greeks. For it is those "unnecessary complications" of thinking about what happens in the world and in human hearts that makes us European, though European—and not just European—mass culture does everything it can to make us forget those "complications."

In one of his poems the Polish poet Zbigniew Herbert writes: "Nike is most beautiful at the moment/when she hesitates." I would like to make it clear: the real Europe is for me the Europe that hesitates. And that, despite hesitations, can act effectively. The Europe that can, therefore, move through that difficult space between a consciousness of the world's lack of transparency, which (we sometimes think) weakens us, and the necessity of unambiguous decisions, between doubt that is full of scruples and hard certainty that one is right, between critical self-irony and fervor. It is a moral space that many simply call the space of the European conscience.

It is in this that I see her true spirit.

May it never desert us.

And I will do all I can that this spirit remain the light that guides my writing.

— Translated by David Malcolm

Aleš Debeljak

The legal framework for cosmopolitanism is to be found in civic
identity. One's choice of civic identity differs sharply
from a "natural" ethnic identity to the extent that it is based
on a respect for differences and their active public articulation
rather than on liberal tolerance.

Aleš Debeljak

Slovenia

Born in 1961, Aleš Debeljak studied philosophy,
comparative literature, and cultural sociology in his native
city of Ljubljana and in Syracuse, NY (United States),
where he received his PhD. The poet, cultural critic, and
translator has won many international awards, including
the Slovenian National Prize for Literature. He is
considered one of Central Europe's leading poets and his
works have been translated into many languages. He is an
associate professor of cultural studies at the University of
Ljubljana in the capital of Slovenia where he lives with his
American wife and three children.

Further Reading:
Twilight of the Idols: Recollections of a Lost Yugoslavia.
Translated by Michael Biggins. White Pine Press, 1994.
Anxious Moments. (Poems) Translated by Christopher
Merrill and the author. White Pine Press, 1994.
*Modernity: The Institution of Art and Its Historical
Forms*. Rowman & Littlefield, 1998.
The City and the Child. (Poems) Translated by
Christopher Merrill and the author. White Pine Press,
1999.
Dictionary of Silence. (Poems) Translated by Sonja
Kravanja. Lumen Press, Inc., 1999.
*The Hidden Handshake: National Identity and European
Postcommunism*. Rowman & Littlefield, 2004.

Concentric Circles of Identity

*Rad bi poudaril, da kozmopolitizem črpa svojo
privlačnost iz empatičnega potenciala, ki ga je morda
mogoče prevesti v povišan občutek za potrebo, da bi se
videlo, četudi le za bežeči trenutek, svet skozi oči
drugega.*

King Arthur and the Knights of the Round Table; the *Nibelungen-lied;* the long campaign of Russia's Prince Igor; the royal bones moldering in the crypt of Krakow's Wawel Castle that dully animate the Polish imagination when the calendar of national rituals calls for a performance: most European nations are able to find meaning in a narrative about their history that, in moments of crisis, lends support to their worldly endeavors, cultural pride, and collective identity. History, as is well-known, means a story or narrative. A *story* helps shape the space of *hi-story* from inside. There is nothing surprising in the significance of an individual biography, his and her story that can reach, I suggest, its full expression only within the circle of a particular collective tradition. A story of this tradition is able to bring meaningful order to a seething chaos of facts. In public confrontations between its multiple versions a narrative about the past assumes centrality for a community's current sense of itself. The way you look over your shoulder determines the way you look at the present.

What do I see when I look over my shoulder and into the reservoirs of collective tradition? I see Slovenes that find the gentle murmur of inspiration not only in the positivism of cultural history, but, perhaps most strongly, in "national mythology" — even if it is held together by a modest roster of figures such as: Beautiful Vida, tearfully longing for a homeland in her wet nurse's exile; Črtomir, the leader of a pagan army, defeated by encroaching

Christians; King Mathias, forever waiting with his soldiers of liberation in the heart of a mountain; Martin Krpan, a victorious peasant who defended the Viennese royal court against the Turks; and, last but not least, Serf Yerney, a rebellious proletarian, and Martin Čedermac, anti-fascist Catholic preacher. They entered the public mind straight from traditional Slovene folklore and early modern literature.

But their symbolic meaning is far from fixed, as competing public interpretations negotiate the conflict between grand public deeds in the name of a larger group and the private desire for a good life. These heroes reveal how the collective dilemma of the Slovenes has been consistently linked to the dilemma of a cultural identity that is unacknowledged by their adversaries—just as it went unacknowledged by the Germans and Austrians, under whom the Slovenes lived for eleven long centuries, or by the Serbs, with whom, and often under whom, the Slovenes lived for seventy years in a "common Yugoslav house." The heroes of Slovene national mythology first had to carve out an identity for themselves and then take pains to make it publicly recognized. Thus in Slovene culture, especially with regard to literature, the modern substitute for mythology, the archetype of "the rites of passage," is palpable. Within this archetype are locked allusions that serve to retain its relevance for Slovenes, though I admit that in this day and age collective inspiration may be drawn more from international icons of the culture industries than from locally published novels.

Metaphorically speaking, the Slovene nation-state exists so that the Slovene language, together with the culture it expresses as the basic structure of thought and emotion, can be used for purposes beyond that for which the Austrian emperors condescendingly used it: to communicate with their horses. The leading voice of Slovenian poetry in twentieth century, the prophetic Edvard Kocbek (1904–1981), fashioned this pregnant metaphor in his poem from the 1960s, "The Lippizaners," which appears in *Embers in the House of Night* (1999):

> Others have worshiped holy cows and dragons,
> thousand-year-old turtles and winged lions,

unicorns, double-headed eagles, and phoenixes,
but we've chosen the most beautiful animal,
which proved to be excellent on battlefields, in circuses,
harnessed to princesses and the Golden Monstrance,
therefore the emperors of Vienna spoke
French with skillful diplomats,
Italian with charming actresses,
Spanish with the infinite God,
and German with uneducated servants:
but with horses they talked Slovene.

Slovene, then, is more than just an instrument of formal communication, it is more than the language one happens to speak. When its public use is neglected, disdained, or infringed upon, the truth of the collective mentality goes steadily to waste. That which is poorly expressed is also poorly thought, remarked Theodor W. Adorno. Most likely one can "think well," that is, with the totality of being, only in the language that allows one to express himself intimately, using the vocabulary of love, prayer, and poetry in which bodily urgency overrides critical reflection. It should thus not be impossible to see the mother tongue as the primary element of cultural identity, which an integrated Europe should honor and uphold. If we do not use the mother tongue for all the complex forms of discourse (commerce, science, administration, medicine, and so on) in which one can express only a complex view of reality, then it will remain nothing more than the language of a handicapped nation.

I need to emphasize, however, that the separation of ethnic and civic identities is especially important. I recall that multiple identities had, up until mid-1970s, a considerable degree of public currency in the country of my birth, a member-state of the former Yugoslav federation. In it, undemocratic as it was, an individual citizen could have at least dual identity, as an ethnic Croat, Slovene, Serb, or Macedonian, and, at the same time, as a member of a larger political body. This was not only possible, but broadly accepted. In the wake of Yugoslavia's disintegration, this historical lesson seems to have been almost entirely lost on the national communities that rose from its ashes, which have opted for the definition of their respective nation-states in terms of exclusively ethnic, rather than inclusively civic, identity.

The recent history of Slovenian struggles to maintain ethnic identity against the perceived threat of being swallowed up in a larger ethnic framework clearly demonstrates the continuing relevance of sensitivity to the rights of ethnic minorities and to the need for multicultural competence. If anything, the refusal to attribute value to the *argument of size*, i.e., the size of ethnic communities as the ultimate standard of participation in international affairs, should be a necessary building block in the development of Slovenian civic identity. Why? Because the very argument of small numerical size has often been used to deny the Slovenes' right to existence as a distinct national collective.

I rush to add that having a small number of people does not necessarily make a nation small. It is not too sentimental to say that the "smallness" of a nation may be measured, first and foremost, in regard to how much its citizens believe into their nation's creative potential and the richness of their shared cultural tradition, regardless of whether it is increasingly recognized as an "invented" one. The argument of the small numerical size, understood as a suggestion about the inevitable, if gradual, absorption of the Slovenian nation in the larger body, is often used today in Ljubljana, the capital city of the nation, as well as in Brussels, the capital city of European Union. It is, alas, far from being new. A quick glance at Slovenian history reveals a long tradition of this erroneous, albeit politically potent, *argument of size*. Such was, to name but one example, the nineteenth-century *Ilyrian tradition* of literary writers like Stanko Vraz and Ljudevit Gaj, who called for the unification of the Slovenian and Croatian languages on the basis of alleged linguistic pragmatism. After World War I, this argument, advanced by the communist central authorities of the federal state, manifested itself in the ideological straightjacket of "integral Yugoslavism," as Andrew Wachtel pointed out in his lucid book *Making a Nation, Breaking a Nation* (1998).

However, it was precisely the numerical limitation of the Slovenians as a people that forced its key national players in the realm of culture to interact with foreign strategies of imagination and reason, assimilating them in accord to their local needs and conditions. A productive, if troublesome, geographic location at the crossroads of the Romance, Germanic, Hungarian, and Balkan cultural traditions has ensured the impossibility of bucolic Slovenian "sameness." The concept of self-absorbed and uncontaminated culture, in which national *ego in Arcadia* might be quietly nurtured is, of course, a mirage. Slovenian creative minds have been traditionally engaged in a dialogue with the gospel of Western civilization, drawing upon the linguistic self-confidence of Protestantism, the Italian Renaissance, the Central-European baroque, French rationalism, German Romanticism and Expressionism, Secessionist Viennese architecture, English rock 'n' roll, American pop-art, not to mention the ubiquitous attraction of the Hollywood screen and the intricacies of Balkan folk blues. Art and culture, if understood only as a dispensable ornament to the public life, can facilitate neither collective freedom nor unfettered flight of the individual imagination.

Both as a literary artist using universal codes of expression to present what I believe is a personal vision and as an ethnic Slovenian with a particular collective experience in my background, I gradually learned to cherish attractions of cosmopolitanism. Cosmopolitanism implies that one's mode of expression, indeed, one's being, has become enhanced precisely because of the cross-fertilization with other languages and cultural traditions. Perhaps cosmopolitanism lacks the emotional appeal of a collective identity, such as nationalism; but it gains in its accommodation of an individual attitude: it is, to a large extent, a matter of ethical choice. It may very well be true that this is one of the main reasons why cosmopolitanism does not enjoy broad attraction, though pursuit of it is crucial if we are to not only survive, but live meaningful and secure lives. "Which also entails acceptance that we are not sufficient onto ourselves, that we are inseparably tied to the destiny of everyone else on this planet, and that only with them can we construct the world of dignity and humanity. But it entails, furthermore, that only if we are totally ourselves will we be able to do so. Cosmopolitan globalism and patriotic localism are therefore two inseparable faces of the present world situation, with a degree of tension that cannot be erased," wrote Alberto Melucci, encouragingly, in *Coexisting with Differences* (1998).

The legal framework for cosmopolitanism is to be found in civic identity. One's choice of civic identity differs sharply from a "natural" ethnic identity to the extent that it is based on a respect for differences and their active public articulation rather than on liberal tolerance. The latter camouflages its essentially passive character, which merely allows other, different and diverse, traditions to exist side by side. As such, it cannot be fully divorced from a self-congratulatory, yet profoundly patronizing, attitude to which I will return later in this paper. Here I want to stress that cosmopolitanism actively links without unifying. As such, it contributes to a transformation of "natural," "inherited," "genuine" identities into a civic identity based on the common body of laws accepted freely by free and equal individuals. This acceptance of rule of law can only be performed in modern, secular, democratic nation-states.

In post-communist Central and Eastern Europe, two types of parochialism assault the cosmopolitan habitus. The first was borne by the frequently violent "navel gazing," i.e., the mentality that cannot, would not, and is unable to learn from others, much less accept such ideas into public life. The *bona fide* liberal "internationalists" represent the second kind of parochialism. They shy away from each and every aspect of national cultural identity, recoiling in fear from the possibility of being lumped together with the local conservatives. As a result, they uncritically approve of each and every idea that comes from the West. Such minds wish an ingratiating *bless you!* when this or that fashionable cultural guru sneezes in Paris, London, or Berlin.

The velvet revolutions of 1989 produced a semblance of renaissance to national ideas in Central and Eastern Europe, invigorating the debates regarding the validity of the collective experience, while teasing the various peoples with the cheap promise of miraculously resolved conflicts in newly independent countries. More than a decade after 1989, however, it has become rather clear that only a very few original approaches to the relation between the national and global facet of collective identity have crystallized on the ruins of communist *ancien régime*. Many intellectuals from Central and Eastern Europe have grudgingly accepted the role of "poor relatives" that only compete with each other in efforts to impress their rich cousins in Europe, that is, Western Europe as embodied in European Union.

However, what kind of Europe are we really talking about? I, for one, remain convinced that the discussion must concentrate on the following difference between two aspects of the European idea. On the one hand, one must regard the project of integration of diverse nations in an "ever closer" European Union as primarily an economic and technological enterprise. As such, this is a goal that is as interesting as it is unavoidable. On the other hand, one must take measure of Europe as a common, if elusively shifting, cultural and mental landscape. What is the price of the first aspect taking over the second? Modern Europe does not reveal itself solely in the noble traditions of Greek philosophy, Roman law, Renaissance humanism, Romantic poetry, and in the politically crucial Enlightenment legacy of universal human and civil rights. The contemporary idea of Europe is increasingly portrayed in popular right-wing politics as *fortress Europe*, the *barricaded society* that often amounts to *fascism with a human face*. This staunchly conservative gatekeeping is used to fortify that which is perceived to be a "natural" ethnic community into one is either born or does not belong. *Tertium non datur.*

For me, a poet by vocation and a critic by choice, it is poetry that reveals the character of human existence in its most distilled form. Not unlike many other poets, I imagine that poetry is my true motherland: only within its geography and history can I really be at home. In the fragile palaces of poetry one could find the primordial text of life ready to release its secret. With its strange and beautiful simplicity of tender feeling and throbbing pain, it is poetry alone that could tune my heart to the grace and wisdom born where spiders silently weave their webs in the gutters of rotting dreams, to paraphrase Ben Okri. And because its social marginality makes it commercially irrelevant in today's corporate world, only poetry could freely uncover the fear and hope that reside in those corners of the heart where only desperate adventurers dare go.

Lyrical poetry, however, is wedded to the mother tongue and thus to a specific ethnic tradition. Divorces do, of course, happen, though they seldom improve the partners. For a poet, the native language is of primary importance; this is beyond dispute. For instance, the preoccupation of Czesław Miłosz's poetry has never yielded to the temptations of career benefit; and even after half of his life spent living in California, he has never been tempted to exchange his native Polish for the ecumenical reach of English. While there are a number of excellent twentieth-century expatriate writers (Samuel Beckett, Emile Cioran, Vladimir Nabokov, Milan Kundera, etc.) who successfully switched to the language of their adopted countries, these are themselves exceptions that prove the rule. A true poet is born into his native language, both its burden and inspiration. Little wonder that these expatriates are known primarily for prose, not poetry, which stems from an awareness that the totality of formative events through which the *genius loci* is expressed — symbolic, historical, social, and metaphysical — lie buried in the layers of a single mother tongue, suggesting a more or less hidden anchorage in ethnic tradition.

But we don't live ensconced in one tradition only. Concentric circles of identity emanate from most local and fecund surroundings, from the neighborhood to a region, rippling outward in an ever more abstract manner to national, state, and European identities and, for those with the most finely honed reflective instruments, perhaps ending in a common humanity.

The cultural context of the former Yugoslavia was, for Slovenians, one such concentric circle. For Slovene writers in the fifties, sixties, and seventies, when travel abroad was still difficult and the limits on communication between Yugoslavia and the West still daunting, getting translated into Croatian, Serbian, or Macedonian was a legitimate, if not perfect, surrogate for reaching the "outside world." The fact that Slovene literature was reaching readers in Zagreb, Sarajevo, Belgrade, and Skopje mitigated the focus on an ethnic tradition alone. In the Yugoslav context, most of the important works of Slovene literature found interested readers beyond the borders of Slovenia. These readers could sample not only the standard translated classics, but also a multitude of small publishers, special book series, magazines, and anthologies, which frequently and willingly published Slovene writing throughout the former Yugoslavia. In short, there can be no doubt that Croatian, Macedonian, and Serbian readers know Slovene literature better than anyone else outside of Slovenia. Let me be precise, however, and note that a decade after a dispersion of this concentric circle this familiarity is increasingly dubious; with increasing frequency, former Yugoslavs read each other in English, in ephemeral magazines like *Erewchton* in Amsterdam and *Stonesoup* in London, on the Geocities web sites, and elsewhere in the consolations of virtual connection.

In the eighties a different concentric circle of identity made itself felt. It was then that Milan Kundera, in his essay *The Tragedy of Central Europe* (1984), issued a passionate plea for a recognition of a common historical experience for former Habsburg lands, an experience of victimized small nations caught between the self-involved West and the despotic East. Though these days hardly anyone talks about this vigorous and far-reaching debate on Central Europe, this call for a larger common identity still seemed extremely liberating. It provided a welcome impetus for Slovene literary culture, which was trying to shake off one context and hopefully place itself within another, perhaps more amiable, context offering more support for autonomous growth.

My generation of writers, who came of age in the eighties, had few illusions about either of these broader contexts. We could overcome the once cozy, but now ever more suffocating, cloak of Yugoslavism less comfortably than our older Slovene colleagues, wearing our Central European culture nattily, like a cap of pride, that is to say, as a mark of self-esteem that was necessary, but hardly sufficient in itself.

But even with such efforts, Slovenes cannot simply close their eyes and hope that the legacy of Yugoslavia will disappear the way villages and towns did in the wars of the nineties. The same is true of the communist political and social heritage. It would be utterly naive to think we can put it in historical brackets. No use pretending that communism was nothing more than an accidental, if lengthy, nightmare from which Central and Eastern Europe awoke at the time of the velvet revolutions in 1989. Nor should we think it possible to go back to the pre-communist state of the nation. What a mistaken illusion! Our communist heritage will be with us for some time, since it colonized not only institutional structures and the fabric of society in general, but, most importantly of all, penetrated habits of the heart and customs of the mind that cannot be removed swiftly and with ease, in the manner of public monuments to disgraced leaders.

In any case, it must be admitted that communism provided the reading public in the West with an immediately recognizable context. The price writers paid for this elementary recognition was linked to the fact that Slovenes belonged to a certain larger community—the Yugoslav federation and communism. Of course, this community necessitated the use of pain and melancholy, decrepitude, and resistance in its literary works, which both confused and attracted Western readers. My friend and fellow writer, Andrej Blatnik, the author of the collection of subtle stories *Skinswaps* (1998), might be justified in saying that the Western literary market, forever on the lookout for the unknown and the exotic, likes to "import suffering." And although I agree that this factor plays a part in the business logic of the book trade and should not be disregarded, this tariff on imported suffering is paid only once, in the first attempt at winning the attention of Western readers and critics.

But once a writer establishes a presence in the international arena, the factor that counts most is a highly individualized imagination: the depth and originality of the aesthetic world the writer presents. Ismail Kadare, Zbigniew Herbert, Ivan Klima, Dubravka Ugresic, Peter Esterhazy, Evgeny Popov, Ana Blandiana, Dzevad Karahasan: I don't want to believe that the appeal these modern Central and East European writers hold for Western readers rests solely on the fact that they describe a certain historical curiosity, or that the interest in their works depends solely on external political events. We can assume, with a good measure of certainty, that in order to achieve international success and sustain interest, these writers had to create coherent literary worlds revealing multilayered images of integral experience—not only historical, but also metaphysical—and that these experiences intertwined aesthetic and ethical concerns in ways that are different from the texts of Western writers. These Central and East European writers, ultimately, present us with different moral struggles, different national cataclysms, and different involvement with emotions.

Such writers demonstrate, each through his or her own personal style, that in order to create art that will survive its time, it is not enough to chase after fashionable new trends. Art that is faithful to its existential purpose embodies nothing less than the longing to transcend human mortality. This is what any reader seeks in a literary work that will endure even after most contemporary literature will have turned into fodder for some future palimpsest.

But Slovene collective existence is more or less anonymous internationally. This fact hit home one summer during the mid-nineties, when I accompanied a foreign cultural journalist on his travels through my country. Post-communist Slovenia is gradually, and somewhat bashfully, opening itself to the wide world. Each year it receives more visitors: inquisitive Western journalists, adventurous students, businessmen, and international con artists. Slovene émigrés also return. Their children enroll in summer language classes and, in Australian, Latin American, or German accents, struggle to speak the mother tongue of their parents or grandparents. Little and irritatingly homogenous Slovenia will of course never become a Tower of Babel. A concert of foreign tongues nevertheless echoes off the cold walls of the renovated mansions that hug the river banks beneath Ljubljana Castle. This testifies to an interest in novelty, the kind of attention foreigners pay to a country that, with its newly won sovereignty, appeared so unexpectedly on the map of Europe.

As I travel around Slovenia with some of these foreigners, I often notice that things self-evident to me appear bewildering to them. After all, have I not for several years now been explaining the peculiarities of Slovene culture and mentality not only to my American wife, but to numerous visiting writers from abroad as well? Christopher Merrill, in his *Only the Nails Remain: Scenes from the Balkan War* (1997), certainly found some of my stabs at explanation valuable.

Still, I am somewhat disturbed by how provisional my accounts can be, rolling off many facets of communal life like water off a duck's back. The seductive gesture of a woman's hand and her down-turned eyes in a courtyard in the Mediterranean town of Piran; the collective obsession with the dangers of flu-inducing wind draft; the crowds of pilgrims at the Savica Waterfall in the Alps, where, according to a locally famous epic poem by the Romantic poet France Prešeren, the Slovene people converted to Christianity, the first of many historical conversions in the name of the collective survival: in the barefoot anthropology of foreign visitors, all these things represent a kind of encrypted mental code that might just explain this unusually small, yet perseverant, "tribe."

These joint trips proved to be a most interesting cultural experiment. They were itineraries of both pride and guilt, outlining the peculiar nature of contemporary Slovenian reality in which remnants of the old communist regime crossbreed with the achievements of the emerging democratic order. I had mistakenly thought I knew this country simply because I lived within its borders. It was thus sobering to accompany foreign visitors on their travels, for I was forced to briefly explain the history and customs of the various regions we visited. I soon discovered just how difficult it is to explain in concise, clear, and simple terms the differing political opinions regarding Slovene ethnogenesis, the faded glory of the seventh-century independent state of Carantania, the religious grip of the Roman Catholic Diocese of Aquileia, and the unquestioned Slovene identification with Alpine farming culture. I had attempted to provide a literary map of my country in an essay, *Slovenia: A Brief Literary History* (1999), largely as a response to my frustrations with curious visitors and their lack of information. Filling the void was necessary, lest get filled with condescension that fast-track journalists frequently mouth.

I remember one particular journalist well. He stood there, eyes wide open, out of breath after our brisk descent from the Renaissance castle in the town of Ptuj, about to step into a pub with a chrome-plated bar. The dust on the visor of his baseball cap had barely settled as he turned it around in a kind of studiously casual gesture so that the late summer sun shone on his bronzed face—a face that had seen Sudan, Ukraine, and Nepal. He was one of those visitors who get so inspired by beautiful landscapes, captivating small towns, sophisticated city life, and the easy-going local population, that when they return home they write a laudatory article about it all for the travel section of their newspaper. Now he was content simply to deliver a bit of honest, well-meaning praise: "Stay just as you are," he approvingly said, "hidden beneath the Alps, and don't let anyone know you're here!"

This is just a benign variation on that horribly persistent image of a nameless bucolic realm, where people live in fecund contact with nature and thus are not fully exposed to the harmful effects of Western technological civilization. This paradigm attracts nostalgic leftists, who for the most part still feed on the mistaken concept of "nations outside history." In a misguided flight from the alienated society of the postmodern West, they take refuge, possibly against their own inclinations, in the ideology of "blood and soil." The Austrian writer Peter Handke, in his provocative critique of Slovenian independence, *Dreamer's Farewell to the New Country: Memories of Slovenia* (Süddeutsche Zeitung, 1991), was perhaps the first to set forth this paradigm explicitly. I do not think I am being overly pessimistic if I say that this obnoxiously patronizing attitude will probably shape the Western perception of Slovenian creative efforts for a long time to come.

References

Blatnik, Andrej. *Skinswaps*. Evanston: Nortwestern University Press, 1998.

Debeljak, Aleš. "Slovenia: A Brief Literary History." In *Afterwards: Slovenian Writing, 1945-1995*. Edited by Andrew Zawacki. Buffalo, N. Y.: White Pine Press, 1999.

Kocbek, Edvard. *Embers in the House of Night: Selected Poems*. Translated by Sonja Kravanja. Santa Fe: Lumen Press, 1999.

Kundera, Milan. "The Tragedy of Central Europe." *New York Review of Books*, 31, no. 7 (1984): 33-38.

Melluci, Alberto. "Co-existing with Differences." *2B: Journal of Ideas*, no. 13 (1998): 140-141.

Merrill, Christopher. *Only the Nails Remain: Scenes from the Balkan Wars.* New York: Henry Holt & Co., 1997.

Wachtel, Andrew. *Making a Nation, Breaking a Nation: Literature and Cultural Politics in Yugoslavia.* Stanford: Stanford University Press, 1998.

Jörn Donner

Political decisions and actions are necessary
in order to establish a European community
of values. This is a difficult process, which, in the
long run, requires that we acknowledge one
another's differences and diverse experiences.
Literature plays only a marginal role in this process.
© Vidar Lindqvist

Jörn Donner

Finnland

Born in Helsinki in 1933, Jörn Donner is a writer,
politician, actor, and film director. Having completed his
studies at the University of Helsinki, he worked, initially, as
a film critic, writer, and author of travel books. In the
1960s Jörn Donner founded his own production
company, and from 1978 until 1982 he headed the
Swedish Film Institute. Until 1995 he was a member of the
Finnish Parliament (as a representative of the Swedish
People's Party) and in 1996 he was appointed to the post
of Finnish consul general in Los Angeles and elected as a
Social Democratic member of the European Parliament
until 1999. Since then he has worked as freelance writer
and producer.

Internationally, Donner is best known as a film director. He
considers his early works to be his best films: *En Söndag
i September (*A Sunday in September, *1963; Opera
Prima Prize, Venice 1963)* and *Black on White (1968)*.
Nevertheless, he is primarily a writer, having published 52
works (above all fiction, essays, and travel books*)*. His first
book appeared in 1951. He received the Finlandia Award
in 1985 for his novel *Far och Son* (Father and Son*)*.

*The following is a link to more detailed information on
Jörn Donner:*
http://www.kirjasto.sci.fi/jdonner.htm

Further Reading:
Report From Berlin. Translated by Anderson, Albin T.
Indiana University Press, 1961.
The Personal Vision of Ingmar Bergman, Indiana
University Press, 1964.

Europe from the Fringe

*För att en europeisk värdegemenskap skall bli
verklighet i vardagliga termer krävs politiska beslut och
politisk handling. Det är en lång process. Början har
blivit gjord. Det förutsätter att vi har kunskap om
varandras olikheter och olikartade erfarenheter.
Litteraturens roll är marginell.*

For my entire adult life I have been preoccupied with Europe and I
have visited every European country. And yet, apart from the Euro
that now unites twelve EU countries, the term "Europe" would
hardly be important in my everyday life. Although I live on the
fringe, I can imagine the sea (in front of my house) reaching down
to the Mediterranean, thus embracing a part of Europe. Europe also
borders on that ocean whose opposite coast incessantly influences
us and sometimes threatens those values that we would like to call
European.

The big difference between the European center and its periphery is hard to comprehend for those living in the center, which
includes a fairly big area: from France to Poland, from the northern
coasts of Germany to parts of Northern Italy, including the city of
Trieste, which has been eloquently depicted by Italo Svevo and
later by Claudio Magris.

Finland, Ireland, Portugal, and Greece belong to the periphery.
According to de Gaulle, in geographical terms Europe usually is
said to extend from the Atlantic to the Urals. However, to include
big parts of Russia in our discussion on Europe would make it
fairly complicated. Although Finland, during its process of na-
tionalization in the nineteenth century, was partly influenced by
European ideas imported from St. Petersburg, legislation and the
judicial system were the products of Western influences.

The cultural impact from the European center to the periphery was at its strongest during the years before World War I, when intellectuals and academics used German, French and, to a certain extent, Latin as their *lingua francae*. This trend came to an end with the increasing influence of Anglo-Saxon, especially American, culture following World War II. In most of the more developed European countries English replaced German and French as the first foreign language, a process that accelerated in the age of the computer and internet. Everyday European life has become dominated by music, film, and TV from the United States. No "defense" has yet been found against this.

Migration within Europe, sometimes voluntary, sometimes forced, has always been significant. For example, as a punishment for the inhumanity of Nazi Germany, more than ten million Germans were forced to migrate to the West, leaving regions where their families had lived for centuries — and far from each of them actually shared Marion Dönhoffs elevated and sympathetic attitude. Although the German migrants did not have to adapt to a new language, they moved to a diminished country that would be divided for a long time.

Contrary to the Germans, millions of Hungarians, who were punished for Hungary's support of the Central Powers during World War I, were forced not only to change their citizenship, but to endure a new linguistic hegemony as well, though in most cases this did not entail leaving their homes. Alsatians changed citizenship in the same manner, without geographical displacement, four times within a period of seventy-five years.

Migration from within Europe has been at least as important as that from without. Until 1918 Finland was a mere agrarian society, having undergone immense demographic changes during the previous four decades, which involved migration from the countryside to the villages, from the villages to the cities, from north to south, and even to Sweden, where the language was different, but the living conditions similar. As throughout Europe, the process of urbanization was dramatic.

Before the birth of modern nationalism, when Europe was more open, enterprising Europeans set off to foreign lands in pursuit of a better future. My own family history serves as an illustration. In 1694 a German from Lübeck moved to a fortified Swedish town, which was later to become St. Petersburg, to work as a school-teacher. He later fled with his pupils via Viborg to Helsinki, and then went on to Stockholm. His offspring, however, married into a family from Gamlakarleby, on the west coast of Finland, as a result of which my grandfather went to study in Helsinki, the site of what at the time was Finland's only university. There my family settled.

Migration, voluntary or otherwise, results not only in geographical change, but in linguistic change as well. In the United States, which is monolingual in theory, but in fact multilingual and multicultural, neither academic nor economic success can be achieved without knowledge of English, whereas Europe, with its variety of national languages, has remained a Tower of Babel. However, we often forget to acknowledge the existence of linguistic enclaves on our continent. These fragments are far too often overlooked, their survival depending primarily on the benevolence of the nations to which they belong. An example of this is Sami, a language spoken in Norway, Sweden, and Finland, which has recently experienced a renaissance.

European languages are often said to enjoy equal rights. This is not true. Especially in the field of literature, we can see a one-way street leading from bigger to smaller languages. To be familiar with the European literary and intellectual heritage implies the knowledge of Montaigne, Goethe, Shakespeare, and Cervantes, but not a thorough knowledge of the Polish literary tradition. Every now and then the periphery can have an impact on the center, as in the case of James Joyce, who, like Musil and Proust, nonetheless wrote in one of Europe's major languages.

If, especially after the expansion of the EU, linguistic unity proves nearly impossible to achieve, what about focusing on something else, such as a common European ideal or idea?

Against the background of a Europe that caused both world wars and the deaths of some tens of millions of people, such an idea might seem bold.

Furthermore, the practical problems involved in achieving this cannot be easily overcome; to illustrate this I would like to describe the evolution of my attitude toward Europe, an attitude that is full of paradoxes arising from various historical experiences. I am fully aware of the fact that familiarity with both the history of one's own country and that of Europe will generally diminish, since the school system tends to focus on market-oriented skills and further education. What does an adult Greek actually know about us?

In spite of widespread migration, people relate primarily to a region, or even a locality, and only secondarily to a nation or a continent, which in our case happens to be Europe. Because identification with a continent is by no means natural, I do not believe that the majority of people understand Europe as a vivid concept; instead they might associate Europe with certain countries with which they happen to be familiar through books or travel.

For me, as a Finnish-Swede, the term *Europe* became defined only gradually, as I will try to explain. I entered adult life during the Cold War years, in the early fifties. By coincidence I first encountered the European continent in Berlin during the summer of 1952. The city was still in post-war condition, which I discovered when I later visited those parts of Europe under Soviet custody, would last until 1989. As early as 1952, the contrast between the two parts of Berlin was striking, though some of the differences could still be explained by the fact that the three united western sectors were the recipients of generous subsidies, while East Berlin already bore the burden of a repressive political system. One of my first conclusions was that political dictatorship did not get along well with the European idea. In that case Europe would be small.

In 1952 Helsinki hosted the Olympics, in which the Soviet Union participated. In that same year Finland paid the last installment of fairly burdensome war reparations, imposed because the Finns had fought two wars—the first, in 1939–40, in defense of their country against Soviet aggression and the second, between 1941 and 1944, as *co-belligerents* in Nazi Germany's aggression against the Soviet Union. According to the terms of the armistice, Finland was forced not only to pay harsh economic indemnities, but also had to promise to expel the Germans from the north of Finland. On April 25, 1945 the last German troops withdrew from the country.

The Finno-Soviet "Pact of Friendship and Mutual Assistance"

cast a shadow over Finland's connection to Europe. It implied that Finland, allied with the Russians, was supposed to defend itself against an attack from Germany or a German ally, which clearly suggested that Finnish integration into Western Europe would be nearly impossible, both then and in the future.

In spite of this pact, whose influence on daily life was minimal, Finland underwent a process of development resembling that taking place in Western Europe. Trade relations expanded with the most important export countries, especially Germany. Increasing Anglo-Saxon hegemony left its marks not only on Finnish culture, but on the sciences and technology as well. When traveling became a more general phenomenon thanks to charter tourism, Spain, Italy, and other countries of southern Europe became popular destinations; however, the travelers went in quest not of profound knowledge, but of sun.

In politics the situation was rather different due to the officially declared "eternal friendship" with the USSR. Any attempt to gain Moscow's sympathy for the concept of Finnish neutrality in the conflict between the great powers was in vain. Through clever diplomacy, however, the Finnish government eventually managed to convince Moscow to assent to free trade between Finland and Europe, marking the birth of the country's economic and political integration, though it would take until 1989 before Finland dared to apply for membership to even such a harmless organization as the Council of Europe in Strasbourg.

The question of where we stand and why would become more and more important to me during the Cold War years. Writing was a means of taking a stand on crucial ideological issues. This (but not only this) prompted me to travel around Europe as much as possible. Again, my focus centered on Berlin, which I depicted in my book *Report from Berlin*, published in 1958. Four years later, in a book about the countries situated along the Danube, I offered a conclusion that seemed natural to me: "The two systems that have been contrasted in this book, communism and liberal Western democracy, are incompatible. They have almost nothing in common; to claim anything else is an illusion. Our Europe is divided by a frontier reinforced with barbed wire, a wall, trenches, death zones." Many people believed that these two antithetical systems would gradually come closer. The term "peaceful coexistence" was coined to assuage the fear of war.

Under these circumstances Finland's unique balancing act seems understandable: on the one hand the official politics that kept the Soviet Union at bay in a loose embrace of friendship; on the other a society that actually subscribed to Western European ideals. In the mass media Finland became a victim of self-censorship, which gave rise to the frequent allegation of "Finlandization." This might be interpreted as a critique of the fact that Soviet demands were taken into consideration and, above all, that the socialist system had not been the target of open criticism. Finland remained officially neutral, that is, abstained from taking a stand regarding Germany in 1953, Hungary in 1956, and Czechoslovakia in 1968, though the news coverage of these events was sufficient.

Neither then nor later were officials ready to admit what should have been evident: that the country profited from the NATO policy that implied "up to here, but no farther" at the time of the erection of the Berlin wall in 1961 and later. The nuclear threat provided protection against the Soviet Union. At the same time economies in Western Europe expanded at an unprecedented pace. The Russians tried many times to gain diplomatic recognition for their vassal state, the GDR, though Finland gave in only after East and West moved closer as a result of Willy Brandt's politics of reconciliation.

During the years I am describing here, many young people espoused more radical political opinions, especially in Germany and France. In Scandinavia these changing attitudes were often reflected in criticism of US policies in Vietnam, as symbolized by Olaf Palme. This student radicalism produced the events of 1968, though, strangely enough, in Finland we had a leftist movement that supported not only China, but the Soviet Union as well. The naiveté was phenomenal. The GDR served as a model for many.

As in other Western European countries, young Finnish radicals attempted to secure key positions at colleges and universities. They succeeded to some extent. People who held different opinions were labeled "anti-soviet," a term that was applied to me as well because

I had offered outspoken support for the values for which the Western European community stood.

One of my novels deals with a young man, who resembles me to a certain extent, from whom the Russians wanted to gain information regarding the attitude of intellectuals toward the Soviet Union. This, in fact, happened—and in my case it was accompanied by lavish amounts of food and drink. The Russians quit trying when they realized that I did not know anything that could be of any use or interest to them. However, I became aware at an early stage that the East German secret service was able to recruit a number of Finns as IM (Unofficial Collaborator) and furthermore, that it would likely require a long time for the extensive network of contacts that the GDR had established in my country to be exposed. Information that Western diplomats and journalists could gain through mere conversation, others tried to procure with money and other bribes, though instances of ideologically motivated treason occurred as well.

Our European reality did not change suddenly during the crucial years between 1989 and 1991, when Hungary opened its borders with the West, the Berlin wall came down, and the Soviet Union collapsed. As for Finland, these events enabled the country to act autonomously, which eventually resulted in its joining the European Union in 1995. In my *Report from Europe* (1990) I predicted the coming of a period of insecurity, due partly to the enormous social and economic gaps existing between European countries and regions. This insecurity still exists.

Literature plays only a minor and, in fact, totally subordinate role in this process. Vaclav Havel's status in Czechoslovakia has often been cited as a counterexample, though this cannot be ascribed primarily to his writings, but to the ideological dimension of his actions and to his symbolical position as a spokesman for change. Although writers did act as a mouthpiece for change in East Germany in 1989, the Monday prayers in Leipzig and the mass demonstrations were actually grassroots phenomena.

The basis of all of this was the complete failure of socialism as a political and economic system, its effort to standardize opinion, which you could easily observe in Germany just by watching TV, in the same way as Estonians, who were able to watch Finnish TV and were thus able to see the abyss that separated the two even linguistically related countries. Had it not been for the collapse of the Soviet empire, to free the people of Central and Eastern Europe without bloodshed would not have been easy. The words of Willy Brandt came to my mind: "You don't live of freedom, but in freedom." That was the crucial point.

Marx, Freud, and Churchill were ideologues whose writings directly and indirectly exerted a strong influence over Europe, at least if you believe in the historical role of the individual, a fact that is relevant in regard to a destructive role such as Hitler's, which is based on a single text, written in prison. Still, in spite of the poetic power of the *Communist Manifesto*, the clairvoyance of Freud's cultural criticism, and the majestic prose of Churchill in his depiction of the English-speaking world or of World War II, it would be difficult to call these men writers.

From early in my adult life I have been aware of the limits of writing when it comes to the creation of a more humane society, which is why I later decided to go into politics. In view of the enormous destruction Europe has endured, it would be imperative for us to establish a common ground of values, which is probably defined most succinctly in Karl Popper's *The Open Society*, or civil society. However, not even the EU countries seem to agree on the implications of this term. The Copenhagen Agreement of 1993 was an attempt to define the criteria for membership, though not all EU members accept these criteria wholeheartedly.

What about equality under the law, equal education, a media free of political pressure, the right to unhindered travel, reliable tax systems, and equal income regardless of gender when enormous gaps between the countries and the regions still exist, when the income gaps between rich and poor are still increasing, and when some of the members view with expansion towards the east with thinly concealed animosity because they are afraid of losing some of their subsidies, mainly those to support agriculture? Solidarity reaches as far as one's own nation, but no further.

A central question in this context is how people relate to the state and public power. Should our relationship to the state be defined by benevolence or dislike? It is understandable that those who were living under a repressive Soviet system still regard the state with suspicion. However, even in Western Europe there is an increasing tendency, based on the apparent success of the American model, to diminish the role of government in society, maintaining state control only over those functions deemed to be absolutely necessary and leaving to individual citizens complete responsibility for managing themselves and their incomes.

Two groups suffer directly from such politics: the sick and the unemployed, for whom the state functions as a social and economical security net; and the artists and intellectuals. Especially in a small country it is absolutely impossible to maintain important cultural institutions such as theatres and libraries and media such as television without considerable public subsidy; this is not to mention the work of individual artists, who rarely achieve economic viability in a total market economy on a small national territory.

This was another reason why I entered politics.

But what does European openness actually mean when open borders (at least in the Schengen countries) are proclaimed and put into practice, while migration from countries outside the EU, especially from the Balkans, Africa, and Asia, is discouraged, albeit with limited success, because it is believed, though rarely said, that EU-Europe, with its variety of lingual and ethnic minorities, cannot bear further immigration on top of that which it has already absorbed over the last three decades and which has, in fact, transformed several Central European countries, in which assimilation is often nearly impossible, into multicultural societies.

Europe applies an economic double-standard as well through its trade barriers against countries that would presumably gain greater profit through free trade than through the marginal subsidies given in the form of foreign aid.

To work with words presupposes that you are part of a linguistic community or a country. However, there is a complication. I write in Swedish in a country in which ninety-four percent of the population is Finnish-speaking. Though I write in Swedish, the market for my books is not in Sweden, but in Finland, translated into Finnish, because the historical experience my writing mirrors is Finnish, not Swedish. This is a specific experience that cannot easily be transferred. This is why, when talking about Europe, I must use political terms in order to describe an imagined community. The fact that I was also inspired by German writers as diverse as Musil, Brecht and Thomas Mann is another story.

Political decisions and actions are necessary in order to establish a European community of values. This is a difficult process, which, in the long run, requires that we acknowledge one another's differences and diverse experiences. Literature plays only a marginal role in this process. To understand all this, it is necessary to listen to what Titus Petronius Arbiter said two-thousand years ago: "Those who step on the sand of foreign shores shall grow in stature."

— *Translated by Dagmar Brunow*

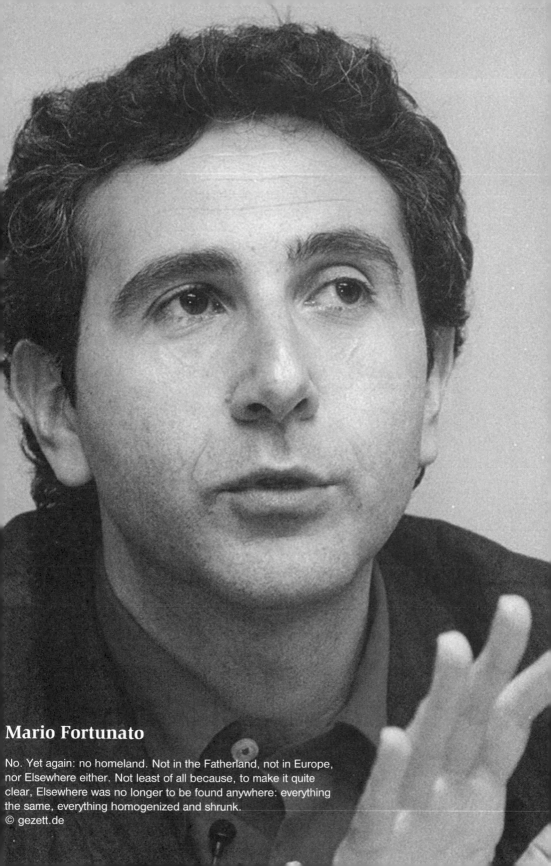

Mario Fortunato

No. Yet again: no homeland. Not in the Fatherland, not in Europe,
nor Elsewhere either. Not least of all because, to make it quite
clear, Elsewhere was no longer to be found anywhere: everything
the same, everything homogenized and shrunk.

Mario Fortunato
Italy

Born in Cirò, Calabria in 1958, Mario Fortunato studied
philosophy in Rome. He is the author of poems, short
stories, and novels. He has worked for radio and has
contributed to several screenplays. Since 2000 he has
been director of the Italian Cultural Institute in London.
Authors such as Doris Lessing and Salman Rushdie
signed an appeal against his planned removal by the
Italian government. Mario Fortunato publishes regularly in
the weekly magazine *L'Espresso* and the daily newspaper
La Stampa.

Europe?

*No. Ancora una volta: nessuna patria. Non in Patria, né
in Europa e neppure Altrove. (Anche perché, detto per
inciso, l'Altrove non si trovava più da nessuna parte:
tutto uguale, tutto uniformato al basso.)*

I was born in the south of Italy. Cirò, province of Crotone, Calabria. A
middle-class family, agnostics for many generations, with a little
Jewish blood hidden in there somewhere. The landscape—not yet
sullied by eight-story buildings right there on the water's edge, but
on the contrary, still well-preserved by poverty—suggested, in every
sense, silence and sobriety. It was a rugged, rather harsh, and unen-
ticing landscape. The sea (the Ionian Sea) possessed the same characteristics: to reach it, tremendous odysseys of a few kilometers on
dirt roads, real, heavily sweated excursions under an overhead sun;
on the beach not even a shadow of a bar, or dancing, or beach huts.
The village: works in progress everywhere, which made it seem like
the most ill-fated banlieu of Tripoli. And all Catholic, ever so Catholic: with the habit, very typical of these parts, of embarking on great
discourses and world systems, while the roof of the house, look here,
it's falling in, or while the neighbors ("but how's it possible?") literally wander about with proverbial patches on the seats of their pants.
Few young people: those who could fled, or better, emigrated.
Whereas a lot old folk awaiting other worlds.

But if the context (in every sense) prompted silence if one
wanted to make a quick getaway, the family did not. The family, (a
blessing, given the atmosphere) spoke mostly the language of irony
and discretion. At the time this language seemed to me, in sum, to
be that of all refugees, which one can be—and how—without even
leaving one's own country.

Well then: a very liberal and witty lawyer father, a housewife mother with a sincere passion for hypochondria, brothers and sisters already adult, flown off to study or marry. And long, memorable afternoons reading everything at the advice of this same family. But for the most part with a preference for the literature of other countries: the French, the English, the Germans ... and with the complicity of a centenarian grandfather of vast European culture, tall, somewhat a snob, I made plans: shall I live in Paris, Heidelberg, or London? (Budapest and Prague, given the times, seemed decidedly inaccessible: I was already on the Left, but within reason).

There you have it: Europe was still a mental space. A space in which to travel far and wide in one's imagination. Rapidly and with great desire.

But what do I mean by that? That in the period of childhood and adolescence, both by origin and descent, I really knew very little about the concept of fatherland, and I didn't care. Or rather, to tell it all, every time I heard it being mentioned, I thought there was definitely some swindle involved. Or again: the fatherland was the thing with a capital F in whose name, at eighteen years old, you were quite possibly flung to the other end of Italy, to Trent or to Aosta, for twelve months, all expenses paid, to "serve the fatherland" of all things. Or again: the fatherland (but here it shaded off into that somewhat more diabolical concept of State) was what imposed, at least once a year, the payment of taxes and surtaxes, scots and imposts, while they could also boast of: widespread unemployment, with proportionate emigration (to the North or to Germany), prehistoric public services, school attendance *au degré zéro*, highly dangerous hospitals, and a jolly, well-organized criminal underworld on a first-name basis with the politicos, then mostly Christian Democrats.

In short: as a boy, I did not like the very concept of fatherland. It was something alien and suspect. And I continued to think of it like this as the years went on.

I wasn't living in the poor and deep south anymore, but had

taken a step this way, towards Europe. Rome was large and tepid —
not only because of the climate. Advantageously anonymous. But
then, looked at carefully from the privileged observatories of university dining halls or from the ever-so-pleasant student dormito-
ries, Rome didn't comfort me a great deal. Nothing worked de-
cently here either. Not a show or a concert to see at all costs
(making sacrifices, but useful and profitable ones). Not a lecture at
the university that began on time and with enough seats. And also
outside the lecture halls: a city barbarized by terrorism, where
everyone took his own, wretched faults out on to his dumbest
neighbor.

Meanwhile, I heard it being said around me, the era of television
had been born. The medium had existed for some time, but only
now was it unfolding in all of its geometric potency. Television was
the true social glue of Italians. The new twelve-inch Fatherland.

Now it was proclaimed that everything was spectacle, fiction,
unreality: the same thin soup warmed up again for the consumption of a new public of users who, thanks to commercial TV, could
now democratically bring on their own misfortunes before foot-
lights and "open the debate." While the imperious popularity rat-
ings and audience-share only made one regret the passing of the
time when aunts did not wander about television studios outlining
the sociocultural causes for the screwing they'd done in their
younger days, when grandparents, grandchildren, nieces, nephews,
and cousins did not yet tear each other apart live from Studio 5, but
washed their dirty linen with dignity in their own homes. And if it
wasn't long-time drug addicts explaining twice a day "what we are
not, what we do not want," it was intellectuals and critics making a
fine display of obscene language, stupidities, and insults learned in
the course of so many years of study. Or else it was ministers and
politicians appearing on the small screen, omnipresent, with their
inanities, ever more wondrously esoteric and vapid.

This then was the Fatherland: a cock-up (metaphorical) between
a put-down and a set-up.

I convinced myself that there was a great disaster all around me,
but well-publicized on the hour by newspapers and journalists,
without there being even one who, now and again, absent mind-

edly, would stand up and say: you build a subway like this, you manage a museum like that, and you make a hospital function like so. Nothing. One became ever more confused and out-of-it from the painfully detailed stupidities of behavior and economic crises resolved by firing people and deregulation. So, thanks also to the odd good book, I adjusted myself to living in a "Country without," as a title of those years put it, and also maybe without a Country. From which I fled as often as possible and whenever I could: by air, by train, hitchhiking. In any case, away: a lover of abroad as all true provincials are, and discovering with some horror that our "model of development" was spreading, flooding all over Europe.

So, after my early infatuation with efficiently run subways and competent bureaucracies, while running left and right in an attempt to escape from the Fatherland, I began to come to grips with the sinister and threatening London of the fearsome Mrs. Thatcher, with Berlin unified and economically devastated, with Paris lecturing everyone and then voting for Le Pen, with the medium- and small-sized cities which, on the glorious American model, exalt blacks who beat you up to the sound of rap because you're white, and vice-versa.

And certainly the Maastricht Parameters weren't enough to soothe me. Perhaps I was still too young, but honestly I didn't see the benefits.

Already faded by the passing of a few, regretted seasons, a time of going to seek and make up new homelands almost everywhere in Europe, I found myself trapped, always and everywhere. Always uncomfortable. Everywhere: as Christopher Isherwood and a whole pack of books had warned.

No. Yet again: no homeland. Not in the Fatherland, not in Europe, nor Elsewhere either. (Not least of all because, to make it quite clear, Elsewhere was no longer to be found anywhere: everything the same, everything homogenized and shrunk).

And even during the Gulf War, where I went among the ruins and the tragedies, among journalists who frequently refused to leave their hotels, where they fattened themselves on their expense accounts, this sense of planetary homogeneity, of creeping cynicism, struck me, when between one bombardment and another one only heard discussions about going on live television and of: "Is war a just or unjust instrument? Pre-emptive or therapeutic?" As if they were all at a communal meeting. Still the same, even today.

Uprooting, therefore. And a certain prejudice against sayings of the type: "My fatherland is writing," followed by dreariness and mockery. Those little frigid, freezing, schoolmarmy squeaks, so very modern, never convinced me. And then I never gave a fig for "the text-as-listening," or for "fictional-space," or for "the word-which-dwells-in-silence." Taken over by more sordid tasks (bills, rent, dermatitis, and South-American prices), I was looking instead for the strength to ask myself, with sincerity: but why replace one rhetoric with another? To go and join the queue of status-symbol literature, of intellectual pret-à-porter? My God, no. So as not to have to listen to conversations of that kind, I felt driven to seek the company of dentists, real estate agents, lawyers, office-workers, hairdressers. At least instead of the usual generic, empty nonsense, I could hear more scintillating and secular discussions about pooh and pee.

So, by now, living in London, the doubt finally comes to me that it is not in search of homelands that one should go, but of a little good and simple civility—not much of it about. And I began, as in the old days, to see it in some trusted friend, from whatever point of the compass. In fact belonging is nothing more than this: the affection binding us to persons, or to things.

In the meanwhile, economic Europe is born. The euro is born. But in England it's not a done deal. I still need exchange rates, banks, even my passport. It will seem strange and unfriendly to say so, but I don't mind it. It's like an antidote to the prevailing rhetoric. It reminds me that Europe is something more than a simple coin.

— *Translated by Bettina Gabbe*

Eugenio Fuentes

If, as a writer, I try to grasp what Europe
means for the people who walk its streets,
it is my duty to warn that the concept holds
both promises and threats.
© Luis Casero

Eugenio Fuentes
Spain

Born in Montehermoso (Cáceres) in 1958, Eugenio
Fuentes studied Spanish literature and worked as a
teacher. He has published many short stories in
magazines and anthologies. Since 1997 he has written
commentaries for *ABC* and other newspapers. For his
novels set in his home region of Extremadura, he has
received numerous awards, including the Premio Cáceres
de Novela Corta in 1990, the Premio Internacional de
Novela Ciudad de San Fernando in 1993, and the Premio
de Novela Extremadura a la Creación in 1997. In 1999 he
received the Premio Alba/Prensa Canaria for *En el interior
del bosque*.

Further Reading:
The Depths of the Forest. Translated by Paul Antill.
Independent Publishers Group, 2002.
The Blood of the Angels. Arcadia Books, 2004
(forthcoming).

The Western Bloc

*Si, como escritor, intento aprehender qué es Europa
para los personajes que recorren sus calles, advierto
que es al mismo tiempo una promesa y una amenaza.*

I

When navigators from my country arrived in America for the first
time they were searching for a new maritime route around the
world from the west to reach the spice-rich East Indies. It didn't
take many more journeys for them to realize that what they had
found was a new continent, which they called the West Indies before it was eventually given its definitive name. European colonial
expansion into the new lands and the imposition of the colonizers'
languages, doctrines, and customs meant that Europe and America
ended up forming a bloc called the West, to differentiate itself from
the East. Ever since, with the passing of the centuries, history has
cited Europe and America as a unit with a more or less similar attitude towards the rest of the world, sharing more or less similar
culture, beliefs, and customs.

However, in this third millennium it may be necessary to establish another, more detailed geographic entity, because the traditional division into two cultural hemispheres has become imprecise. It is still too early to say, but the latest political orientations
and changes may be introducing significant differences that distinguish two different poles of gravity in the West: the European and
the American. Although this has not yet caused a short-circuit between the two sides of the Atlantic, there are already sparks of
dissonance warning of a clash of attitudes.

After the terrorist outrages of September 11, the United States changed its political outlook, becoming more globally and unilaterally aggressive. It now appears intent on creating a new world order in which Europe, speaking metaphorically, could find itself tied to two runaway horses galloping unchecked in opposite directions and threatening to tear it to pieces: on the one side, Bush's warmongering policies—I don't think we should use the word *doctrine*—and his decision to impose military and political hegemony on the rest of the world; on the other, the terrorist movements, with their spectacular, bloody, and grisly acts. In the face of both, the European option should be, more than ever, to consolidate and defend its identity.

Among other things, the twentieth century has bequeathed to us a fundamental lesson: a country can only be at peace within its own borders. In the past, under colonialism, dominion over other peoples brought wealth and prestige to the dominant power. Today things are less simple. With the onset of globalization and the newfound ease of transporting goods and people, any nation that is bent on the domination of other peoples is exposed to risks, to an uncomfortable state of alert, to huge expenses that cannot be offset by whatever benefits it derives from domination, to cruel attacks, to fear amongst the civilian population. In short, to instability.

Fortunately, Europe appears to be free of this temptation. Although Europeans watched with horror the attacks against the Twin Towers, and have cooperated in the subsequent efforts to ensure that it could never happen again, they did not use these events as an excuse to mount a permanent crusade. I believe that in spite of all the inevitable implications, September 11 was not, nor should it be considered, the starting point of a new world order in which Europe distances itself from the principles that shaped its identity, its personality, its very essence.

Our culture is made up of the sum of Hebrew theology, Greek tradition, and the social, geographic, and legislative organization of Rome, all of it superimposed on the previous cultural capital of each people. It is the sum of these influences that defines us; and although there is still unfortunately room for the occasional welling up of barbaric tendencies, these three main sources of our historic heritage contain everything we need to define ourselves as a continent of peace and civilization.

I have selected a few ideas derived from these sources that, in my view, have made Europe into a privileged place in which a large part of the population lives in freedom and contentment: the civic awareness that a community must be guided by political representatives elected at the polls and not by a shady oligarchy of powerful men; the outright separation of church and state and tolerance toward others' beliefs and customs; a healthy respect for the shared history of Europe's peoples — to quote the words of Ortega, "European society predates the existence of the European nation state"[1]; scrupulous respect for human rights and a ban on the death penalty; the memory of atrocious wars, both civil and national, and the subsequent pain of atonement; skepticism toward any kind of utopia; the maturity to surrender legally held territory and submit to the international legal order of which Kant used to dream[2]; the determination of governments and society not to allow citizens' social well-being to be governed by market forces; the requirement of neutrality; punishment of corruption in bureaucratic and administrative systems; consensus in developing the Third World; a concern for the environment, for protecting forests, rivers, and seas and making cities habitable; the primacy of knowledge over opinion; the certainty that science and technology alone cannot meet all of man's needs; the acknowledgement that Culture is not a mere ornamental or ancillary aspect, but the very foundation upon which the basic institutions by which we are governed have been built; the tendency to resort to the vast body of culture handed down to us over the generations for inspiration and support in dark times, in the knowledge that there will always be a book, a piece of music, or a painting in which to find solace.

II

When writing, I always ask myself, "what is happening on the streets that doesn't find its way into books?" Or, to put it another way, how much does what takes place on the streets of Europe affect the content of its books? To answer this question, the writer must constantly query the interface between his mind and the outside world.

In my case, this process of questioning has expanded from a regional to a European level as my own outlook has gradually expanded.

Practically all the books I have written up to now have been set against a single background, a fictitious place whose geographic location could be situated in northern Extremadura, the region where I was born and where I live. Its genesis corresponds to the ancient idea that the entire universe is contained in the tiniest stone, that the entire animal kingdom is to be found expressed in the most modest butterfly, that a single tree contains the potential essence of an entire forest. So when one speaks of a stone, one is speaking of the world itself.

The name of that imaginary place is "Breda," which, as you all know, is also the name of a Dutch town. I gave it this place name, which is a departure from regional and customary names, because in the story it is founded by a veteran of the wars in Flanders. Breda is a place where no one can call me to account for my actions, where I can grant passage to whomever I choose, where I banish characters or create their descendants; the story unfolds in 1985, a few years after Spain emerged from an interminable dictatorship and a few months before it joined the European Union. At the time the Pyrenees Mountains were still something more than a mere geographic barrier. However, even then the influence of European history was already coloring my writing; I was well aware that Spain's relationship with Europe had made the country what it was and what it is now. In the words of Gadamer, himself pondering on the Europe of 1985, I was "looking backwards in order to be able to look forwards."[3]

The novel I have been writing over the past two years features a woman who is looking for the father of her son. Her journey begins in Madrid and takes her all the way to Cadiz, Europe's southernmost point, where she contemplates the masses fleeing north from wretched and teeming Africa, before traveling all the way up to the northern Baltic. The Greek geographer Estrabon once noted in amazement that a squirrel might cross the Iberian peninsula without ever coming down from the trees; today, two-thousand years later, the descendants of the men who lived at that time can criss-cross almost all of Europe—from Tarifa in the far South to the Norwegian fjords, from Finisterre to the banks of the Volga, from Hamburg to Sulina, without getting out of the train or car to cross a border.

I believe that were it not for some of the journeys I have made in the past, were it not for the new political and social integration of Europe and the newfound feeling of being at home in the other countries of Europe, I would never have written this novel.[4]

However, the transition from a regional to a continental outlook has not been without its upheavals. If, as a writer, I try to grasp what Europe means for the people who walk its streets, it is my duty to warn that the concept holds both promises and threats. Europe is promising for many people because being part of it en-sures they have a stake in the progress and the security that I men-tioned earlier. It is threatening for others because they feel that the European Union constitutes a rejection of everything traditional, rural, and manual in favor of things new, urban, and technological. Thus a polarization is emerging between the opposed yearnings of escapism and permanence; Europeans are split between loyalty to their roots and the temptations of a multicultural population. The ability of leaders and thinkers to show people that belonging to a Whole do not necessarily imply betrayal of their unique origins will be crucial in order to ensure the future of this dream.

I come from a poor region, in a country not known for its riches, where this tension between tradition and progress is in constant evidence. Part of my book is therefore dedicated to describing a number of characters who, moved by the unease that stems from hardship, become embroiled in an internationalized world that is completely alien to them as the old order wanes forever.

— *Translated by Stephanie Carmona*

1 José Ortega y Gasset, *De Europa meditatio quaedam,* Complete Works, vol. 9 (Revista de Occidente, 1971); Sir James George Frazer, in his

monumental work, *The Golden Bough*, shows examples of how the same ancestral rites and customs are repeated throughout ethnographic Europe.

2 Jürgen Habermas, "Political essays" (Peninsula, 2002), p. 128.

3 Hans-Georg Gadamer, *Die Vielfalt Europas—Erbe und Zukunft* (Stuttgart, 1985), p. 20.

4 It will be my small contribution, covering all the distances, to the current abundance of European authors who travel, observe and write about countries in which they were not born. See Claudio Magris: *The Danube;* W. G. Seebald: *Saturn's rings*; Cees Nooteboom: *The Detour to Santiago*; Rafael Chirbes: *Mediterraneans.* All of them speak of European soil as if it were their own, almost with familiarity, without seeking exotic or outrageous facts like the romantic travelers.

Jens Christian Grøndahl

We are all storytellers rather than representatives of this
or that common, but limited, cultural kinship, that we are
indeed the narrators of those intertwining tales that form
the ever-changing web that is human civilization.
© Maxim Segienko/PHOTOMAX

Jens Christian Grøndahl

Denmark

Born in 1959, Jens Christian Grøndahl studied philosophy
in Copenhagen. He trained to be a film director and wrote
radio plays and essays. He has received many awards for
his novels, which have been published in over twenty
countries. He achieved a breakthrough in 1996 with his
novel *Tavshed i oktober* (*Silence in October*).

Further Reading:

Silence in October. Translated by Anne Born. Canongate
Books Ltd, 2000.
Lucca. Translated by Anne Born. Canongate Books Ltd.,
2002.
Virginia. Translated by Anne Born. Canongate Books Ltd,
2003.

Notes of an Escapist

Literature travels well, and it does so because for individual writers, writing, as life itself, is a journey that releases them from the confinements of hereditary identities, taking them into the unknown.

I was in St. Petersburg a couple of years ago and read from my novel *Lucca* to a group of students. After the reading, one of them asked, rather fascinated, how it was that Danes could leave their partner and find a new place to live just like that. It wasn't the leaving part that seemed to intrigue her, it was the question of finding an apartment. I suppose that she had no choice but to live with her parents, whether they got along or not. This is possibly the widest gap of understanding I've encountered since being translated into other languages.

The young Russian reminded me that my characters belong to the privileged Western middle classes and have freedom as their major problem rather than material necessities such as a roof over one's sinful Western head. Our gap of understanding was social rather than cultural. Once married, young Russians may not be able to move out on one another just like that, though I am sure some of them would like to.

Apart from that afternoon in St. Petersburg, I am usually asked the same questions in Paris, Amsterdam, New York, Barcelona, or Hamburg, and quite often I struggle to find new, ingenious answers. This probably testifies to my general lack of ingenuity, but I also take the recurring questions as a token that somehow people can relate to what I have written, no matter who they are, where they live, or which culture they belong to. (We shall see about that, though, when some day I am published in Afghanistan.)

It is possible that I talk like this because I, myself, belong to that secular, globalized, relentlessly alienating Western middle-class culture, which has practically no culture left at all. But I don't think so. I think that I am also touching upon what novels are and what they do.

We are constantly being told that people cannot understand one another because of their cultural differences, and these days I have to remind myself all the time that understanding is less about what people can do than about what they are willing to. As I see it, there would be no novelists in this world without the will at least to give understanding a try, allowing for how much there is to know and how little of it all we shall ever fathom.

Writing is a strange operation, adding to culture by revolting against it. Most of us write in our mother tongue, and that may seem like a comforting notion; but then again, who can imagine himself spending a lifetime under his mother's skirt? For the writer growing up means finding a voice of one's own, an approach to language that will almost make it sound like your own invention, interpreting the old words in a way that makes them resonate with personal thought and experience.

This may seem like an overwhelming endeavor since all we have is the language handed down by the cultural community to which we belong, including what others have written before us. What we write, having become literature, will eventually merge into that national tradition and hopefully enrich it, perhaps even change it a bit. But if culture is enriched and changed by the work of writers it is because they have challenged the social function of language, that being the affirmation and certification of the values and conventions of this or that culture, or subculture for that matter. Even minority groups and so-called avant-garde movements are often afflicted with conventions, prejudice, and oppressive decorum.

Literature should do the opposite. At least that is the only demand on it that I myself would ever accept: to question those values and conventions, to challenge the communal urge to belong, to transcend the imagined barriers between "us" and "them," and to celebrate imagination as the adventure of individual freedom.

As I write, exploring the endless possibilities of human experience, creating characters seemingly out of the blue, I discover that I, myself, am the product of my own imagination, the protagonist of the ongoing story of my life. This doesn't mean that I could be anyone; it means that identity is closely linked with the very act of storytelling, just as literature reminds us that we are all storytellers rather than representatives of this or that common, but limited, cultural kinship, that we are indeed the narrators of those intertwining tales that form the ever-changing web that is human civilization.

The wonderful thing about literature is that it remains faithful to a personal point of view while at the same time transforming that which is personal and private into narratives that may be read, understood, and interpreted in a million ways across the boundaries of time and space. That is why we are moved by stories from a different age or culture. Literature travels well, and it does so because for individual writers, writing, as life itself, is a journey that releases them from the confinements of hereditary identities, taking them into the unknown.

You may ask yourself what all of this has to do with the European aspects of my work; but I hope that you won't, because what I have already said is just another way of expressing what I have to say about that matter.

Europe is a thing as strange as literature. A Babylonian mumble of languages, a multicolored patchwork of cultures between Asia and the Atlantic Ocean, once connected by an empire, then by a religion, and lately, for little more than a century, by an idea—all of them with a propensity for universalism. In the Roman Empire universalism was achieved by law, but that law was forced upon its subjects by distant rulers. In early Christianity, universalism was a promise, calling upon the followers of Jesus to abandon their native communities and identities in order to share a deeper and wider human fellowship of equals. The Italian philosopher Gianni Vattimo has pointed to the Christian notion of God becoming Man as the very origin of secularization. He sees Christianity as a religion that has slowly secularized itself, thus laying the foundations for humanism and modernity.

After the Enlightenment, democracy could no longer be thought of as a local affair, like the original Greek version of the *polis*. Vattimo's German colleague, Immanuel Kant, dreamt of a worldwide community of free people united by shared, universal human rights—a vision more generous than anything fancied by the bureaucrats and politicians of our present day EU. Though Kant's notion of a world community may still be a distant dream, we may get there some day. However, the remarkable thing about Europe is not, I think, the fact that this divided continent has seen an abundance of cruelty and terror committed by one people against the other, or by totalitarian elites against their own populations, or by Europeans against the peoples of the Third World. Cruelty is a rule rather than an exception in human history, and the universalism of terror is part of our European heritage, though so is the notion that we are individuals, persons in our own right, and equals, before anything else.

With democracy now established throughout the continent, this has become less a dream than it was fifty, or even ten years ago; but even so, talking this way about universalism and the European individual may sound rather lofty, even a bit naïve, except when it comes to literature.

From the troubadours of Medieval Provence to the dissident writers behind the Iron Curtain, literature has expressed the sensitivity of individuals, the individual life of the mind, and its resistance to the tyranny of imposed ways of life and thinking. From its very conception, the European novel has staged and interpreted the conflict between private and public life, between individual hope and fear, on the one hand, and social or historical forces on the other. The novel was a European invention, as was the notion of private man and the inviolable right to privacy. We have no reason to be ashamed of this or to fear the charge of eurocentrism. Mind you, both inventions are cherished by writers and citizens in countries outside Europe where civil rights and the freedom of imagination remain luxuries to be fought for.

If the history of democracy is also the history of the individual and how the notion of selfhood has emerged from the warm, comforting, and utterly suffocating embrace of cultural identities, then the novel is a way to tell that story. So many great novels delve into the real or imaginary chasm lying between the pressure or indifference of society and the thoughts and feelings of individuals. There are so many novels about individuals who take leave of their homes and kinsmen, despairingly or in an act of rebellion, either forced into exile or exiling themselves as a consequence of self-creation. Freedom and despair, loneliness and chance encounters, unsought and sometimes utterly improbable: the novel connects the social sphere and the intimate life of the soul in its dramatization of their conflicting perspectives, that of culture and that of one's secret fears and obsessions.

But the notion of personal freedom as opposed to acceptance of the identity offered or imposed by society and culture is not only a story told in novels. A story like that is only told by someone who has discovered that he or she doesn't fit in with the overall cultural pattern of values and behavior inherited from one's ancestors. To write, and to have chosen to become a writer, are indications that somehow you feel like a stranger, even at home. It has been said that writing amounts to a form of mental exile—and I think it's true. I think that writing itself is triggered by, and may indeed produce, a loss of innocence, a deep sense of not belonging.

Once you start writing, you turn into a stranger because you realize that becoming your own self is tantamount to rejecting and denying what others would like you to be. But writing as writers do, searching for the intimacy of a personal voice, also leads you to the simultaneously terrifying and terrific, proud and shameful, discovery that your own self will remain undisclosed—that you will always be a stranger, even to yourself.

In the process of writing, you appropriate common language according to your personal needs, finding words within yourself for that which you hardly know how to express. In doing so, you discover the otherness of your true self, and in the end you may even discover yourself in others. It is called fiction, but it has to do with the very business of being human—separate and lonely because of that, but capable of escaping loneliness and entering into a more true relationship with the world around you. What literature may thus communicate is the strange recognition that what we have most in common is also precisely that which divides us: that we are separate minds and bodies who can only share our innermost selves by becoming and remaining free individuals.

It is unbecoming, though, for a writer to generalize too profusely in regard to the blessings of literature—and this is the perfect place to stop myself. Fiction is nurtured by detail, invoking the life and outlook of this or that specific person. Novels are usually written in the singular, and singularity is their whimsical claim to such a thing as universal truth.

What a writer may have to say about The Novel is usually nothing but a plea for his own personal way of going about it. I am no exception, and my writing has grown from among one of several modern traditions: that of setting plots aside in favor of introspection, memory, observation, and reflection, articulating the adventures of the mind rather than those unwinding out there in Reality. I would concur with any writer who shares the hunch that nothing is more real than the mind's way of interpreting and responding to the flux of appearances.

My private literary tabernacle hosts an eclectic range of idols who might well grumble about the company they're in since form rather than topic is what brings them together: Marcel Proust, Patrick Modiano, Thomas Bernhard, Saul Bellow, just to name a few. What they share in spite of all differences is a penchant for soliloquy, leaving the writing itself to become the vibrant cord stringing thoughts, emotions, impressions, digressions, and events together in the narrator's effort to equalize world and self.

Most of them are French, by the way—and none of them is Danish. How come? Perhaps it is easier to point out inspirations that have required an effort. Anyway, I have come to acknowledge that inspiration is often a matter of productive misunderstanding. Obviously there are Danish masters who whisper in the back of my head, but I don't hear them, so much are they part of the atmosphere I breathe. There is the soft-spoken intimacy and subtle, ironic inversions of perspective in Hans Christian Andersen and his universal way of losing himself in the world of detail. There is the

melancholy sensitivity in Herman Bang, a certain mildness of in-
flection, a hush despair, always so close to his characters that you
can hear them breathe in the silence of their rooms, where a clock
chips away at eternity.

The living room, not the world, is our stage, for Denmark has
spent most of its days on the outskirts of History. We were only
grazed by the tragedies of the century now behind us, hence our
strangely numb sense of distance between our emotional interiors
and the thunderbolts on the horizon. This, if anything, is my Danish theme for you, political as well as philosophical. But more often
than not my novels could take place in any modern Western society where rigid cultural patterns have given way to the bewildering
impermanence of urban life.

This is why being translated has been such a redeeming experience. I don't see myself as a particularly Danish writer—European
perhaps, but that sounds far too pretentious, especially for a Dane.
Escaping labels is the concern of any writer, and I am just as touchy
as everyone else. "Escapism" would be the only reliable exception;
so please, don't read me for the rustic charms of my exotic
"Danishness." As the very cosmopolitan, yet very Danish, poet
Henrik Nordbrandt—himself a great escapist—once said: "What's
wrong with running away if you can afford the ticket?"

Another major poet has defined poetry as that which is lost in
translation. But I am just a storyteller, therefore for me it is the
other way around. If there isn't something in there that will survive
even a lousy translation, I don't think it is worth bothering. Writing
in a small language such as mine is really to act out the paradox of
the novel, if you will allow me one last generalization. Most of us
write in our mother tongue, yet there is an ambition in any novel
worth writing or reading to transgress the contingency of one's
own kinship, culture, etc. to become recognized, in any sense of
that word, for the way you explore the singularity of personal experience.

Durs Grünbein

Born either too early or too late for Europe, all I had was
its myth. I am one of those dispatriated people, who saw
only the wreckage of the old Europe, in ruins like my
birthplace Dresden, and to whom the new was nothing
but the expressionless façades of Brussels bureaucracy.
© Maxim Segienko/PHOTOMAX

Durs Grünbein

Germany

Born in Dresden in 1962, after a short period of study he
became a writer, translator, and essayist in Berlin. After
the opening of the Iron Curtain, he made journeys to other
parts of Europe, Southeast Asia, and the United States.
He was a guest of the German Department of New York
University and the Villa Aurora in Los Angeles. He has
been awarded numerous prizes for his work, including the
Peter Huchel Prize, the Georg Büchner Prize in 1995, and
the literature prize of the Salzburg Easter Festival in 2000.

Further Reading:
Poems on *www.poetryinternational.org* translated by
Michael Hofmann.

Europa's Lovers

Heute erst fühle ich mich, nach mehreren
Amerikabesuchen, wieder als frischgebackener
Europäer. So geht einem die Lieblichkeit der
Lagunenstadt Venedig erst so richtig auf, nachdem
man etwa Las Vegas gesehen hat, die aufgedonnerte
Hure unter den Städten der Neuen Welt.

The first of them was, of course, Zeus. He whisked her away in the typically macho costume of a bull. The place where he first set eyes on her—the beautiful princess who gave her name to our common continent—was on the coast of Phoenicia, which nowadays is shared between Lebanon and Syria. In other words, the girl was not just some unspecified and interchangeable trophy, a mere sex object, something for the young bull to frisk with. She was from the opposite shore, from the Levant. Her home was actually on the western edge of the continent we know as Asia.

Let's listen to the story of the abduction as Ovid tells it in the *Metamorphoses*: "Until the princess dared to mount his back, / Her pet bull's back, unwitting whom she rode. / Then—slowly, slowly down the broad dry beach—/ First in the shallow waves the great god set / His spurious hooves, then sauntered further out / Till in the open sea he bore his prize." Once on the other side—you'll not find this in Ovid—the god did to her what he liked best to do, and then he left her to her fate. One wonders whether her nomination as playmate for an entire continent can have been sufficient compensation for what she was put through: abduction, rape, and presumably life in exile. The only thing we know is that her case took a sudden turn, and became a typical instance of the etiological, or founding, fable. No girl's name can ever have caught on more dramatically. However elusive the connection between this daughter of Oceanus and the subsequent naming of a continent, that's what happened. Whole countries and regions identify themselves by her name. It takes up its own space in the world atlas. And, furthermore, we've recently even named a currency after her.

At first, when the wicked act was fresh in memory, the name was only applied to the Greek mainland, as opposed to the wind-swept Aegean islands. Only subsequently was its cover extended to take in all of Hellas, and thence the entirety of that landmass that stretches from the Peloponnese peninsula in the South to Lapland in the North, and from the Aran Islands off the coast of Ireland to the much fought-over milestone on the banks of the Volga, in deepest Russia. But in the beginning, the name was far from having a continent in its grasp. It took extreme pressure to spread its suzerainty. But once the aggressor had been sent packing to the desert from which he came, then the barbarian belle — or belly — began to spread. The new shape resembled the swelling of pregnancy. The continent's self-confidence grew with the geographical distance from its original birthplace.

To say it again, by today's standards Europa was an Oriental gal. That, in and of itself, is already more than a little unexpected. Then, not only did she bestow her name in all perpetuity to the place of exile to which the wanton god had dragged her, she also left the stamp of her own origins on the area. Would that not help to explain the persistence and obsessiveness with which cavaliers born on her native soil have sought to woo her? *Cherchez la femme.* Maybe not all the robbing expeditions, but a good many, certainly can be laid at the feet of the lady. Beginning with the Greeks — the only people in history that got double value from their mythology, once as philosophy and once as poetry (and then both in the form of tragedy, and as individual poem) — through the Romans — their natural heirs and policemen of the continent — on down to the colorful tournament of nations that formed as the Middle Ages came to an end, this wooing process was always the bloodiest imaginable. In the pre-Christian era, it usually took the form of — no pun intended — defensive engagements. On several occasions, it looked as though Europe were about to be gobbled up from the East, a recurring nightmare for her young defenders. Some violent breed of Assyrians, or Persians, or Mongols, or Huns was forever rising up out of the depths of space, fleet as the wind with their horses and their scything chariots, and it was always a near thing. The delicate seeds of civilization on European soil were always within an ace of being trampled by despotic armies and nomadic hordes. The cute beauty would surely have been stolen away and repatriated by her admirers, if the small troop of confident beaux that were the European nations had not, on each occasion, somehow managed to surmount their numerical inferiority, and, in some utterly improbable way, win the day. On each occasion, something happened that, like the sea-battle at Salamis, was all but miraculous, and that in turn created something like a special historical aura.

What does this aura consist of? It's possible that it was just a sort of mirage, a fata morgana; yet it's striking how regularly such a manifestation showed itself over European soil. But there was this eerily promising intimation of a mixture of intellectual adventurousness and an almost erotic predilection for personal liberty. As rough and approximate as that is, it seems to express a pan-European attitude. You could also call it existential curiosity or a desire to think the unthinkable—there are lots of possible labels. A certain imaginary site from which the cultural life of this multiple and heterogeneous continent could at any time be rebuilt and extended, in continuation, as it were, of its geological substratum. Every dark age was followed by a renaissance, every Hieronymus Bosch Inferno by a Botticelli Spring. This appetite for freedom, this lightness and facility in starting afresh, even amidst the worst catastrophes, is a quality that in the individual is called charm, and in the life of the sexes, gallantry. Once more, it would seem as though the ancient Greeks had set the standard. It is to them that we owe certain crucial words—Goethe called them *Ur*-words—and still more the concepts to which they are attached. It is to the Graces (the *charites* in Greek), the goddesses of beauty, that Europe still owes its essential nature, the *charisma* of its various cultures, the *charm* of its best natives. A tireless clear-sightedness, the ability and the will to understand and to shape, a brave readiness to step up to the board—here is the particular capacity of Europe, transmitted on occasion across all five continents, for ill, as we have sometimes been forced to see, as much as for good. The extraordinary intellectual ferment that typified the awakening of Europe in the centuries, let's say, from Sappho to Ausonius, was like sea foam from which there arose, Aphrodite-like, the idea of the individual, the person, in which we have since come to see as the center of creativity. And, however often its names (and qualities) would change over time, this eerie apparition emerged from the same circles of seducers and kidnappers.

If it's true that a woman blossoms through her lovers, then Europe was in a most fortunate position. For centuries, she was desired, as much in the most crude and rapacious way, as with the most refined etiquette. And she it was who taught manners to those who came to court her. Those young men in the paintings of the Venetian and Florentine masters that you see leaning against a pillar, with their well-turned stockinged legs, their buckled shoes, and their slashed doublets. Before or after the chase, the crossbow casually dangled over one shoulder, a winning smile on their lips, lounging around on the edge of some piazza, these dandies, watching some grim procession, bored witnesses to some martyrdom. All of them suitors, and with an eye for beauty, it is they, in their *sprezzatura*, or in their *cool*, as we nowadays say, who courted Europa. Them of all? Granted, only a minority of them were moralists. Baldassare Castiglione's noble dialogues on the courtier were more their cup of tea than Pico della Mirandola's universal *pensées* on human dignity. And yet, however dandified they might be, they had in them the germ of what, to be elitist, one might call the flower of culture or the acme of creation. For the lover, in Latin, was many things: he was the troubadour, the man of learning, and the philosopher as much as he was the servant of a cult in which the most refined traits of social life found expression. That's him, the European man, the one proudly portrayed in those Italian paintings. You see him everywhere, in various guises, as you trawl through museums and libraries, the worshipper with the blatant desire to conquer visible on his forehead like a brand, the mark of all Europa's enthusiasts. Of course, he changed in the course of time. After the Roman legionary, he was the Christian, the wandering monk mapping out for himself the extent of the continent. He was followed by the mercenary in service of various potentates, then the traveler on his *grand tour*, finally the surveyor, the entrepreneur with his beady colonialist's and geostrategist's face. The last time you saw him, it was in the portrait of the bearded nineteenth-century theory lion, in whose life's work, unrepeatably, old Europe found its culmination. In every one of these, there lived and breathed something of the continent's enduring founding myth.

As I say, after two thousand years of getting used to it, it may not be much more than a phantasmagoria; something everyone who was born and grown up here has encountered in one way or another, even if he's only read about it. And won't now forget it. I am talking about the desire for personal autonomy that has been vouchsafed to some, while for others it was the object of lifetime's striving. That—in a word that combines myth and advertising— was Europe's "halo." It comes at you out of historical terms like humanism and enlightenment, even if not much seems to be left of it now.

You may wonder: what has all this got to do with the girl from the Levant? Well, the myth the Greeks handed down to us, the account of the founding of our territorial identity, involves not only an act of violence, but a unique historical maturation, generosity, self-determination, and tolerance. (To return to the Persians: can you imagine a people prepared publicly to contemplate the lot of its defeated enemy, who, moreover, had been the aggressor, without glee, and with self-critical insight? But that's precisely what was shown in the Greek amphitheatre, with the production of Aeschylus's tragedy *The Persians*.) Differently expressed, and returning to the myth, Zeus compensated for his insatiable sexual appetite by giving us a model of European dynamism, on to which the philosopher Hegel later slapped the brand *Weltgeist* for believers in history.

Granted, it's a strange thing to name a whole continent after a naked woman. Others, following in the hoof prints of Zeus, chose to see Europe similarly as a sex object. That explains the violence that the struggle for her possession engendered in her suitors. What promises to be fertile and enjoyable is generally liable to the occupational hazard of conquest, and a serenade only anticipates a future land grab. That Europe, conversely, might be able to take her destiny into her own hands was a twist in the tale that it took later times to come up with. It wasn't the assertion of boundaries so much as the cunning curiosity about something utterly foreign that was the spur to the criminal act of continent-building. Admittedly, it took a long time, with repeated lapses into the worst excesses of patriotism (which Goethe said spoiled history for him), till international agreements, national self-restraint, in a word, true courtesy became the order of the day.

It was Osip Mandelstam, the Russian poet and one of the troubadours of Europa who wrote the important line: "O Europa's tender hands, take—take everything!" His poem, written in 1922, describes the abduction as a foaming sea voyage with caprioles of dolphins and wild green water. It is remarkable that, in his telling, the princess on the bull's back appears in her dual role—both as the stolen woman and the meek trophy, embracing the neck of her ravisher. That schism is there from the start, and the poem draws its tension from the ambivalence that is present in the story, and has been present throughout the entire history of this continent. The trauma of the story and its extraordinary promise have *both* contributed to its historical destiny. The poem begins with a snapshot of the god in his disguise: "The pink foam of fatigue on his soft muzzle, / the bull snorts his way through the green sea, / it's not oarstrokes he loves, it's women— / the burden is unfamiliar and hard to bear." The author—it's no accident—was Russian. At the time of writing, in the fifth year after the so-called October Revolution, he was further than ever from his ideal of world culture on European soil. With the clear-sightedness of disappointment and exclusion, he was one of the first to understand what was happening in the East. The Socialist steamer was pushing off from the European dock. The twentieth century brought an end to the cherished dream of union. Mandelstam was bereft. He saw, as not many did, that the European man was the man of antiquity *par* excellence. The great schism, the loss of the East, was the outcome of a titanic battle fought out between Hitler and Stalin, the two anti-European rivals. Each in his own fashion, they worked to destroy the common foundations. One with his idée fixe of a pan-European state under German rule, the other with his Assyrian tyranny dressed up as Socialism. The result was the post-War world into which we were born, with, on the one side, the West and European–American civilization, and on the other the East, a prison house of nations that, under Soviet influence, congealed gradually into a block of ice. But this division, this toughest test of the old Europe, also had its paradoxical good side. It wasn't just that this continent in wartime tended to get above itself, only to have to relearn humility afterwards; no, in the long run, war, the divider of peoples, proved to be a way of bringing peoples together. The Thirty Years' War, the Napoleonic era, World Wars I and II, all dug up and loosened this soil. After each bout, the warring nations understood more about one another than they did before. Behind the fraternal fisticuffs was what Mandelstam described as the appreciation *of a European consciousness as a common mother.* At the end of each jealous and murderous fight, there was less isolation than there had been, the patchwork of frontiers seemed more unnecessary, and communication was a little easier than heretofore.

Finally, I want to declare that I, too, count myself among Europa's lovers. And that's saying something for me, because I'm not generally a joiner or a belonger. Until recently, for someone like myself, Europe was almost a byword for the unattainable. The very word made me feel a bit solemn. Born either too early or too late for Europe, all I had was its myth. I am one of those dispatriated people, who saw only the wreckage of the old Europe, in ruins like my birthplace Dresden, and to whom the new was nothing but the expressionless façades of Brussels bureaucracy. And yet I always viewed myself as a native of this continent. I say this because I was not alone, growing up as I did among people for whom a Wall had eclipsed all sense of Europe. What did you do if you were a European at heart? You looked for solace; and in the camp of daily life under Socialism, you got by on what Nietzsche called love, not of the nearest and dearest, but of the "furthest and dearest." So great was this love, in my case, that it transported me way beyond the recently established German unity. They say travel cultivates, but sometimes it's like root canal treatment. It's really only now, and in the wake of several visits to the United States, that I've begun to feel myself truly European. It's as though you can't realize the loveliness of Venice until you've been to Las Vegas, the painted harlot of New-World cities. It was the poets, people like Ovid or Mandelstam, who professed their love of Europe over the centuries, each in his own commensurate fashion. For one man it was the purlieus of Athens, the area under the Acropolis; for another, sent to live among Scythians on the Black Sea coast, it was Rome, the Eternal City, the center of a crumbling empire; and for the last of them it was what he majestically expressed as *nostalgia for world culture*.

Perhaps you will let me end with a suggestion. Whenever you're next in Greece, take the change out of your pocket. Perhaps the national bank of the most southerly of the European nations has made you a present. Hold, if you have one, a two-euro coin in your hand; don't look at the denomination, but turn it over, maybe for frugality's sake, and examine the embossed motif. You will see a familiar constellation of figures—and a slim, long-legged woman. She is sitting, feet together, side-saddle as it were, facing you from the back of a charging bull.

— *Translated by Michael Hofmann*

Daniela Hodrová

And it is in this narrative web of literary Europe that the writer is caught. No sooner does he touch it with his own lived and written story than he spins a new loop and radius, a new cocoon.
© Maxim Segienko/PHOTOMAX

Daniela Hodrová

Czech Republic

Born in Prague in 1946, the writer, scholar, and translator
Daniela Hodrová studied philosophy in Prague, receiving a
doctorate for a thesis on the Russian writer Andrei Belyi. She
worked as an editor for the publishing company *Odeon* and is
currently a literary scholar at the Institute for Czech Literature
of the Czech Academy of Science. Her main literary work,
Città dolente (Podobojí, Kukly, Théta), a trilogy written
between 1977 and 1984, could be published in Prague only
after the political changes of 1989. Daniela Hodrová lives and
works in Prague.

Further Reading:
"In Both Species." Excerpts. Translated by Tatiana Firkušný and
Veronique Firkušný-Callegari. In *Prairie Schooner: Czech and
Slovak Writing in translation,* University of Nebraska Press,
1992 (Virginia Faulkner Award for Excellence in Writing 1992).
"Inner place." Translated by Charles Townsend. *Czechoslovak
and Central European Journal,* vol. 11, Winter 1992, no 2.
Edited by Paul I. Trensky.
"I See a Great City..." Excerpts. Translated by Paul Wilson. In
Prague: A Traveler's Literary Companion. Edited by Paul
Wilson. Whereabouts Press, 1995.
"The Kingdom of Olsany." Excerpts. Translated by Tatiana
Firkušný and Veronique Firkušný-Callegari. *The Prague Revue.
Jáma Revue,* Winter 1996, no 1.
"Perun's Day." Excerpts. Translated by Tatiana Firkušný. In
*Daylight in Nightclub Inferno: Czech Fiction from the Post-
Kundera Generation*. Edited by Elena Lappin. Catbird Press,
1997.
"Theta." Excepts. Translated by Tatiana Firkušný and Veronique
Firkušný-Callegari. In *Allskin and other tales by contemporary
Czech women*. Edited by Alexandra Büchler. Seattle, 1998.

Woven Into the Web*

*A do této narativní sítě vyprávějící Evropy je lapen
spisovatel, sotva se jí dotkne vlastním žitým i psaným
příběhem a přede v ní nové oko a zauzlinu, zámotek.*

In Johannes Putsch's woodcut of 1537, Europe is depicted *in forma virginis*. Queen Europe is garbed in a robe of green, the color of life and regeneration. Scattered about in a bizarre pattern are the names of her countries, their capitals represented by emblems. Mountain ranges, too, are illustrated here, and flowing across her body from top to bottom is the Danube. Perhaps the fact that Bohemia is located at the very center of the Queen's torso, in the solar plexus region, site of the sunny chakra, captures the unique status of this land, in which the knot of European history has been tied more than once in the course of the twentieth century, as well as in those previous.

If I may, then, I will use this personification as a point of departure. My other point of departure will be the notion, from four centuries later, of a universal cosmic material that forms an envelope around the earth, "imprinting and retaining, recording in some fashion, every one of our mental processes, deeds and thoughts ... every action whatsoever ... There is a record of all that has happened," as the Czech psychologist Břetislav Kafka wrote in the 1920s. It was for this special material that he invented the concept of "protonation."[1]

In the spirit of these ideas, then, I imagine Europe as a living thing cloaked in an aura, an invisible mental substance woven out of every thought, memory, notion, illusion, dream, anxiety, obsession, and trauma that has ever passed through the head of this maiden, or rather lady, of an uncertain age. She has experienced every one of these and spun them into stories, individual and collective, ancient and contemporary. And it is in this narrative web of literary Europe that the writer is caught. No sooner does he touch it with his own lived and written story than he spins a new loop and radius, a new cocoon.

By its nature, this narrative mesh, ever expanding, thickening, tearing here and there, is different at every moment, and yet in a sense it is the same, in that it grows in accordance with a "genetic" program, and pulses in regular rhythms. However, those inside the cocoon, eagerly awaiting transformation, may only with difficulty, if at all, distinguish its outlines and discern the processes governing its dynamics. Not only that, but simply by their looking at it, it changes into a story. Another characteristic of Europe's narrative web or body is that the holes in the stories from various eras are interconnected; stories flow along invisible threads over and around one another, even within the same work, which itself in small form mirrors the larger web.

And what sort of stories are they? The stories of Oedipus, Odysseus, Tristan and Isolde, the search for the Holy Grail; the stories of Christ, Don Quixote, Robinson Crusoe, and Faust; stories of lost illusions, delusion and insanity, crime and punishment; of inconceivable acts and misconceived guilt, of lost time and recollection, of alienation, and consecration unfulfilled.

European writers of the last century were spellbound by all of these stories and many more, weaving together old and new alike, often questioning them, and not infrequently even parodying them (storytelling Europe has known all of these methods for ages), in the process transforming, if not completely reversing, their meaning. Gullible Hans Castorp, Thomas Mann's modern-age Perceval, leaves the magic mountain for the slaughterhouse of World War I. Kafka's surveyor searches in vain for a way into the Castle; while in *The Trial*, K. fails to recognize his own guilt and so falls short of redemption. The travels of Bloom, Joyce's Ulysses, take him on a tour of the modern city, lasting but a single day. And in Robbe-Grillet's *Erasers*, the Oedipus myth does double duty as a pseudo-detective story about the fatality of knowledge.

Kafka's novels also illustrate another distinguishing trait of "European text," and above all that part of it which is linked with the chest of the allegorical being that served as our starting point: incompleteness. Citing Musil, Kafka, and Hašek, the Czech critic Václav Bělohradský has pointed out how the great novels of Central Europe share this trait. What he had in mind was not the incompleteness resulting from the circumstances of the writer's life, but incompleteness as a result of his doubts about the ending, about the possibility of knowing, of creating a story with a single, unambiguous meaning. Such occurrences, if rare, are indicative nonetheless.

In recent decades, however, European narrativity, or European narrative discourse, to use a modern-day term, is in my opinion characterized by still another, more weighty incompleteness—an internal one. Instead of the expected event, a "hole" yawns in the story, as in Beckett's *Waiting for Godot* or Dino Buzzati's *The Tartar Steppe*. The rigid structure of the novel, traditionally divided into chapters, collapses; the text is often composed of a sequence of loosely connected paragraphs, riddled with ellipses. This fragmentization corresponds to a descent into the past, foregrounding the text and recording the fleeting present. This is the case, for instance, in Milada Součková's *First Letters*, Nathalie Sarraute's *Childhood* and *Between Life and Death*, Marguerite Duras's *To Write*, and Bohumil Hrabal's *Too Loud a Solitude*. Examples of it in "women's" prose in particular are legion. Also disruptive to the traditional continuity of text is hypercontinuity, in which the text is conceived as a stream, composed as a single, never-ending sentence (Hrabal's *Dancing Lessons for the Advanced in Age*), or constantly branching off and digressing (*Song of Youth*, by Josef Hiršal), coiling and collapsing in on itself—the technique known as *mise en abyme* is common, in the "new novel" and elsewhere. The narrative in these cases is frequently conceived as a search for narrative and story, as well as its "destruction" and "cleansing." The Austrian Thomas Bernhard offers the reader stories that are formally complete, but destroys them from within, his fragmented themes repeating insistently throughout the text. The use of variations—the primary compositional and noetic approach of Milan

Kundera, self-declared savior of the European novel—strikes me as another prominent trait of European discourse in those works that cast doubt on the existence of a single, "easy" meaning.

It seems that those who come into contact with the body of Europe are infected by the internal incompleteness and discontinuity of its stories (though in reality, on closer examination, there are actually multiple continuities), and are carried away by the stream of European stories, visited by their characters, possessed by the demons of memory and forgetting. I was struck by this recently while reading *The Invention of Solitude* by the American writer of Austrian origin Paul Auster. For as soon as the narrator finds himself in Paris and Amsterdam, he plunges into the European narrative element, drawing on stories and themes both old and new (e.g., the story of Anne Frank). The typically European theme of memory even lends its name to the novel's second part, The Book of Memory, placing Auster's work in the context of the great European novels of memory, from Proust's *In Search of Lost Time* to Peter Nádas's *Book of Memories*; the wandering through Amsterdam, too, echoes the wandering through the city of canals in *The Erasers*. And I was amazed to come across the story of the insane Hölderlin, who wanders a Prague cemetery in the novel *Comedy*, I am now writing.

The same mechanism that operates between continent and writer exists between city and writer, too, in an even more obvious way; the aura of the city exerts its pull on foreigners as well as natives. *The Weeping Woman on the Streets of Prague*, by the French author Sylvie Germain, who lived in the city for several years, is written in an almost medium-like contact with Prague's narrative aura. From this aura emerges a being without name, age, or face, with "a body of tears and memory," an apparition born of the city's stones, like Gustav Meyrink's Golem. Germain's text, like Paul Auster's, gravitates toward internal incompleteness and, also like Auster's, makes a theme of the act of writing. At first, this approach may seem like a postmodern play on story, yet hidden behind it, here and elsewhere, is the existential anxiety and ontological uncertainty of the narrator: "Who am I when I write this novel? Who do I want to be? Am I the one descending into my past, or the one standing off to the side, watching the descent?" (Forgive me for quoting myself, from the novel *Theta*, part of the loose trilogy "Città dolente.")

So how is it then with the European story, itself a substory of the macrostory of Earth and a metastory of the stories of individual European cities? What will it look like in the next two or three decades, and what meaning does it offer? And why is it that the story— my personal story, as well as the collective one, of which my own story is a part—is so attractive to us, or to me, even though, or in spite of the fact that, it is falling apart (my own trilogy from the Prague district of Olšany remains unfinished), that these stories are questioned and ridiculed?

Perhaps what makes the story so attractive to European writers, including myself, is that it creates, as the French philosopher Paul Ricoeur noted, a conscious (or even merely potential) context of meaning for individual action in history. If it can be said that mankind acquires a narrative, in its essence dynamic, identity through the story, which tells itself about itself or someone else, then the same is true in another sense about the space it occupies, and its stories. Europe certainly acquires its identity not only through its landscape, but also, unremittingly, through the stories it rescues from forgetting, shaping, and relating them. None of this is changed by the fact that in the postmodern situation the story is diminished, breaking down, fragmenting, called into question. To some the story may seem ailing, and perhaps in a sense it is. Nevertheless it is precisely this story that best corresponds to today's changing conception of the world, to the nature of knowledge. In short, a story that is ragged and incomplete is still a story; more difficult to access, perhaps, but intended to lead us to a meaning that is also less accessible. In any case, it becomes part of my memory, contributing to my self-knowledge and, with luck, to my transformation.

Some dreams are as significant as stories in our lives, replaying for us in images our current situation, the momentary state of our soul. Clearly, this is not true of every story, only of those we might describe as archetypal, such as Greek myths. We keep them tucked away in our unconscious, through their repeated telling effecting a

transfer of primal epic information, of the initiatory human experience that is encoded in these stories. The significance of the story
in psychotherapy is well known: once a person can tell his story—
in other words, can conceive of and view his life with detachment—
he is nearly, if not fully, cured. This was Tristan's problem in the
medieval novel *Tristan et Iseut*, recently published in a new edition
by Pléiade, with all of its variants and extensive commentary. True,
Tristan remained "crazy," despite telling his story; but the reason
he failed to be cured of his tormented passion was that his storytelling and self-revelation were nothing but a ruse, a role he played
in the court of King Marc, lacking true detachment and a genuine
desire for atonement.

I believe the story can have therapeutic, restorative significance,
not only for the individual, but for society as a whole. Who can say
whether the fact that Europe today has an urge to retell the stories
that once established it as a geographical-spiritual formation is not
a sign that the ailing maiden is back on the road to recovery?
Maybe "crazy" Europe is beginning to realize that her fragile identity exists only through the stories she remembers and tells, and in
which she attempts to understand herself. Stories such as Tristan's
offer us moments of great wonder and high emotion, a way of per-
ceiving that has long been neglected, covered over and suppressed
in recent centuries by Europe's restrictive rationalism. And yet it is
these very stories, "great" and "small" alike, that constitute an irreplaceable tool of knowledge, and self-knowledge, for the individual and humanity as a whole. Faith in the story, despite being
questioned by some modern novels and philosophers, has made a
visible comeback in Europe in recent decades, with the story and
its telling beginning once again to be viewed not only as a metaphor for humanity's lot in life, but as a real and fundamental dimension of human existence.

— *Translated by Alex Zucker*

*The title of the symposium in Czech (Evropa píše) is such that the word
Europe, grammatically speaking, functions as a subject ("Europe writes"),

whereas the official translation into English ("Writing Europe") makes Europe an object, rather than a subject. As a result, I had to leave out a phrase in Hodrová's essay in which she refers to this (the translator's note).

1 Remarkably, this concept was later echoed by the French Jesuit priest and paleontologist Pierre Teilhard de Chardin, who wrote of a "thinking layer" or "noosphere."

Panos Ioannides

Europe is the cradle of modern humanist civilization. Its foundation stone lies in the saying of Protagoras: "Man is measured above all in money."

Panos Ioannides
Cyprus

Born in Famagusta, Cyprus in 1935, the writer, essayist
and playwright Panos Ioannides studied at the Pancyprian
Lyceum. He worked as a journalist and a civil servant. In
1967 he won a scholarship to Syracuse University in the
United States and then taught sociology and
communication at York University, Toronto. From 1955
until 1995 he worked for the Cyprus Broadcasting
Corporation, ultimately as head of television and radio
programs. Panos Ioannides is president of the Cyprus Pen
Club. He has been awarded several prizes for his fiction
and plays.

Further Reading:
Panos Ioannides. Cyprus PEN Publications, 1995.

Europe in My Prose and My Theatrical Work

*Η Ευρώπη είναι η κοιτίδα του σύγχρονου
ανθρωποκεντρικού πολιτισμού. Θεμέλιός του λίθος η
Πρωταγόρεια ρήση "πάντων χρημάτων μέτρον άνθρωπος.*

The question we have been called upon to answer at this conference, the way I understand it, could be put like this: what is the core of our literary work and how is it expressed in terms of topic, questioning, form, and structural material?

In order to answer this question properly, I sought the elements that constitute Europe, apart from the geographical region and the peoples who reside there. From my list, I have singled out as most important the following three: history, religion, and culture.

Having specified my objectives and defined my coordinates, I will examine these questions through the spectroscope of my own work. But, before doing so, I feel the urge to attempt a brief historical retrospective. I consider this essential for those of my readers— and I presume there will be many—who are not completely familiar with Cyprus.

The island has been populated since the fourteenth century B.C. by the Achaeans and other Greek tribes, which brought with them their languages, cultures, and religion—the twelve gods of Olympus. According to mythology, the goddess of beauty and *eros*-love, *Aphrodite* (Venus), or *Cypris,* was born in Cyprus. It is also known that for many centuries celebrations and mystical religious festivities were held in honor of this goddess, attracting visitors from all neighboring countries.

In Cyprus Christianity was taught by the Apostle Paul and his travel companion, the equal-apostle, Barnabas, the Cypriot from Salamis, beginning in the year 45 AD.

Due to its geographical position and rich natural resources, the island had always fallen prey to plunderers from the East, such as Persians, Arabs, and Turks, but also to many Western European kingdoms or knightly orders. Throughout the entire period of the Middle Ages, the latter occupied the island as a maritime base-of-operations for the Crusades and a huge protective shield against Asian invaders. They exploited its key position and its riches and enslaved its native Greek inhabitants. In ancient times, Cyprus was occupied, in chronological order, by the Egyptians, the Persians, and the Romans. During the Middle Ages it became a Byzantine province, which was then occupied by English crusaders, the Naites, the Hospitallers, the French Lusignans, the Genoese, and the Venetians. In 1453 it was conquered by the Turks, who retained sovereignty over the island until 1878, when they sold it to the British. During the four centuries of Ottoman sovereignty a Turkish minority emerged, which has remained on the island since then and, by 1974, had come to comprise eighteen percent of the native population. After two centuries of British dominion, and as a result of the liberation struggle of the EOKA (National Organization of Cypriot Fighters), Cyprus won its independence in 1960. Then came the secessionist mutiny of the Turkish Cypriots in 1964, the creation of a small pseudo-state in occupied northern Cyprus in 1974 following the coup of the Athenian junta against President Makarios, which the Turks used a pretext for invasion, occupying approximately forty percent of our territory, a state of affairs that continues to weigh heavily upon Cyprus.

The recent European Union summit meeting, held in Copenhagen on December 13, sanctified incorporation of the Republic of Cyprus, for now simply the free Greek-Cypriot region, into the EU. So the century of discordant relations between the island and Europe at large has come to a happy end.

During its twenty-five centuries of recorded history, Cyprus has kept its Greek language, religion, and identity intact. Despite the tragic events and the inhuman conditions its population has endured, Cypriot culture never ceased to evolve and develop. There were chroniclers from ancient and Byzantine times, medieval poets, such as Stasinos the mythical father-in-law of Homer, philosophers, such as Zinon Kitieus, the founder of Stoicism, the chroniclers Leontios Mahairas and George Voustronios, the unknown medieval poet, who composed flawless, erotic Petrarchan sonnets, the first in the Greek language, Constantinos Eusevis Anagnostis, who wrote the *Circle of Passion*, one of the oldest and most important Byzantine mystical works. And there are a lot more, older and contemporary, writers and scholars, who, having produced a significant literary corpus in the Greco-Roman tradition, have marked the cultural map of Europe with a Cypriot stamp.

This long and turbulent history and the recent violent upheaval and attendant sociopolitical changes that we Cypriots have experienced over the past years, especially since the beginning of the liberation struggle and territorial claims of the Turkish Cypriots, have served as an important source for my themes. The plays, *Thy Were Killed for the Light*, *Fotinos*, *Onisilos*, *The Ventriloquists*, *Petros A*, *Mass/Liturgy For Kyriakos Matsis*, as well as the stories contained in the collections *In the Aerial Cyprus* and *Cronaca I and II*, all refer to the period I have mentioned. I deal with the *a priori* doomed efforts of the Cypriots to gain their rights and freedom, either through peaceful means or gunfire. I simultaneously gain comfort from the prosperity and the Sybaritism of our Eastern and Western conquerors and share the misery imposed on the natives: "My daughter, my Arkyri, was exchanged by her master, porno-Mostris, for three oxen and a bond, written and sealed, for her new master Count Montolif to give her back to her old master in case she becomes a widow," complains a common woman, in *Petros A*, which refers to the Frankish domination of the twelfth century.

The language used by the protagonist in the metrical play *Fotinos* is different. Being a prisoner of the Turks, the young hero, nailed on a rock like a new Prometheus, advises his fellow prisoners:

> We don't beg for what is rightfully ours
> to stand up for our own home

> this is the right we claim
> once we feel free and worthy
> of the freedom we demand. And willing we are,
> for the future of our descendants,
> to spare our own miserable today.

In addition to the riots in the name of freedom, I devote many pages to the conflicts of the native and foreign inhabitants of the island with the Eastern invaders, the Turks, the Saracens, the Mamelukes—in other words, the whole Islamic world of those days, which devastated not only Cyprus, but also many European countries. Being inexperienced in war, the Cypriots are called forth, dragged violently into combat in which they are slaughtered in defense of the throne.

I am also accustomed to developing history in other ways, for example, by seeking people and events that have obvious similarities to current people and situations. I have no difficulty in finding these people and events, which very often seem to be reincarnated from one millennium to another, in order to underscore some eternal realities.

Reading about the mythical archpriest and king of Pafos, Kinyras, who lived during the Trojan War, I detected astonishing similarities with the sociopolitical and religious aims of the Archbishop Makarios, first President of Cyprus, also from Pafos. In my attempt to comment on Makarios' life and work objectively, I wrote a novel for Kinyras, trying to link the distant past with the present. These are its first lines:

> The Archpriest King of Pafos played with his beard and smiled to his interlocutor. This is one more thing that characterizes a true leader. The ability to replace, when necessary—and it is necessary often enough—policy with fluency and consistency with generosity. Talthyvios, Agamemnon's ambassador, may not have yet agreed with his recommendation to have a bath, rest, meet the new priestesses in the temple of Aphrodite or the cheerful adolescent from Phoenicia before he pres-

ents all the disagreeable reasons that brought him to
Cyprus, but he could not have guessed the deepest
thoughts of Kinyras. He waved to have the cups refilled
... The wine of Pafos, he thought, is more intoxicating
for the foreigners than for the locals. Why shouldn't he
use this very wine now, to prevent, while he can,
Talthyvios from indicating that neither the treaties nor
the libations can be lapsed?"

The tragicomic development of the myth, the way Robert Graves
presents it, and of course my own novel's development, in spite
of all the differentiations, having the benefit of poetic license, jus-
tifies the effectiveness of the political philosophy and the pragmatic
of the two immortal Kinyras, reminding us of Elliot's classic verse
from the "Four Quartets": "Time present and time past are both
perhaps present in time future." I have also attempted to perform
similar connections, between General Grivas Digenis' revolution
of 1955–59 and a medieval rebel farmer, Rigas, or "Wolf," Alexis,
who engaged in the same romantic and heroic foolery as the
general. Rigas Alexis, who was hanged by the Franks, dragged
down to hecatombs of innocent Cypriots. George Grivas, involuntarily, due to his arrogant patriotism, brought on the coup, which
brought about devastation. These millennia-long connections can
only be made in countries with great historical depth; this is why I
consider it to be a characteristic of the art of the old, much more
than the new, world. Robert Graves in *I Claudius*, Jean Anouilh in
Antigone, Margueritte Yourcenar in the *Memoirs of Adrianos*, and
many other European writers performed similarly formidable
strides towards a "perpetual" past, of course with their own, unique
targets.

The second principle European element I am dealing with is religion. Like History, religion holds an important place in my work.
Both the twelve gods of Olympus and, mainly, Christianity, can be
largely found in the story *Kinyras* and in the plays *Thy Were Killed
for the Light* and *Onisilos*. The protagonist in one scene of *Thy Were
Killed for the Light* is the Apostle of all nations, Paul, who com-
menced his mission of Christianizing Europe from the small island

of Cyprus. The first European citizen baptized by Paul was the Roman Proconsul of Cyprus, Sergios Paul.

Both in sociopolitical and religious terms, the rivalry between the Cypriots and the European conquerors in the Middle Ages was intense, because they were both Christians. The conquerors were Roman Catholic and the conquered Orthodox. However, the Vatican, throughout the Middle Ages, had the unrelenting aim of imposing Catholicism by any means. This arbitrariness elicited the resistance of the Cypriots, sometimes through peaceful means, at other times through war and struggle. They both resulted in torment and death. This revolution is preserved in the chronicles of Leontios Machairas and took place during the rule of King Pierre de Louisinian I, known as Roi Pierre. It is mentioned in my homonymic play. The Commander of Nicosia, Sir Jean Viskountis, writes in the Haut Cour:

> Riots broke out in the capital, outside the Cathedral. The Legatos of the Pontiff and the Monsenieur imprisoned ... the Cypriot Bishops. If they wish to retake their bishopric, they should agree to be subject to the Holy See. The orthodox refused, so the papists have been inflicting upon them the torments of hunger and thirst, for days and days on end. Dometios Salaminiotis, who dared to talk back, had his palms and soles and all the openings of his body parched.

Such scenes of intolerance and cruelty are also found in the play *Thy Were Killed for the Light* and the story *Gregorios and Euthimios*. Nevertheless, there are also moments of reconciliation between the conqueror and the enslaved Cypriots. Roi Pierre de Lousinion fell in love with the humble freed Cypriot woman, Aradafnousa. Their love affair was turned into a folk song and a fairy tale. It also inspired sociopolitical reforms for the benefit of his enslaved subjects. Here are a few lines from the love confession of the Frankish governor to Aradafnousa taken from my play *Petros the First:*

> The petty man you see, not Roi Pierre, but a simple man,
> if you want him fair and prudent, save young Aradaf-
> nousa for him ... If you want me wise, sympathetic, not
> tyrannical and tax enforcing, give me your love. Other-
> wise, if you leave me, I swear to God, my fierceness will
> be the most hideous and repulsive in the years to come ...

Queen Eleanor d'Aragon, with the assistance of her lover and other courtiers, kills Aradafnousa. The king becomes insane from the torment and violently takes as mistresses the wives and the daughters of those who took part in the crime. He throws in the dungeons and puts to death hundreds of Franks and Cypriots. Furious at that insult and the reforms he had performed, the queen and the knights conspire against him and kill him. Even this love story ends up in a blood bath. Allow me to mention that this story inspired George Seferis to write the *Demon of Harlotry*.

Let us now examine the third major European constituent that we noted at the outset: the universal theory, the intellectual and ideological basis of the perennial European, as well as the manner and the extent to which this can be found in my writing.

Europe is the cradle of modern humanist civilization. Its foundation stone lies in the saying of Protagoras: "Man is measured above all in money." Along with it the values and rights man embraces are of great significance, for these he has struggled and sacrificed himself: political and religious freedom, democracy, equality, justice, respect for human life, and the right to be different. In other words, whatever was taught by the Greco-Roman civilization. Christianity, before weakening into dogmas, Roman legislators, Justinian with his Civil Code, and numerous other contemporary European philosophers and writers. These values comprise the ideological pattern of my works and are externalized either as clear, visible aims of "enlightened men" or as their absence and the instinctive search for them by the common man, whom I describe.

At the same time, in both my prose and plays, my attention is drawn to the barbarity of today's "civilized society," whose only difference, compared to the Middle Ages, is its superficial sophistication, the loneliness and alienation by the Epicurean and Sybaritic lifestyle as expressed by uncontrolled overconsumption, power and its relation to the individual, the position of art—if art has a place in the age of internet and the modern mass media that flattens everything. An identity at a personal and collective level, the cheapening of values and so on. Everything, in other words, that my compatriots and I have lived through in all these years on our island and in the neighboring, tragic Middle East, outdistanced, for the most part, compared to the rest of Europe, which already lived through and overcame these ordeals about a half century ago.

So these are the motifs, illuminated either on their dark or bright side, that permeate my work. The guerrillas, heroes of the short story "Gregory" to which I referred at the beginning, by putting their lives at stake, place their friendship and compassion above so-called "national duty." Onysilos and Kyriakos Matsis, in the homonym theatrical, sacrificed themselves in order to set an example, to create a symbol. The thirteen orthodox monks of Kantaras, by refusing to espouse Catholicism, suffered the torment of being bound from the tails of the papal horses, dragged along a riverbank, and burnt at the stake. They went through all this fully aware that their actions would strengthen orthodoxy on the island. Roi Pierre, whose love for the humble Cypriot girl led to generous reforms, pays a heavy penalty for his political courage. The solitary hero of "The Meal," who believes that if he exposes his body to the bright light of the day he will be transformed and gain Faust's gift of youth, continues his experiments in complete isolation despite the fact that he ends up being a laughing stock. The simple foot soldier in "The Silent Infantry-man," who, hurt by the cruelty of people, isolates himself for decades in a mountain cavern, is eventually defeated by silence and loneliness, thus he abandons his dark cave to seek human company. The low-ranking priest in "The Literate Man," who plunges to his death from the archbishop's balcony, underscores, through his suicide, his repulsion towards hypocritical piety. Kriton Stefanis, the hero of the story "The Bath," is tormented by feelings of remorse and guilt due to his avarice, which made him fleece many people as a wholesale merchant of medicine, now in the twilight of his life, locks himself in the bathroom for eight hours a day, trying to rinse himself of the imaginary filth that distresses him.

Here are some of the recurring motifs of my work, none other than the quintessence of my experience, which we, as Cypriots, have endured over the last decades. Similar experiences can surely be found in the works of hundreds of European writers of the by-gone years or even in those of the contemporary ones, but also in the works of fellow craftsmen from nearby or more remote "neighborhoods of our world." This is because, in final analysis, the terms "Europe" and "European" not only define the specific geographical area and its history, but something bigger and wider: they define man himself.

Concluding this essay and apologizing for its omissions and im-perfections (I have never been an essayist or critic), I would like to add a couple of words about the method of writing, the structure, aesthetics, and language employed in my work.

I attempt to make my narration simple and coherent in its meaning. Many critics call it modernistic and elliptical, whatever these terms may mean. Perhaps the avoidance of verbiage in some parts of my novel *Census* and in a number of short stories in which words and sentences are abused and the straightforward narration is interrupted. I frequently attempt a deep introspection inside the consciousness, obeying the call of psychoanalysis. At other times, being a secret worshipper of poetry, I replace prose with a more substantial and succinct poetic word.

In the novels *The Unbearable Patriotism of P.F.K.* and *Census*, I invert normal narrative conventions. In the plays *Counterpoint* and *Key Made of Nacre*, I interweave reality with a dream or a night-mare and realism with allegory and metaphysics. In the satirical play *Leontios and Smyrna*, my hero first disguises himself and is eventually transformed internally and literally into a centaur. The metrical description belongs to his mistress:

> Leontios Leontiou, of the Immortal parentage,
> Robust centaur, fully mature,
> More than the Earth's navel, a wise man,
> Poet Laurel-crowned and sacred,

As for the rest,
From the loins to the foot
A very rare specimen of a vigorous bull.

The structure of much of my prose is that of the theater. In this I am prompted by my love for the theatre, with its strong Hellenic-European roots. Indeed, after I have completed and published a story, I often rewrite it as a play, looking into its new potentials. Many of my plays emerge in this way.

My language is multifaceted. I use a vocabulary originating from all "branches" of the Greek language: ancient, Byzantine, medieval, and of course the modern spoken language. Thus, I strengthen my efforts at the extension of myth into the eternity I always pursue. Neither do I hesitate to use words of foreign origin, the remnants of Frankish, Turkish, and English occupations, which have found their way in the Cypriot culture.

To conclude, I would like to say, that I give myself the right to fulminate and inveigh against every evil, by using satire, sarcasm, and self-criticism. I do this perhaps more frequently than the small Cypriot community would permit me to, and as a result, I once became the object of fierce criticism, and my life was even threatened on one occasion. I believe that such methods are familiar to European writers. The above-mentioned technique started with Aristophanis and Meandros and went on to Plautus and Poplios Terence, reaching its peak with Molière, Chekhov, Gogol, and others, and arrives at our own times, revived and enriched.

Summing up, I would like to add that in all my work, my prose, drama, and poetry, I try, using the heretical words of literature, to compose a modern fresco on which the current sociopolitical reality of Cyprus, but not only of Cyprus, is imprinted, a fresco whose ideal seal is nothing more than the anguished quest for a world ruled by the very values that give man substance and identity.

— *Translated by Atreas Tsiflakos*

Mirela Ivanova

Europe is part of my biography, my
poems, and my freedom. It is not
one continent, but a state of mind
and of words. It is one person uniting
an infinite number of people.
© Maxim Segienko/PHOTOMAX

Mirela Ivanova
Bulgaria

Born in Sofia in 1962, the poet, journalist, translator, and
editor Mirela Ivanova studied Bulgarian and Russian
Philology at the University of Plovdiv and worked as a
curator at the Ivan Vasov Museum. To date she has
published seven volumes of poetry including "Stone
Wings," "Whispers," "Lonely Game," "Memory for Details,"
"Dismantle Toys" and "Eclecticism." Mirela Ivanova writes
essays, reviews on fiction and theater performances,
deals with literature history, writes scenarios for
documentary films and translates from German. In 1994
she translated and published an anthology of modern
German poetry, entitled "The Wandering of Stones." She
has also translated from German works by Shara Kirsch,
Elke Erb, Gregor Laschen, Ernest Wicner, Durs Grünbein,
Uwe Kolbe, as well as Ernst Gombrich's popular work
"History of Mankind for Young Readers."
Mirela Ivanova is one of the most famous modern poets in
Bulgaria. Her poems have been translated into English,
German, Spanish, Czech, Hungarian, Turkish, Serbian
and Latvian. In 2002 she was awarded the Hubert Burda
Prize for young writers.

Further Reading:
*Window on the Black Sea: Bulgarian Poetry in
Translation*. Edited by Richard Harteis in collaboration
with William Meredith. Carnegie Mellon University Press,
1992.
Carnage: New Writing from Europe. Edited by Michael
Blackburn. Sunk Island Publishing, 1993.

Europe—One Way of Reading It

Европа е част от моята биография, от стиховете ми
и свободата ми. Не континет а държава на духа и
думите. Човек, у когото живеят безброй хора.

The first time I came across the term "Europe" was in a poem by our national poet, Ivan Vasov. In this poem he addresses Europe as a person who is dear and close to him and whom he would like to continue to trust, mainly because it knows the price of freedom. Therefore the attitude of indifference that Europe displays toward the brutality and the atrocities of the Turkish oppressors of our country is incomprehensible to him, and he is provoked to passionate rebuke in the face of this apathy. Right in the middle of this dramatic and, in all its cruel detail, epic and pathetic polemical poem, Vasov calls out in the name of his people, "Europe! Hold out your hand to me and I will be saved!"

I grew up in a village, free and without restraint. At night, when my mother came home from work, tired and downcast, she read me poems by our classical Bulgarian poets. Presumably this opened up for her a parallel world where she could be happy—a world beyond a reality that was so unjust to her, the young dentist plodding wearily along amid the country dirt and her own poverty. Thus, at an early age, I grew accustomed to the parallel existence of two worlds. During the day there were the open fields, the dusty roads, the wild games, the climbing of trees, and the unsentimentally crude language of the peasants; and in the evening, by contrast, there was the magic of the big words—their emotional luster, the tragic spirit of the lament with its dizzying pathos and the aureole of verse recited with pathos and resounding around the rich hair of my beautiful and sad mother. Vasov's Europe, too, demonstrated the existence of two parallel worlds: "What kind of Europe is this, great because of its humanity, / yet unfeeling at the sight of these atrocious pictures ..."—the idea of freedom of the people "luminous like altar candles" existing side by side with conceited indifference and economic interest, inevitably provoking "the awful guilty verdict" of the "enraged muse."

At the time I was four or five years old and, to my mind, Europe was indeed a person who failed to grasp the reality of our unjust suffering and did not even want to understand it. A person with whom it would be hard to find a common language, for striving to understand the other is the only bridge that can lead the way into foreign fields with the aim of them becoming our own. But I was also made aware of suffering and held tight to the word "freedom," thinking of it as a kind of stigma of my own fate. Later on, in my geography lessons, I learned all the boring facts about the continent of Europe, the square miles of its land mass, the number of states, the natural wonders and ore mines, the highest mountains, and all the rest of it. Yet those accumulated facts remained just that and did not stir my easily aroused childish imagination, where freedom and suffering shouted cacophonously, yet inexplicably, with the voice of a single person whose name was Europe. The old Hellenic myths were of no use to me, apart from confirming my childish notion that Europe was a person, and this notion joined up with the sensibilities of adolescence, the period in life where the gods fail us, too.

It was not until I started at the German Grammar School and had to memorize close to a hundred words per day during the first few weeks that I became aware of the fact that Europe must also be a language by means of which new worlds would eventually speak to me. Whereas it was no more than an inkling at first, I later discovered the German expressionists, both painters and poets. I played hooky from school and hid in the library, where I abandoned myself to their force, to their all-consuming and mysterious passion.

Much later I was to discover a similar intensity in the works of the Spanish poet Federico Garcia Lorca and the Bulgarian poet Geo Milev, both of whom were cravenly murdered in a Europe of revolutions and utopias of justice.

By the age of twenty I had learned a lot about Europe, and when I was twenty-five I had a map of Europe pinned to the wall of the basement room where I lived in Sofia. I was convinced I would only ever be able to know Europe by means of my imagination and through literature, and so I traveled the continent in the company of the great Greek poets Kavafis, Seferis, and Sikelianos and visited the beautiful and mythical Arcadia, an impossible, yet fervently coveted, world beyond. By this time Europe was no longer a geographical entity, but a state of words and spirit. Today I remember the many romantic gestures that served as my refuge, as compensation for my lack of freedom. I took French lessons in order to read the French symbolists in the original. I spent days comparing the various Bulgarian translations of Baudelaire and Rimbaud with the originals, or reciting the poems of Apollinaire aloud to myself in order to learn them by heart. With its damp walls and dark austerity, my "ivory basement," as I came to call it later, helped me open my inner self to the manifold and never-ending tragedy of European poetry. Hölderlin and Zwetajewa fascinated me, the dark side of the word that makes exiles of all of us, and I was obsessed by the idea that I had to join my lot with the fates, and the follies, and the suicides of these poets. Those years when Europe was not accessible to me as a reality, when I had to create a Europe for myself in order to learn to love it passionately, seem, in retrospect, like a gift. My self-education was unplanned, greedy; I devoured knowledge and sadness in order to find the courage to be my own true self. Today I realize how much time I had then—how much loneliness to be peopled only with words. I kept a diary, I wrote and read, I sought to form my character and hunted for clues to show me the way. Of course, at the same time I was also looking for work, for life is also a concrete and mundane affair and, in addition to beauty and the sublime, it requires food and clothing. Thus I continued to live in parallel worlds, though they were far less compatible than those of my childhood. Moving from one to the other was achieved either by an enormous effort on my part, or it pulled me down into the depths of despair, as into marshy land. I remember not leaving the house for days on end, staring at some point on the map of Europe and drawing up mental lists, to the point of insanity, of all the restrictions under which my life had been decreed to unfold. But, of course, youth and poetry are stronger than any despair they manage to bring forth; they have enormous resources of energy, imagination, and pride at their disposal and are willing to master obstacles of all manner.

In 1988, after encountering innumerable humiliating barriers, I finally succeeded in finding employment as editor of a magazine on children's literature. At the same time I was working on my second volume of poetry. The title, *Lonely Game,* I borrowed from an essay by Hermann Hesse. I had to go through endless and almost hopeless discussions with an otherwise supportive editor regarding notions of pessimism and optimism in my poems. I defended each and every word, rejecting any suggestion of cuts. Eventually the publishing house for "Bulgarian Writers" accepted my book for publication, and I received a small advance on my royalties. It was enough to allow me to buy my first painting, and to sign up for a trip to Greece organized by the publishing house. It was a fascinating and exciting journey, and at the same time shameful. One member of our group, Angel, a member of the translators' association, was a state spy. He had a good sense of humor and brought with him several bottles of brandy, but otherwise had no distinguishing features. A number of people in the group brought things they wanted to sell in Greece: sheep's cheese, terrycloth towels, even inner tubes for tires. Officially we were allowed to change only thirty leva, a ridiculously small sum no matter what one wanted to buy. This trip to Greece was my first real live contact with Europe. Basically we traveled through parts of Greece that had formerly belonged to Bulgaria, visiting towns whose names and stories also existed in my mother tongue. But what I marveled at was something else: the brightness of it all, the great variety of things, the different colors, the liveliness of it, life going on day and night. In a poem about Kavala I wrote: "This town is a veranda with a view of freedom." The Europe of my imagination corresponded to the reality of Europe, and all my senses and sensibilities trembled with enthusiasm during those few days, while a colleague, who had previously visited a cousin in West Germany, kept saying to us, "But over there—if only you could see what it's like over there!"

Thus, in an elated mood, I was stunned by the news of the fall of the Berlin Wall and by my first invitation to the *Literarische Colloquium* that, at the time, was still situated in West Berlin. At first it was not an endlessly complicated and humiliating procedure to obtain a visa. All you had to do was to present the required documents and pay the fee. Later on, however, when I had to stand in a long line thinking that my turn would never come, I frequently remembered that poem by Ivan Vasov. Full of vengeful thoughts, I reflected on the conceited indifference of a Europe that scorned even those measures that it had introduced as protection against the locusts from Eastern Europe, which threatened its cozy privacy. I took my own small revenge by going to Amsterdam and Paris illegally for a few days, places that I had ached for with longing during my enclosed youth. Through the railings of a bridge, I stared at the flowing waters of the Seine or the Neckar and let myself be carried away by my favorite poems. As soon as I stepped onto a street in Berlin, London, or Paris, I became one with its freedom and let my self drift in its immensity; sitting in a café, I looked out on those streets for hours and enjoyed them endlessly and insatiably; walking through galleries and museums I became familiar with them and the people in them.

The spiritual variety that Europe carries around constantly, like a rucksack, has not made me unaware of the tangible order and rules that govern life, the smiling day-to-day here. With meanings and symbols creating an inner tension, I am traveling from city to city, knowing that I am basically traveling to my inner self, to my childhood, where two parallel worlds were united harmoniously and without complications—the infinity of the word with the infinity of the fields and meadows, the buildings of civilization with the dust of our games, the celebration of human closeness with the metaphysical pain of man, "who is on his own in the heart of the Earth," the "lightheartedness of the poet," as Unamuno describes it, with the stress of modern man, who is preoccupied by innumerable, mutually exclusive, tasks.

Europe presents a complexity of life and of the mind, a semblance of order uniting all our human and national imperfections and talents; it is a perpetual invitation to practice tolerance towards others, a good place for parallel worlds that are mutually dependent for their existence. Europe is part of my biography, my poems, and my freedom. It is not one continent, but a state of mind and of words. It is one person uniting an infinite number of people.

Vasov, our national poet, in whose museum I am presently working, mentioned in his poems the names of those who "are luminous, like altar candles in ubiquitous darkness."

— *Translated by Susanne Höbel*

Lídia Jorge

Tthe most important thing that Portuguese
literature has to offer is what it has to say
about its relationship to the Other, those
that are different, at least half of an essential
dialogue that the future is urgently seeking.
© Maxim Segienko/PHOTOMAX

Lídia Jorge

Portugal

Born in Boliqueime, Algarve in 1946, Lídia Jorge studied
Romance languages and literature in Lisbon and spent
several years in Angola and Mozambique during the
colonial wars. After her return to Portugal, she taught at a
grammar school, worked for the Portuguese Ministry of
Education, and taught literature at the University of Lisbon.
Her first novel *O Dia dos Prodígios* (*The Day of Miracles*)
was published in 1980. It was followed in 1982 by *O Cais
das Merendas*, for which she was awarded the Lisbon
Prize, and in 1984 by *Notícia da Cidade Silvestre* (*News
from the Other Side of the Street*), which was celebrated
as a masterpiece of contemporary Portuguese literature.
For her novel *O Vento Assobiando nas Gruas* (2002),
she was awarded the 2003 Grand Prize for Fiction of the
Portuguese Writers' Association. Lídia Jorge lives in
Lisbon.

Further Reading:
The Murmuring Coast. Translated by Natalia Costa.
University of Minnesota Press, 1995.
The Painter of Birds. Translated by Margaret Jull Costa.
Harcourt, 2001.

A Sort of Huge Portugal

...aquilo que de mais importante a Literatura
portuguesa tem para oferecer é o recado que dá de si
na relação com o Outro, o diferente, enquanto metade
da voz de um inevitável diálogo, a que o futuro
clamorosamente obriga.

1

There was a well-known anecdote in the early seventies about a Portuguese student, who, standing in front of the Café Flore in Paris, raised his arms and began to shout, "Europe! I've made it to Europe!" The next day he failed to turn up for a university outing, disappeared from his hotel room, and began to live clandestinely in France. Of course, the young student in question didn't want to stay in France just because he recognized the role that Café Flore played in the mythology of a certain period of European thought nor because it was in Paris that European and world history had been engraved most powerfully in the collective memory. Like thousands of others during this period, the student didn't intend to return to Lisbon; he was fleeing his country, a nation seriously deprived of the culture of freedom. He was fleeing from dictatorship, from university closures, from a cruel colonial war, from the prohibition on meetings, from travel restrictions, from scarce financial resources, from an archaic infrastructure and from a lack of freedom of expression. The café window next to which Sartre drank his coffee had become a potent symbol, gleaming like a beacon of light. Other Portuguese exiles did not become legends or shout in front of cafés, though they almost certainly harbored the same hope that their country, if only for geographic reasons, would one day belong to a free Europe, that then existed only in our imagination. This situation would not last long, however. Within three years, the Carnation Revolution would erupt. Within fifteen, Portugal would be integrated into the European Community. And from then on, words and expressions like *adherence, integration,* or *the strength of convergence* would become the key terms in the new political dictionary.

2

But the heart together with memory or intuition about the future, doesn't beat exactly in time with agreements or the signing of contracts. The special nature of Portugal's past and its relationship to the old empire survived and endured beyond the historic moment of the official changeover, affirmed in 1985 at the Monastery of Geronimos by Mario Soares' signature. Portugal's isolation, which had progressively distanced us from Europe (democratic or otherwise), could not be eliminated overnight. The image of frightened people, arriving from Africa every day at Lisbon Airport—an exodus of Biblical proportions unleashed when their countries became independent—was too disturbing to be overcome by simply turning a page.

No treaty joining us to the European community, however auspicious, could wipe away the memory of the extraordinary scenes of the mountains of boxes lining the river Tagus. It was as if a giant wave, more than five-hundred years old, had swept back, with both weapons and baggage, the Portuguese who had once sailed from there. The bemused delight of receiving subsidies to build bridges and carve out motorways became mixed up with the images of civil wars that had broken out in the meantime in the newly independent countries recently freed from Portuguese colonialism. The daily bloodbaths in Angola, Mozambique, Timor, and later Guinea aroused uncomfortable feelings of disorientation among all those who had predicted the creation of stable nations, eager to move towards progress and peace, in these newly independent states. It is true that Portuguese girls grew ten centimeters taller than their mothers did twenty years earlier and that young people could travel throughout the world without restrictions. But at the same time, they became conscious that Portuguese territory had shrunk to the size it was during the Middle Ages—the period when the concept of nationality first came into being. Throughout the nineties the idea persisted that an important part of the nation's body had been amputated. The image of empire was like an imaginary limb, still felt long after it had been separated from the body.

Nationalism, with its obsolete and rigid structures, was reviewed and re-examined, along with the other tattered components of citizenship. During the last quarter of the twentieth century Portugal was composed of this mass of contradictions that did violence to the soul. Ghosts of the past appeared, holding hands with the personalities of the present, and our dramatic arts took on a new, vigorous life.

It could be said that Portugal lived through a unique emotional history in this regard, without parallel in any other European country. Our losses were so fundamental, the changes so radical — and they all happened simultaneously and out of their time. Within this context the Arts, particularly Literature, whose basic material is that of everyday speech, extended their area of influence, as often happens in such times. Everyone began to speak their mind, and a turbulent, fertile period turned Portuguese literature into a brutal, strange, and unique thing among European literatures.

Thus, in the middle of the eighties, when Portuguese literature began to be translated and read abroad, there was an almost unconditional admiration for its poets. But when it came to fiction, that area of literature which shares so much with history, it was considered to be a "prisoner" of that immovable triangle — *Old Empire, Colonial War, Carnation Revolution*. It took some time for this thesis to become outdated; for what is usually called internationalism, global citizenship or stories from all parts of the world, didn't seem to inspire Portuguese writers. Some talked of a redundant obsession with identity, or the strangeness of Portuguese narrative, which was tied to the African experience and fables from the past. In 1991, for example, at a conference such as this in Strasbourg, Pascale Casanova classified Portugal as an "island of paradox." In reference to Portuguese literature, she said that intellectuals, and especially novelists, were perpetuating a single polemic — that of national identity. She concluded by explicitly proposing a theory of Portuguese separatism vis-à-vis European intellectual life. To quote her: "The references to history and Portuguese culture no longer belong, in any way, to the common and essential heritage of Europe ..." In this way she was trying to say that Portuguese writers had not managed to conform to current standards of literature, global culture, cinematographic writing that they had ignored the grand narrative theme assumed to be contemporary. This is certainly what is being implied in the Strasbourg Notebooks, *The Desire of Europe*, which were dedicated to that conference in which Portuguese writing played a prominent role.

Eleven years later, this analytical approach had become somewhat outdated. Over the past decade it has become commonly recognized that the theme of Portuguese identity was, in the end, not so exceptional in Europe. It became rapidly understood that questioning the relationship between a "marginal country" (ours) with the world was one of the various European forms of questioning itself. The Portuguese world, almost ridiculous in the way it hesitated between spaces in the globe, now bunched together, now scattered, became a respected example of how to conduct relations between Europe and other continents. A slightly tongue-in-cheek anecdote, often told in Portugal these days says, that Europe, so indecisive that it is paralyzed, seems to have been transformed into a huge Portugal. Leaving irony aside, it might not be too misleading to suggest that the most important thing that Portuguese literature has to offer is what it has to say about its relationship to the Other, those that are different, at least half of an essential dialogue that the future is urgently seeking.

This is not because Portuguese literature has changed into something else; it is due to the fact that the world has been obliged to change course. First, in the nineties civil wars broke out all over the place, in former English, French, Belgian, Spanish, and Dutch colonies. Europe's entire legacy to the world was being questioned. Second, because ethnic conflicts that had previously seemed to be confined to Africa and Asia now had parallels in terms of brutality and violence in the heart of Europe itself. Consequently, Europe began to suffer from an identity crisis at the beginning of the nineties, which left her astonished, paralyzed at a crossroads, unable to move forward. It was at this time that the Portuguese factor became acknowledged as a pertinent contemporary issue.

3

In order to gain an understanding of one's own identity it is necessary for someone else to identify us, because no one knows themselves unless they look into another face. The mirror into which we look in the morning is only an intermediary between us and the other. Portuguese writers, inspired by their particular reality, have written obsessively about this relationship with the other. A relationship that has passed through all the shades of interpretation; writing in which colonizers, the colonized, rivals, brothers, lovers, the vengeful and the repentant, friends, and enemies are intermingled.

From this point of view of total involvement and endless association with the other, I would say that the *original* text in the decolonizing, post-colonial mental process came paradoxically from the creative force of a creator of empires, both metaphysically and otherwise. I am referring to a great poem full of magnificent, piratical deeds. The tradition of Portuguese, European, and global piracy that made the world go round, intermingled people, violated nations, wiped out the defeated, and raised flags. I quote from the long poem, "Ode Maritima," written in 1915 by Fernando Pessoa under his pen name of Álvaro de Campos. These passages reflect a sentimental delirium in which the thrill of conquest and the excitement surrounding the pirate's life is intertwined with an amalgam of humanity, as of a whole: You men who plundered peaceful African villages, / Scattering the natives with the roar of your cannon, / You who murdered, robbed, tortured, and grabbed the reward / Of the New Things promised to those who lowered their heads / To rush out against the mystery of the new seas! / He-he-he! / To all of you together, to all of you as though you were one, / To all of you mixed together and interlocking, / To all of you bloody, violent, hated, feared, revered, / I salute you, I salute you, I salute you! (translated from the Portuguese by Edwin Honig, New Directions, 1971)

Written in the beginning of the twentieth century, at the time of the World War I, "The Song of the Great Pirate" thus opens a door on the objective inevitability of history, without remorse or sense of sin. The explosion of European culture was inevitable when,

moving beyond its borders, it made itself the center of expansion
and initiated the process of globalization. As a consequence, subjected to all the effects of today's violent flux of change, we are
contemporary. Recent Portuguese fiction regarding the question of
identity, of the post-colonial and post-revolutionary period, alter-
natively democratic, melancholic, and introspective, began to review the balancing of accounts with the most strident part of this
flow, and in this respect has something to say. For Europe, on the
other hand, whose main concern is the drawing up of its internal
frontiers, in conceiving it's external frontiers, in determining its
new center or various centers, the Portuguese experience doesn't
offer an important contribution. The problem of geographical
frontiers doesn't flow through its veins.

What does flow there is a concern for the frontiers of the other,
the possibility of dialogue with the other, the problem of sharing
with a strange neighbor now that increased mobility has shrunk
distances and made us simultaneously guests and hosts wherever
we may be. How to receive the other in our home, how to go about
being received in the other's home; how to coexist in a mental
space in which we can't even imagine the previous prison orders,
the sending in of police patrols or fighter planes. In this imprecise
space all wars can be moderated, but none can be won. This is the
unavoidable question whose epigraph is "The Song of the Great
Pirate." In the realm of fiction it has been more that twenty years
since Portuguese narrative focused tenaciously and obsessively on
this theme, as if this balancing of accounts, coming to terms with it
in the process, was the inevitable point of it all. That's where I see
myself. That's where I place the core of my books. And these, my
books, I see as savage beings existing between the twists and turns
of fortune. Chance put me among people dislodged by history,
people who move from one place to another in search of rest. It is
also true that I write mainly for another reason, one that exists
outside history and without name. Another thing and another
cause. The theme of brotherhood, personified, offers me a tangible
face behind which I ask life about this mystery; that we are all
people, to be alone on the earth and unable to understand each
other except through conflict. Perhaps for this reason my current

bedside reading is by a European bruised by war, written in segments between 1951 and 1952. It talks of a Europe just emerging
from the last great conflict. Its author was Curzio Malaparte. It is
called *Mamma Marcia, Mae Apodrecida*. That is the title. I don't
read it as someone who dips into a menacing Bible; but I open it
regularly, to think about the way in which it is possible to descend
from peace into ignominy and write about this. Against this.

— *Translated by Stephanie d'Orey*

Dževad Karahasan

If there exists anything on the basis of which
Europe exists as a kind of cultural unity, then
it is time—a shared assumption about time.
© gezett.de

Dževad Karahasan
Bosnia

Born in Duvno, Yugoslavia in 1953, Karahasan received a
doctorate in literary theory from the Faculty of Philosophy
in Zagreb. He was a script editor at Zenica Public Theatre
and an editor at the literary magazines *Odjek* and *Izraz*. As
a professor, he taught at the Academy of Stage Arts in
Sarajevo and was chairman of the jury at Yugoslavia's
largest theatre festival. The siege of Sarajevo is the theme
of his book *Tagebuch der Aussiedlung* and his novels
Schahrijârs Ring and *Sara und Serafina*. He has been
awarded many prizes for his works. Karahasan lives in
Graz, where he is a city chronicler, and in Sarajevo, where
he is a professor of the Faculty of Philosophy at the
university.

Further Reading:
Sarajevo, Exodus of a City. Translated by Slobodan
Drakulić. Kodansha International, 1994.

Europe Writes in Time

*Ako postoji nešto na temelju čega Evropa postoji kao
kakvo-takvo kulturno jedinstvo, to je onda vrijeme—
zajednička predodžba o vremenu koja je u nekakvu
(naravno uvijek otvorenu) cjelinu povezivala sve dijelove
Evrope.*

To write means to relate to time. That was observed by one of the
first great Europeans, G. E. Lessing, in his essay "Laocoon," in
which he pointed out the difference between the "temporal" and
"spatial" arts, defining music and literature as "temporal arts." I do
not remember how Lessing defined the difference between music
and literature in relation to time, I do not remember whether he
defined it at all and I do not know whether it ought to be defined
because it springs from the nature of the material in which music
and literature are realized, and thus it is quite obvious. Music is
time which is heard, it does not need the material world and in fact
it needs nothing outside itself; the ancients were right to speak
about the "music of the spheres," thereby expressing the conviction
that the Universe produces music, that it is music, or at least music
is its fundamental characteristic. Literature, by contrast, could not
exist without the material world or outside it, it is realized in language and that is why one of the fundamental characteristics of
literature, and of language, is reference to what is outside it—a
work of literature, like every other linguistic statement, is a presence which brings with it the absent, a body which bears witness
to the truth of incorporeal existence. Literature is not time which
has been invested with audibility, like music; literature is an attempt to give time a specific form, to shape it in keeping with the
question of meaning, to bequeath a form to human existence in
time, and thereby also meaning, comprehensibility. Music does not

ask and does not affirm, it simply is; literature is above all a question, it asks about the way in which man is present in time and about the value of particular ways of being present.

To write means to relate to time even when one writes in order to deny time. Samuel Beckett, for instance, projects out of space into time the logical paradoxes of Zeno of Elea, endeavoring to deny time the way Zeno had denied movement: if the tortoise had at the outset at least a little advantage, Achilles could not overtake it at a run because space is, logically speaking, infinitely divisible so that the ten steps of distance between the tortoise and Achilles, which was the tortoise's initial advantage, are divided into infinitely many units which Achilles could not overcome except in eternity. Beckett's play demonstrates that logical paradox on the plane of time: if time is infinitely divisible, it is clear that every fraction of it is infinitely divisible, and it is then clear that every smallest unit of time contains the whole of time, that is eternity; hence this moment is equal to any other moment, that is why the differentiation of individual units of time is illusory, that is why there is no movement of time or movement in time. Is there then a symmetry between Beckett and Aurelius Augustinus? Augustine maintained that time was set in motion with God's creation of the world, it had stood still until the moment when the Lord pronounced his first "Let there be...," and from that moment it began to move towards the Day of Judgment, bringing each one of us his age, weariness and death. But Beckett speaks about a world in which time no longer flows, in which there simply is no time. And thus a symmetry is established between authors who endeavor obsessively to understand time and authors who obsessively deny time, a symmetry between entrance and exit. Perhaps a symmetry of the beginning and end of a process or a series?

What fills this symmetry, that is how do these two authors relate to one another "seen from within"? As the beginning and end of a chain based in causality? Did Augustine really "produce" Beckett? Did Beckett's denial of time necessarily originate in Augustine's attempt to understand time?

Mystics and rationalists know that these two authors are inextricably linked and that their symmetry is not merely external. Be-

tween the mystic and the rationalist, between two apparently opposed types of determinism, that is, there are evident different
degrees of one fundamental conviction according to which two
different points of the temporal chain are not mutually connected.
And therefore between Augustine and Beckett there is no
"objectively existing" symmetry and there is no real connection,
but it is I, the reader, who discovers some kind of external symmetry, by reading into what I observe a relationship that exists only in
my experience. As this conviction denies the connection with
which we are concerned here, we can ignore its proponents and
concern ourselves with the mystics and rationalists. Jakob Boehme,
for instance, knows that Augustine, at the moment when he was
writing his "Confessions," made Beckett necessary, he knows in
fact that Beckett is "the other side" of Augustine and that they
make each other possible. When Augustine wrote that he seemed
to know what time was if he was not asked about it and he realized
that he did not know when he tried to explain it to someone, he
"produced," that is made necessary a Beckett who would illustrate
Zeno's logical paradoxes and thus confirm that there was no time
and that there was nothing to be known. Jakob Böhme also knows
that Beckett, when he writes his plays in which he denies time,
confirms Augustine, proves that he lived and wrote, confirms and
proves that he is necessary, summons him and makes him present
in the place where Beckett's play is being performed. I do not know
whether Beckett attended the first performance of "Godot" in 1953,
in Paris, but Augustine was certainly there.

John Stuart Mill maintained that the current state of affairs is a
consequence of the previous one, just as that previous one was a
consequence of the state of affairs that preceded it. The current
state of affairs is always the consequence of what preceded it, this
moment a consequence and that preceding one a cause. That is
why it is enough for a man who knows how to think logically, such
as, for instance John Stuart Mill, to know any one moment in the
infinite chain of time, in order to know, by logical induction based
on the principle of causality, and understand all the preceding and
subsequent moments, all the events which preceded the state of
affairs he knows and all those which will follow. If I know how to

think logically (causally), I understand confidently from reading
Beckett that a Jan Potocki and a Laurence Sterne must have existed
and written, that a Racine and a Rutebeuf must have written and
thus formulated questions about time. If I know how to think logically, if I am let us say J. S. Mill or Claude Levi-Strauss, if I am a
positivist or a structuralist, a Marxist or a follower of any scientist
sect, through Beckett I shall come quite certainly to Augustine,
because Beckett is a consequence of Augustine, just as shards of
glass are the consequence of a ball breaking a window. But, unlike
Jakob Böhme, I shall believe that Augustine was not present at the
production of Beckett's play because everything, including the
dead and meaning, is subject to a mechanical order, and a dead
person cannot appear in the present and nor can a consequence
affect its cause (Beckett Augustine).

That is how mystics and determinists think (that is mystics of
scientist religion). But what do I think? How do I feel Augustine
and Beckett relate to one another, this day to that distant day in
which St Francis of Assisi first felt that a wolf was his brother?
Those are the questions that must be answered by a man who
wishes to write and make conscious his relationship to his craft
and to the culture in which he is writing. At the heart of literature
lies the question of man's existence in time, to write means to give
form to time and to articulate man's relationship with that form, so
that we wonder about time as we write, we wonder even when we
are not aware of it. And that is how it is with culture. Culture is
above all and more than anything else the shaping of time, a system of assumptions and rituals which give form to a day and a year,
which define the thresholds in the life of the individual and the
community, and prescribe the steps by which those thresholds are
crossed. Perhaps the unbreakable connection of culture with time
is nowhere so obvious as in Europe: not for one moment of its history was Europe identical with its geographical limits, not for one
moment of its history did Europe have "spatial unity" which would
define it as a cultural identity, never did Europe have linguistic or
educational unity. If there exists anything on the basis of which
Europe exists as a kind of cultural unity, then it is time — a shared
assumption about time which has connected all the parts of Europe

in some kind of whole (always open, of course), however unclear it always was where the borders of Europe were and what was actually going on within those borders. For all its differences, Europe was always some kind of cultural whole because it was always integrated around an image of time. That is why it is logical that, ever since I began to write, I have been endeavoring to answer those questions.

I have discussed these questions in essays, without succeeding in discovering whether I am sincere when I deny a direct connection between two very distant points in the chain of time or when I maintain that this connection cannot be called into question because it is too obvious. Once (in my essay "Language and History," for instance) I ironized to a disproportionate extent the determinist concept of history, wondering whether Hannibal really did cross the Alps in order for me to be just what I am. Another time I articulated my deepest conviction (which is inseparable from feeling, which is not whole without feeling!), when I upheld the precisely European concept of tradition based on the mechanical orderliness of the temporal chain (for instance in my essay "The Geography of Shadow"). It was only when I knew that the deterministic feeling was far closer to me, that I knew that I was far more inclined to believe the mystical rather than the scientist concept because I could never question the happy presence of ancient teachers in any way. Of course I cannot doubt the mystical presence of Fariduddin Attar when I write about ruins, if I were to call that into question, I would have to doubt also the presence of my theatrical and prose characters, which is really indisputable and without which I could not write either a play or a novel. Of course with every sentence I write I engage in a discussion with some author or work, regardless of whether I know it or not, regardless of whether I do it intentionally or not. With every sentence he writes, a man weaves a new thread into the dense web of senses, which is potentially always present, everywhere where people speak or write.

But concerning myself with this question has not helped me reconcile myself to an image of time as a straight line, as an axis moving, from an immeasurable depth (or distance?) towards naught, and then from naught to the present day and further on, presumably to Judgment Day. It has not helped me to reconcile myself to this image of time (which is irresistibly reminiscent of a series of primary numbers), and still less has it helped me to free myself from it. All "types" of time about which I am capable of speaking—mythic time and sacred time, historical time and mystic time, are in fact forms defined above all by their relationship to that one form of an axis moving from "minus infinity" to "plus infinity," a form which is the fundamental and dominant image of time in European culture (the image which is the foundation of that culture and which distinguishes that culture from all others).

I also concerned myself with time in connection with dramatic form, as a professor of drama, and, "directly," as a writer. I developed a whole theory of chronotopes, demonstrated that the experience of time is decisive for the inner logic of drama, in my plays I intertwined various concepts of time which existed in parallel in the places in which I lived and which I presented in my plays. I based my comedy "It's Good Over There" on the "dramatic comparison" of forms in which the Communist, Catholic and Bosnian-Muslim worlds articulate their images of time. I dedicated my comedy "Concert of Birds" to time, as a theme and a structural principle. But that did not help me make friends with the European concept of time as an axis either, and still less did it help me free myself from that concept.

Time moves infallibly from a beginning towards an end, one moment follows logically and necessarily from the preceding one, as its consequence or at least as its response, each moment can and must be precisely (mechanically) defined on that axis, so that it is perfectly reliably clear how far any given point in the past is removed from this point from which I am looking (the present). And meanwhile, in my (and the European, nota bene) sense of tradition, the entire past is present in every moment. This in itself contradictory, disturbing experience of time, which places me in the center of a paradox and does not allow me to get out of it, was, of course, insupportable, particularly because it is so inalienably mine and at the same time it does not correspond fully to my sense of time.

It was only working on novels that helped me to understand the problem of my relationship to time, a relationship that is not simply rational, nor can it be. My persistent dissatisfaction with what I write, innumerable failed attempts, dozens of rejected stories and sketches for novels which remained mere experiments with narrative structure, the feeling that the text I have written is simply not mine—all that brought me to the problem of time, but not only the problem of time in a narrative work, but the problem of time in my experience. Because my problem was not so much narrative technique, my problem is the precision of the narrated world. And this cannot be achieved if the author is not present in what he has written both experientially and emotionally, without reserve, if he has not tested every word he writes on his own skin; it is only then, when an author is present in his writing, that the work is able to be free of him and the author can confirm whether the world of his work corresponds also to external reality, beyond language; and it is only when the inner reality of a work is certainly genuine, because the author has tested it on his own skin, when the external reality of the world corresponds to the external reality of the work—it is only then that the work has attained the essential degree of precision. And this refused to happen for me in my prose writing until I found a novelistic form in which the spiral image of time characteristic of Islamic culture and the axis image of time characteristic of European culture were connected (completing one another? Linked together in a relationship of tension?).

The spiral is a form that unites the circle and the axis, a form that contains a kind of precise infinity. Perhaps the most exact expression of the spiral experience of time is the arabesque, a visual form that depicts movement which is repeated infinitely (the end of the wall on which the arabesque is painted interrupts it, but it does not end it because an arabesque cannot end; and at the same time, one could say that it is ended when the basic figure, in which all the elements of an arabesque structure are used, is repeated a certain number of times). "The arabesque is the most spiritualized of all lines" maintained Baudelaire, probably sensing that the arabesque was in fact the image of time as it was experienced by classical Islamic culture. I cannot speak (narrate) about destiny, I cannot even think of destiny, separately from the arabesque form of spiral time, all the points of which are potentially present in every place. Forms of destiny or forms of thought can make people from different centuries contemporaries, if they have connected them in experience or ideas. In the spiral experience of time, in my experience, Augustine and Beckett are contemporaries, perhaps even friends, who never cease to quarrel passionately. I adopted this experience of time in my parental home and connected it once and for all with prayer and death, with destiny and truth. That experience of time adopted me and settled in that part of my being from where narrative springs.

But nor did spiral time in itself suit my conception of narration and my experience of time. Augustine and Beckett are certainly contemporaries, there can be no doubt of that, but it must be known that one of these contemporaries comes from the fifth and the other from the twentieth century, just as a story must make it clear that one of them had experience of barbarians and the other of machines, and that is probably why one preached belief and the other hopelessness. Namely, the whole world outside my parental home, all the experience brought me by school and the street, the bar and the stadium, brought me a different, axial sense of the world, which is insolubly linked with an external precision and measurability ("only what is measurable is real," Max Planck explained to us). And that is why my form of narration had to link axial and spiral time, external "measurability" and the inner contemporaneity of moments, which are technically very far apart. Sometimes I think that the search for such a form is that decisive element which European culture has brought me as a writer, the most important of the abundant riches, which it has unselfishly lavished on me.

— *Translated by Celia Hawkesworth*

Fatos Lubonja

The reluctance of Europe to accept writers from
small countries as European writers has had a certain
alienating effect on the creative process in literature.
© Joachim Röhm

Fatos Lubonja
Albania

Born in Tirana in 1951, Fatos Lubonja, who was called *Albania's Václav Havel* by the *New York Times* in 1997, is one of the most highly reported independent writers of Albania. His penetrating analyses are much noted both at home and abroad. Under the communist regime, he spent seventeen years as a political prisoner in detention centers and work camps. He has recorded his experiences in autobiographical stories and the novel *Ridënimi* (*Second Judgement*). Lubonja is publisher of the literary journal *Përpjekja*, which he founded in 1994. He lives and works in Tirana.

Further Reading:
"Neocolonialism and Responsibility. The Western Presence in the Balkans" and "Re-Inventing Skenderbeg. Albanian Nationalism and NATO Neo-colonialism."
www.eurozine.com
"Ahlem." Translated John Hodgson.
www.wordswithoutborders.org

Between the Local and the Universal

*Ky lloj konceptimi thjeshtë si dëshmitar i rolit të
intelektualit të vendeve të vogla në nivel kontinenti, kjo
rezistencë e Evropës për t'i pranuar edhe si shkrimtarë
evropianë shkrimtarët e vendeve të vogla nuk ka mbetur
pa lënë gjurmë alienuese në procesin krijues të
shkrimtarëve.*

When trying to answer the question, "What is European in my work?" my mind goes back to Burrel Prison, where I wrote my first novel, *The Final Slaughter*, between 1988 and 1991, and to the diary I kept during my last year in prison, in 1990–1991, later published as *In the Seventeenth Year*.

I cannot think of Burrel Prison without seeing in my mind's eye the rectangular cell in which I spent the final years of my imprisonment with eight, nine, or sometimes ten fellow inmates, according to circumstances. It had a row of beds placed on a wooden platform leaning against one wall, a narrow passage between this platform and the opposite wall, a slanting outside wall with a window and an iron grille, so high that nobody could see out of it, and in the slanting inside wall a door that opened only a few times a day, with a spy hole kept almost always open. A prisoner spent twenty-two of twenty-four hours on his bed or in the passageway, walking up and down the narrow gap to stretch his legs, and only two hours in the prison yard for fresh air. He spent most of his waking hours with his backside to the straw mattress, which was so narrow that you often bumped elbows with your neighbor. To sit more comfortably he would position the pillow between his back and the cold wall, drawing his knees up to his chest, wrapped in blankets, especially in winter.

In a life of this kind the most commonplace reality coexisted with the highest ideals: physical survival, with a bent aluminum food dish, cigarettes rolled with bad tobacco, and piss pots in the corner of the room went with dreams, love, and the most fantastic ambitions. A prison poet described it in this way:

> I wake at dusk to a gnawing belly
> And soon chew on memories
> That rise in my gorge and I cannot keep down;
>
> I wrap myself in forgetfulness and my blood boils
> I stretch my limbs and cover my desires
> And the lamp of dreams glows all night
>
> (Chronicle)[1]

Time underwent strange distortions under the pressure of this kind of existence. The extreme monotony, with one day exactly like the next, and the absence of any sense of the present, meant that the past shrank into a short space and the future stretched out endlessly. Everything belonging to the past, both historical and personal, seemed to draw very close. This was because stories that had been regurgitated again and again in conversation, reading, or in the revolving mind became vivid, intimate, and part of your life, taking the place of all kinds of routine matters that fill the "normal" life of a free man. So the distant past of Socrates' Athens or Nero's Rome became very immediate. The Crucifixion of Christ and the monks copying manuscripts in the monasteries of the Middle Ages drew very near in time to each other and to you. The Renaissance was still closer. It was as if you had lived through the French Revolution yourself, with the execution of the king, and Danton saying to himself before the guillotine, "Don't flinch!" World War II, with the victory of the Allies and the Communist defeat of the nationalists in Albania, seemed to have ended yesterday. The same compression of time affected personal memories from childhood, school, marriage, the birth of your children, and your arrest: all these seemed part of a two-hour movie. Then came your years in prison, which shrank to a few moments. On the other hand, the future stretched ahead without end. A century would have to pass before your next meeting with your family, and the year of your release lay beyond your own death. It was like the opposite of time in a spacecraft traveling at the speed of light.

Something similar happened to geographical space. The longer you spent in isolation, the more meaningless the geographical borders of states became. A prisoner increasingly felt like a citizen of the world, living more and more in other civilizations, beyond the Adriatic, beyond the Atlantic, or beyond the Indian Ocean, while Albania grew smaller and smaller.

Then there would come a moment when the prisoner's mind stopped, and he would find himself at a still point in the very center of the globe, in hell.

> Suddenly the globe stands still
> Gathers its burden and slips into the abyss
> Sound is caught short and shuns its echo
> And the world speaks to me wordlessly, as if under water.
>
> (The Globe)[2]

I see myself poised between this sense of the universal, a citizen of the world and of all ages, and this point where I sit transfixed, my legs wrapped in blankets and my back against the wall, a notebook and pencil in my hands, writing *The Final Slaughter* and the diary that was later called *In the Seventeenth Year*.

The Final Slaughter

At the time when I was writing *The Final Slaughter* and *In the Seventeenth Year*, my conception of art was nourished by the idea that a work of merely local significance is just as inadequate as one that is purely universal; that is, if a piece is to be really good it must be both local and universal. What I want to say by describing the maturation and subsequent fate of these two books of mine concerns the local and the universal, which I would interpret as the Albanian and the European. Certain thoughts have also come to me on this subject during the years since I disembarked from this "spacecraft" of prison.

The creative germ of *The Final Slaughter* lay in a problem that had preoccupied me for years during my long incarceration: Why was it that the ruling Communists, after they had seen that their idea had failed, did not resign, but clung to power and persisted in their crimes? This was a question of particular relevance to Albania up to 1990, because Albania experienced no de-Stalinization, no thaw, and no perestroika, but on the contrary, only increasing Stalinist terror.

In order to express this concern, I chose my material from perhaps the most universal source with which my background had supplied me: the Greek mythology that, as I have said, felt so much a part of me at the "center of the world" where I found myself. Taking as my point of departure Sophocles' drama in which Oedipus, once he discovers from the Delphic oracle that he is the cause of the curse of Thebes, surrenders his rule, gouges out his eyes, and is left abandoned and banished by the Thebans, I had the idea of recreating the myth of Thebes and of Oedipus, but taking it in the opposite direction. In short, this is the story of the novel:

The rain that lashed men into fury (a symbol I created myself) first waters the dragon's teeth that Cadmus has sown, feeding and bringing forth from the earth the children of the Dragon, who are the citizens of Thebes (the creation myth of Thebes). This rain sometimes falls on Thebes, and the Thebans, drinking the water that floods over everything, are transformed into beasts, turning against each other, murdering and tearing one another to pieces. Meanwhile the rain also brings the Sphinx, who announces that only the solving of his riddles will save the city from the curses and periodical bloody disasters that the rain causes. But the solutions offered to the Thebans as their salvation turn out to be nothing but myths that are sooner or later exploded. The solution that my Oedipus offers to the riddle of the sphinx is also of this kind. And so Thebes falls under a new curse. My Oedipus becomes aware of this; he knows that he brought about the curse by murdering his father and sleeping with his mother, that he has given a wrong answer to the riddles of the Sphinx, and that his continued rule will merely perpetuate the general curse. Yet, unlike the Oedipus of Sophocles, he does not surrender his rule, but on the contrary embarks on a policy of terror in order to retain power, liquidating anyone who reveals the truth.

The power-hungry Oedipus of this story is different from Sophocles' Oedipus in another way as well. The absence during the first year of his infancy of any relation with his mother, the strong affective tie that defines and, indeed, according to one psychoanalytic view, determines a person's emotional disposition throughout life, has created a dark void in his soul that generates only hatred, a desire for destruction, pleasure in violence, and the degradation of others as a pleasure in itself: in other words, the traits of a tyrannical character. Thus, in the Oedipus of this story, incest and a tyrannical predisposition fit together.

The novel ends with the noise of the wings of the approaching Sphinx, implying that the rain of fury is about to fall again. But Oedipus does not end up banished by the citizens of Thebes, persecuted and lonely, as in Sophocles' drama. His destiny is to rule in solitude over a devastated Thebes, imagining himself as a cursed God, who will die as soon as the rain begins. After his orgy of murder, he is surrounded only by the corpses, not only of the sons of the Dragon, but of his other more recent adversaries, including even his closest supporters and most loyal guards. It is worth mentioning here Elias Canetti's idea, upon which Leonardo Sasha has commented, that a dictator, deep down, seeks to resemble God, so that his ego envelopes the entire world at the expense of the existence of other egos: thus a dictator's ultimate dream is to create and rule over a world without people. However, this is impossible because he would not have anybody to rule over, and so he tries to create a world without individuals.

The Final Slaughter was also written as a prophecy of what would happen after the fall of Communism.

In the Seventeenth Year

A prisoner sometimes lived his real life in parallel with the ideal world and sometimes inextricably entwined with it. His life consisted of three types of daily struggle: against the government; against other prisoners; and against himself. A prisoner could never win against all three simultaneously. Most often, he would win one struggle and lose the other two.

In the Seventeenth Year is a prison diary about these three struggles, a description of a prisoner's daily life and his prison memories. It depicts the prisoners' relations among themselves, with the guards, the soldiers in the watchtowers that kept them under surveillance, their family letters and family meetings. It also describes the events of the fall of Communism in Albania in 1990–1991 as experienced in prison. One climactic day is February 21, 1991, when the student demonstrations in Tirana toppled the statue of the dictator Enver Hoxha, who had inspired *The Final Slaughter*. The diary ends with my release on March 17, 1991.

Prophet, Judge, Witness

Both books were published in Albania in 1994, after the fall of Communism.

The book I liked best was certainly *The Final Slaughter*, to which I had devoted so much effort. I had even done research into the language, finding archaic Albanian words to create a sense of timelessness. I loved it so much that after writing it in prison, I copied the whole of it on cigarette papers to hide it from a possible search by the guards. I claimed, as I still do today, that this work was not a simple allegory, but the kind of work of art that might be called an "open parable," which can be interpreted or decoded from the language of symbol to the language of ideas in many, almost infinite, ways. In other words, it was a myth with possible resonances of countless universal meanings, viewing the human world through the perspective of psychological and metaphysical symbolism.

I loved this book because I had created it with the idea that it was written by a writer who was a citizen of the world as much as of Albania, who had lived through the year 2500 in time, and had inhabited the entire world in space.

But when these works were published, both in Albania and abroad, their fate was different from that which I had anticipated. *The Final Slaughter* was passed over almost in silence, while the diary had a lot of success in Albania, and was published, un-abridged, in Italy, with excerpts published in other countries as well.

Regardless of whether *The Final Slaughter* indeed has the merits

I ascribe to it, its failure and the simultaneous success of the diary, by the same author, are not unrelated to a continental shift in the conception of the role of the writer in small countries and of so-called minor literatures as compared to that of so-called European or Western writers of the major literatures of major countries — a shift that, in my opinion, threatens to distort the nature of creativity.

I can explain this idea most clearly by telling a story from a meeting that took place in Budapest in the middle '90s on the subject of intellectuals of the East and West. There the Hungarian philosopher, Gáspár Miklós Tamás, told a joke. Talking about the role of the intellectual, he said:

Now let me tell you what the three roles of the intellectual are:

First, the prophet, who creates and spreads visions of the future, etc., etc.;

Second, the judge, who judges his time, history, reality, etc., etc.;

Third, the witness, who bears witness to his time ...

So, Tamás continued, these Westerners have taken upon themselves the two main roles of prophet and judge, leaving only one role to us of the East, that of witness.

This provocative joke also expresses my understanding of the success of the diary, a work that attempts, above all, to bear witness, and the failure of *The Final Slaughter*. The cause lies in the conception, common throughout the continent, that gives the intellectual in small countries only the role of bearing witness. The reluctance of Europe to accept writers from small countries — here I refer mainly to the experience of my own country — as European writers has had a certain alienating effect on the creative process in literature. The great aspiration to transcend the borders of their own country has led some writers to concentrate on local exotica without any universal dimension. It has led others, especially the young, to the universal, without any local characteristics.

Recalling his conversations with Goethe, Eckermann describes how the German poet read a book about China. Goethe said that he started the book, imagining that he would be delighted and amazed by the exoticism of the Chinese world. Yet, in fact, what surprised him was not the difference, but the similarity between his own world and China. He then advocated the translation of books and cultural exchange. Two centuries later, perhaps more than ever in this era of globalization, this idea of the Enlightenment is fraught with the danger that what is called Western culture might impose its own methods and assimilate other cultures. On the other hand, also implicit in this idea is the demand that cultures should not be of merely local interest, but that their modes of thinking and their truths should also be universal and accessible to the peoples of the greatest diversity in order that every human creature might be able to understand himself through them. Nobody feels this contradiction more acutely than the writer, who seeks less to resolve it than to experience it in the creative process.

— *Translated by John Hodgson*

1 Gjergj Peçi, *Rage* (Tirana: Përpjekja Publications, 2000).
2 *ibid.*

Adolf Muschg

In essence, the Europe I am speaking of is
a common attitude, the fusion of national
memories whose components are no longer
distinguishable. A civilization of memory.
© Maxim Segienko/PHOTOMAX

Adolf Muschg

Switzerland

Born in Zollikon (Canton Zurich) in 1934, Adolf Muschg
studied German language and literature, English language
and literature, and philosophy at Zurich and Cambridge.
Since 1970 he has been professor of German language
and literature at the Swiss Technical University in Zurich.
He co-founded the Swiss Authors' Group, Olten. He is a
member of the Social Democratic Party of Switzerland and
was a candidate for Zurich city council in 1975. Since May
2003, he has been acting president of the Berlin
Academy of Arts. Adolf Muschg has received many
awards, including the Georg Büchner Prize in 1994 and
the Grimmelshausen Prize in 2001. He lives and works in
Männedorf near Zürich.

Further Reading:
Blue Man and Other Stories. George Braziller, 1985.
The Light and the Key. George Braziller, 1989.

Europe or "Eleuthera, City of the Mnemosyne"

*Das begründete Erschrecken Europas über sich selbst
heilig zu halten und eben daraus Gelassenheit zu
schöpfen, ist ein anspruchsvolles Geschäft: Aber seine
Geschichte hat Europa kein geringeres auferlegt.*

You are likely not to have heard of the invitation extended to the
European Union to become part of Switzerland rather than the
other way around. This is what Christoph Blocher of the *Swiss
Tribune* proclaimed two years ago in his so-called Albisgüetli
speech, which is most appropriately compared to the Ash Wednes-
day speeches of the CSU (Christian Social Union) pronounced in
Passau in the tradition of the late Franz Josef Strauß. Here the ordinary party members are being told what's what, while the rest of
the world can discover where God resides: in the unspoiled soul of
the province, neatly segregated, a demonstration of worldwide
diligence. Mr. Blocher's recipe for success is based on a combination of a patriotic self-consciousness and global enterprise. He
represents a miniature version of the political prototype to be recognized today in the person of George W. Bush. Ever since the era
of Jefferson and Madison the explosive force of the Republican
Party has rested in this mixture of patriotic self-interest—at the
time with regard to Virginia—and the claim to universal validity of
its norms and maxims. It is this revolutionary nuclear energy that
prompted the Bush administration to set off on its God-pleasing
unilateralist path toward establishment of a global empire, which
gratified the nationalist conservative Mr. Blocher to such a degree
that he offered his insular Switzerland as a free port and offshore
facility to the Americans for their European business enterprises—
at least before the Jewish World Congress spoiled it all by raising

embarrassing questions about the Switzerland's role in World War II. In 1992 Mr. Blocher managed to prevent Switzerland from becoming a player on the European economic platform, pointing it instead toward the rocky road of bilateral negotiation, which will lead to the predictable conclusion that the tail does not, indeed, wag the dog. And now that the Swiss bankers' obligation to discretion has been called into question, interest in the European Union has reached its lowest point.

It has been a Swiss characteristic throughout the centuries to never trust any kind of peace. The country has learned, almost too well, to look at an emergency situation as the norm and to turn an unequivocally normal situation into an emergency. As late as 1982 the basement of my study had to be equipped with a bunker, complete with six sleeping berths, a chemical toilet, and a ventilation system — just to be on the safe side. A situation free from danger is not something that my country envisages. Any such thing would pose a risk to Swiss identity.

At this point the story of the Japanese Christians comes to mind. Iberian missionaries converted them to the only true faith in the seventeenth century, after which they became the target of persecution by Japanese officials. This had the effect of forcing the community to celebrate mass only behind closed shutters. When the missionaries returned to Japan about 250 years later they couldn't remove those shutters. The blackout had become an integral part of the dogma of the community.

This is not as ridiculous as it sounds. Preventative defiance and unyielding stubbornness have acted as lifesaving forces for my country. Most events in history had the potential, one way or another, of dividing Switzerland. Owing to its diverse cultural composition, the country could have disintegrated in the manner of the former Yugoslavia on several occasions during the course of its history. Is it therefore surprising that the paradoxical weapon of neutrality is one of the instruments used to safeguard the identity of a nation that would prefer to reserve the unloved notion of state for each of its own cantons? If the Swiss are not threatened by any "significant or immediate danger," then simulation of this — the ever useful "danger of suspicion" — must stand in its place. It is the fear of dissolution (like sugar in tea, as Dürrenmatt put it) that frightens the Swiss, and it is this fear that represents Blocher's strongest ally.

The problem is, though, that his image of Switzerland can no longer do anything to save the country—at most it will prevent general recognition of the fact that the country does not need to be saved "from Europe." On the contrary: a Europe that evolves into a federation of civil societies not only represents the best guarantee for Switzerland's security, it would also provide an appropriate political home for my country. What Switzerland has to offer, its historical-genetic dowry of reflexes, customs, and institutions, does not deserve to be buried like the talents in the Bible. Europe clearly could make use of them. Switzerland would not just be a net contributor to the European Union, it would be a donor country.

I am not talking about federalism versus subordination, about direct democracy versus the autonomy of communities. I am talking about something less tangible, an existential minimum so to speak, corresponding to an optimum of European civilization. Switzerland's most reliable characteristic has always been its refusal to be submerged under a single, monochrome identity; in fact, if there is one achievement worth celebrating with regard to this federal state that has recently celebrated its 150th anniversary, it is this instinctive resistance to any rigid form of identification, be it on a national, social, or cultural plane. Not suitable for celebration, yet remarkable in its own right, is the fact that in spite of this blurred identity, the men and women of Switzerland have maintained a common household, that they have mastered the everyday tasks of life honorably, that they have practiced good governance, and they have not, on the whole, put up with injustice; in short, they have established an acceptable society. Switzerland is a federation of the late Middle Ages that did not have to first establish itself as a nation in order to function as a modern federal state. If you like, it is the stubborn decision to muddle through in this way that provides the foundation of its eligibility for membership in a community.

Life itself—if I understand biological science correctly—works on the same principle, that is, it works without principle. In an emergency it finds a suitable niche and jogs along, moving from situation to situation, until it reaches biological equilibrium. It looks for, and finds again and again, that precarious balance between metabolism and survival. God forbid that it should have a fixed identity, or even a plan or a grand design, a living, immanent entelechy. *Bricolage* or patchwork would be other, more fitting terms; a hole is made in a place where it does not matter in order to fill one elsewhere where it does. It looks so simple, the makeshift approach of this trifling people; yet it is infinitely complex, like any tradeoff with the environment that serves nothing less than to safeguard existence itself.

"La Suisse n'existe pas"—this slogan could be read in the Swiss pavilion at the World Exhibition held in Seville in 1992. The national outrage it caused was so great that nobody bothered to read further: if it doesn't exist now, perhaps it can grow into existence. The very fact that its crypt is empty provides Switzerland with the opportunity to join those nations that first had to clear out their own crypts, by force and causing much sadness, in an effort to create a tolerable life. The open definition of a culture is its potential for growth; only if it is treated as a gap to be filled with the waste of legends and the overflow of self-pity will it degenerate into an energy-sapping vacuum. This is the material from which pride and fear are made—the stopgaps of life, its enemies, for they spoil its metabolism, the job of which is to suspend identity in order for it to become created afresh.

Yet nobody can guarantee that as a political life form, as an extension of the Swiss Confederation, Europe will not tend toward the malignant growth that the speaker at the Albisgüetli predicted. But perhaps Switzerland's past can serve as proof that Europe may successfully shape a pragmatic future for itself. I hold the faith, the love, and the hope that exist vis-à-vis Europe to be founded in a gap in its identity that has nothing to do with market needs, but is more like an open wound. "L'Europe n'existe pas"—it disappeared into the blackest of all possible holes, when it dug a grave for its Jews in the skies. But the zero point of its history also became the place of its rebirth. In order for that to happen, it had to put call into question the illusions of man about himself. Two European wars and

Auschwitz have falsified all messianic messages, especially those constructed on the slippery slope of nationalism. After this mass production of death, the societies of Europe were condemned to resist any relativized barbarism under any condition. No economic success could release them from this obligation. For is it not in view of economic success that the concept of "life not worth living"—now disguised as gene technology—is brought into circulation? Without the courage to look back upon its past, which will never be over, Europe would be superfluous, for it failed at its task of filling the basic human needs that Europeans have always had. I confess that I am guilty of hoping that this change will come about. It has made me into a European. As a Swiss I want to go to a place where people are ready for a different history. My idea of Europe is more than a community of interest and economy, though I have to admit that it would not have happened at all had it been less. It is a topography of many gaps that continues to produce radiation. What is required now is the transformation of this deadly energy into the achievement of a common civilization. A topography of gaps is to be transformed into a continent of memory—of remembrance. Each and every scar in Europe demands a memory—it may open up again at any time. Even a fleeting look at the map reveals that Europe cannot be more than a continent, a section of the world. Yet there is no border beyond which participation is no longer required—and that applies to Europeans in global terms just as it does to the Swiss in European terms. In essence, the Europe I am speaking of is a common attitude, the fusion of national memories whose components are no longer distinguishable. A civilization of memory. I honor vision, but it can only emerge from retrospective vision. To keep alive and sanctified in memory the horror and atrocities of Europe and to use this memory as a source of equilibrium is a difficult task; but history demands that Europe not shirk this responsibility.

In one of his later hymns, Hölderlin speaks of a duty "to hold on to much—as on the shoulders a burden of failure": thus the sinister language of the poem dissects the fate of the Occident. The title "Mnemosyne" refers to the goddess of memory, the mother of the muses, and the poem dedicates a city to her, the city of Eleuthera, the free one. That much about the topography of my European hopes. May memory keep watch at the zero-point of history and prevent its fading into oblivion. Only then can history become a source of freedom.

— *Translated by Susanne Höbel*

Péter Nádas

From time immemorial Europe has been
an addle-brained monster slumbering in
her beastliness. Once in a while she
groans and pants, tossing and turning
on her foul-smelling couch stuck
between the great seas.
© Maxim Segienko/PHOTOMAX

Péter Nádas
Hungary

Born in 1942, the narrative writer, dramatist, essayist, and photographer Péter Nádas trained as a photographer and worked for some years as a photojournalist. He published his first novella in 1967 (*The Bible*). His book *The End of a Family Novel*, which in Hungary could be published only in 1979, was praised as the most important manifesto of a new generation of Hungarian authors. For his novel *A Book of Memories*, he was awarded the Austrian State Prize for European Literature, France's Prix du Meilleur Livre Étranger, and the Leipzig Book Prize for European Understanding.

Further Reading:
A Book of Memories: A Novel. Translated by Ivan Sanders and Imre Goldstein. Farrar Straus & Giroux, 1997.
A Lovely Tale of Photography. Translated by Imre Goldstein. Twisted Spoon Press, 1999.
The End of a Family Story. Translated by Imre Goldstein. Penguin USA, 2000.
Love. Translated by Imre Goldstein. Farrar Straus & Giroux, 2000.

In the Intimacy of Literary Writing

Európa az idők kezdete óta állatiasságban szunnyadó,
ködös agyú szörnyeteg. Olykor felnyög, fújtat,
hánykolódik a nagy tengerek közé szorított büdös
fekhelyén.

Europa. With a name of Phoenician origin, which Hesiod mentions
among the forty elder daughters of Téthys and Oceanus and the
four wives of Zeus, Europe emerges from the dim of prehistoric
days, and, naturally, neither reads nor writes. Yet the people living
on the continent bearing her name assume that anyone who masters the written alphabet is able to write. It is probably this embarrassing belief that prevents them from ever really learning how to
write. From time immemorial Europe has been an addle-brained
monster slumbering in her beastliness. Once in a while she groans
and pants, tossing and turning on her foul-smelling couch stuck
between the great seas.

According to some legends, the breath of Europe smells of saf-
fron. Rubens painted her as a wildly plump female, who at the
moment of being abducted, presses the pelt of a panther to her
body. Europe has always had more fat and gold than the knowledge
she would truly need. From the beginning of time Europe has been
illiterate and will remain so to the end of time. And this situation
will not be altered if some individuals, some of whom can also
read, acquire the skills of penmanship. It may not be superfluous
to mention that the Greek word for illiterate (*analphabetos*) refers
to persons who are not only unfamiliar with the alphabet, but who
are also unacquainted with the administration of justice; they do
not know how to enter into a contract, or how to defend their rights
in a court of law. They are panting domestic animals. Even in an-

tiquity such a person or situation must have been a great burden, a weight around society's neck. Judgment in court could be based only on circumstances that had been presented in writing. *Quod non est in actis, non est in mundo.* What is not in the files, does not exist.

Which of course implies that there had been a period of pristine conditions, prior to antiquity, in which proficient oral communication was sufficient to maintain existence in the world. I write. The individual person must have arisen from the enormous mass of primary matter by making use of the written word. For more than forty years now, every morning at ten minutes to eight I sit down at my table covered with my handwritten notes. Individuals have no other means by which to convey their existence to others. And even writing cannot produce more than a mere sketch of a full personality. Personal intimacy is usually felt through the sense of touch. If, however, people fail to convey to one another at least a sketch of the *intimacy of their existence*, then the existence of everyone will remain blind and deaf, insensitive to social contacts, insensitive to bodily contacts, as a result of which they will all sink back into the chaotic primary matter. Something that has already occurred, and most likely will occur again, in the horror-filled history of Europe.

So that this should not occur, everyone, every single day, should lift himself out the primary matter of one's simple-mindedness.

And the person able to prepare a daily written report of this successful or failed effort, at least concerning himself, may begin to hope that after a few decades, perhaps before his death, he might even learn to write.

Learning to write cannot begin with writing. For example, every afternoon after writing I begin my not-writing period, because if I want to be able to write the next day, I must know every day precisely where the division is between my own reality and the reality of my own writing. And this dividing line, given the nature of the thing, changes every day. But no matter what I do without or instead of writing, all further activity must occur from the viewpoint of writing. I must go to bed neither too early nor too late, and I must be aware, whether awake or asleep, just how far I let the unavoidable influence of others penetrate my being: deep enough to reach the marrow of my bones, or let it be stopped at the epidermis. In my youth, for example, I learned to sleep so that I could analyze my dreams while dreaming them, and after waking to fix them firmly enough in my consciousness so as not to forget them later. The reality of the dream ought to find its place in the reality of writing. At the edge of madness one begins to see the structures of one's own consciousness, and this is very important to an understanding of the consciousness of other people. If only for the reason that language, the common mother tongue that tomorrow will become the material and subject of the writing, cannot be understood without the manner in which others use the language.

Since my younger days I have spent the first hour of the morning in exercises of classical associations, classical analyses, in the breaking down and rearranging of the contents of consciousness. I continue where the monks left off at the end of the Middle Ages. Anyone looking at me at such a time would see a compulsively idle man, staring foolishly out the window; and the sight would be almost identical every day. While the mad rush begins outside, I keep life in a high state of eventlessness. In due course the little differences will shed light on many things. But not on everything, and not by themselves.

At any rate, because of the involuntary observation of things, the contents of human consciousness appear to be so rich and so full of detail that one would need several lifetimes to process them and write them up properly.

There is no point or circumstance in one's thinking of oneself at which one wouldn't have to step out of oneself, and therefore place everything in a conditional mode, to continue thinking through the system of parallel connections. Something that only a computer would be able to do. As if while thinking one would constantly have to ask oneself: do other people think what I think, or conversely, am I thinking what others—because of other people—are thinking?

You haven't even started writing and you can already tell that you wouldn't get to the end of it, because the end cannot be reached; but you shouldn't be frightened by this. One could easily start the whole thing from the beginning and, if needed, once again from the beginning. The use of language by strangers contains strange references to the contents of strange consciousness, and these varied linguistic signs will produce at least the sketch of a structure. Following this trail, however, may make it difficult to find the points where the writing should start and end. Because there is no such thing. This realization paralyzes one only in one's youth. Your own life, and that of others—oh, horror—consists of eternal repetitions. What else can there be? One eats, purges, makes love, and then starts all over again. Others before you have already searched for those starting and terminal points. If you can't find God either, or an explanation for God's absence, then perhaps it is enough for you to recognize the structure of repetitions, to evaluate them, and to bring them in some connection with the particular structure of others' repetitions. Then you've at least had a tiny insight into the nature of creation. If every morning you can deal with and take care of part of this task, and if you manage to surprise yourself a little with the result, then with this knowledge you may slowly approach the manuscript where you had left it the day before.

It is important that you should write for decades only by hand, and thus see immediately in your handwriting the differences and similarities between today and previous days. A writer must be able to distinguish between these different levels—something he'll never be able to do on a typed page or on the monitor of a computer. A handwritten manuscript of the previous day opens dimensions that, led by the deepest instincts, no one likes to look into. One would see something that requires immediate correction. You may improve the quality of the manuscript, or make it worse, with corrections; but there is nothing to be done about the previous day's written form. Whether one is satisfied or dissatisfied, the written form must be accepted as the only reality.

The written form is personal; however, the personal way of writing takes its place in a larger tradition that has continental peculiarities, but no continental borders. Although my own way of writing is strongly locked into the system of secret connections and intricate references of European literature, these connections and references cross naturally over ethnic, linguistic, religious, and national boundaries. And they do so even when the Continent falls on its own sword of ethnic, linguistic, religious, and national distinctions, and sinks back into the state of precivilization.

— *Translated by Imre Goldstein*

Emine Sevgi Özdamar

In both parts of Istanbul one often heard people discussing: Are we Europeans? Where does Europe begin? How European are we? To become genuine Europeans we must eat all the bread from two hundred bakeries. We'll never belong to Europe. Where are we and where is Europe?
© Maxim Segienko/PHOTOMAX

Emine Sevgi Özdamar

Turkey

Emine Sevgi Özdamar was born in Malatya, Turkey in
1946. After graduating from the Istanbul School of
Dramatic Art, she had engagements at the People's
Theater of East Berlin, in Paris, and Avignon, and in the
Bochum Theater under the directorship of Claus
Peymann. Besides working on her own plays, she has
been a free-lance writer since 1986. Her first volume of
fiction *Mother Tongue* was chosen by the *Times* as
International Book of the Year. She has received
numerous other awards for her literary work, including the
Ingeborg Bachmann Prize in 1991.

Further Reading:
Mother Tongue. Translated by Craig Thomas and Alberto
Manguel. Coach House Press, 1994.
*Life Is a Caravanserai, Has Two Doors, I Came in One, I
Went Out the Other*. Translated by Luise Von Flotow.
Middlesex University Press, 2000.

Guest Faces

Als junge Frau in der 68er-Bewegung in Istanbul hielt
ich auf den Schiffen zwischen Asien und Europa wieder
die europäischen Toten als Bücher in meinen Händen
und in meinem Herzen, und der Mond über Istanbul
schien in den Nächten auf diese Bücher und
beleuchtete sie.

As a child in Istanbul the first European word I ever heard was: "Deux-Pièces." Every Monday my parents used to go to a cinema called *Teyyare Sinemasi.* In English this means "airplane cinema." The cinema only showed European films. My mother told me about the owner of the airplane cinema: he dressed like a film star and would stand at the entrance of his cinema and welcome the patrons. He knew that some of the European films featured would bring tears to the eyes of his audience. So he had handkerchiefs specially made from the finest textiles, which he handed out personally in front of the cinema when sad films were on the bill. My mother gave me one of the handkerchiefs that she used to wipe away her tears in the cinema. I placed this handkerchief, infused with the tears of my mother, between the pages of my school atlas depicting Europe.

Every Monday my mother and father used to don their best clothes. "What are you going to wear?" they would always ask. And once my mother replied: "I am going to put on my 'Deux-Pièces.'" I asked: "Mother, what does Deux-Pièces mean?" "Deux-Pièces is Deux-Pièces," answered my mother.

My grandmother was a superstitious woman. She was afraid that the shadows on the screen would spirit away the faces of my parents. One morning I inquired of my parents about the film they had seen at the cinema the previous evening. My father answered: "I've forgotten what the film was called, but the actor Jean Gabin smoked like this," imitating Jean Gabin smoking a cigarette. The burning cigarette hung in the corner of his mouth until ashes fell to the floor. In the ensuing weeks my father continued to smoke like Jean Gabin, until one Monday when he went to the cinema and saw a film starring Rossano Brazzi. By Tuesday he had switched to Brazzi. Consequently, the first European guests to enter our wooden house in Istanbul were Jean Gabin and Rossano Brazzi. As a child I experienced difficulties pronouncing the names of our European guests. So I found the Turkish word *can*, which means "soul," for Jean and the word *biraz iyi*, which means "a little better," for Brazzi. Thus I had already become acquainted with "Soul Gabin" and "Rossano A Little-better" in the face of my father before I had the opportunity to see them in person at the cinema. My mother's face also bought two European guests into our house: Silvana Mangano and Anna Magnani. I also found similar words in Turkish for their names: *Silbana*, "wash me up," Mangano and *Ana*, "mother," Magnani. The first faces exchanged between different countries were film faces.

One day a hat with the name "Borsalino" turned up in our house in Istanbul. Every morning my father would stand in front of the mirror carefully adjusting his hat, casting a last glance at himself before unlocking the door and leaving. He considered the matter of having this hat perched properly on his head to be of vital importance, standing in front of the mirror for so long that I still saw his head and the Borsalino in it even after my father had left the house. Atatürk had introduced the hat as a part of his "Europeanization" drive. In photos Atatürk is seen either wearing a hat on his head or holding one in his hand. He always wore a hat as he traveled around Turkey greeting people as part of his endeavor to win popular support for his policy of Europeanization. In one small town on the Black Sea the men gathered to welcome Atatürk turned up wearing Western-style women's hats. Having run out of men's headwear, an astute trader began selling old-fashioned women's hats to these men, who were not yet aware of the difference.

After my parents had invited "Soul Gabin" and "Rossano A Little-better," "Wash-me-up" Mangano" and "Mother Magnani" as guest faces into their own faces, and got on famously with them, I gained my first European friends. As a child I fell ill with tuberculosis. In our street there lived a mad woman. Sometimes she would invite me on to her balcony, whose floor was covered with fallen mulberries. Once she told me how I could enter paradise before I died: "If you cut a pomegranate into two halves and are able to eat one of them up without allowing a slice of the unpeeled pomegranate to fall to the floor, you will enter paradise." The mad woman and I then ate a pomegranate. One half of the pomegranate lay in her hand, the other half in mine. The mad woman ate her half without allowing anything to fall to the floor. I had almost eaten my half successfully when, in my joyful anticipation, I hurriedly ate the last portion and dropped some on the floor. So I could not enter paradise. But I wanted to go there because I thought that my grandmother, whom I loved deeply and who told me fairytales every night, would also enter paradise. She had lost eight children and believed that everybody has two angels in life. Perched on one shoulder is the angel who documents your good deeds, on the other shoulder the angel who records your sins. After you die, these angels read out all your sins and your good deeds before they are put on a pair of scales to be weighed. You are then taken to a bridge, a bridge as thin as a length of hair and as sharp as a knife, over which you must run barefoot; if you reach the other side you will enter paradise—otherwise you fall into hell, which is located right under the bridge.

My grandmother was convinced that she was full of sin because, in her grief over the death of her children, she had smoked many cigarettes. However, she believed that her eight children, who all died young and thus had committed no sins, would fly as angels to the bridge and carry her into paradise before she fell into hell on account of her smoking. "How can I enter paradise with you?" I asked. She replied that I should never forget the dead and must pray for their souls. Sometimes my grandmother took me to the cemetery. She would stand in front of each gravestone and pray for the unknown dead. Since she was illiterate, I used to read the names of the dead to her out loud, eventually learning them by heart. And at night I would pray, going through all the names, devoting my prayers to their souls. Soon I had a long roll call of the dead. Initially the list only contained the names of dead Turks, though later it was include dead Europeans as well. I used to read novels to my grandmother and her illiterate friends. My first dead European "guest" was Madame Bovary, who used to bring the old women to tears and whose name I added to my list of the dead at night. They were joined by another dead European — Robinson Crusoe. As I read *Robinson Crusoe* aloud to my grandmother, she would always ask me: "How did his parents endure it? What did his wife do? What did his children eat?" Grandmother was continually preoccupied with Robinson Crusoe's children. In order to allay her concerns, I concocted lies about what the children ate: rice with lamb, maize, and chestnuts. And at night I prayed for Robinson Crusoe. My third dead European guest was Isadora Duncan. One day a neighbor, the actor, asked my mother if she could borrow a scarf because she was planning to take her convertible on a drive along the coast. My mother offered her a long scarf, which the actor refused, explaining that in France a very famous dancer got strangled with one like that. Her name was Isadora Duncan. She had been driving in her convertible, wind in her face, when her scarf became entangled in the car's rear wheel and choked her to death. My fourth dead European guest was Molière. I was finally cured of tuberculosis and was performing at the State Theatre in a play by Molière. The older actors had informed me that Molière had died on stage, so I included him in my nighttime prayers as well. I prayed every night for dead Turks and for Madame Bovary, Robinson Crusoe, Isadora Duncan, and Molière — until one day I fell in love. After I fell in love I rather began to neglect the dead.

It is not only film faces that people of different countries first exchange, but also their dead.

Istanbul, the Half-European, Half-Asian City

In Istanbul one is unsure whether it is the sea that holds the city in its arms or the city the sea. If the sea holds the city in its arms, then it holds the European side in one arm and the Asian side in the other. And if the city holds the sea in its arms, then the European arm and the Asian arm hold the city together. Generally speaking, both arms are still. But sometimes the two arms will join together to stir the sea dividing Europe and Asia. When the arms of Europe and Asia begin to toss the sea to and fro it becomes dangerous to board the ships moored on either bank. The ships are dashed back and forth against the quay wall. One could be easily hurled into the sea and crushed by them. This is why mothers warn their children everyday: "Don't jump onto the ship before the landing-stage has been extended. Whether from Europe or Asia, the power of the waves must be respected."

During my childhood my parents moved several times between the Asian and the European side of Istanbul because they had fallen in love with Istanbul and wanted to live in all areas of the city. When we lived on the Asian side, my father would look over to the European side and proclaim: "Europe is over there." Then he fell silent. I used to gaze up at his face to see Europe there. Sometimes he would count the lights of the houses on the European side that shone across the hills towards Asia. The cars drove on the European side, resembling a trail of stars twinkling constantly in the direction of Asia. Some evenings my mother would say to my father, "If you can count the stars in the sky, you can also count the lights of the houses in Istanbul." When my father announced to my mother that he had business to do on the European side of Istanbul the next morning, they would carefully choose his shirt and trousers and hang up them together that evening on a coat-hanger on the balcony. During the night the white of the shirt would shimmer before my eyes, and it seemed as if the trousers and the shirt were so excited about their forthcoming trip to Europe that they were unable to sleep. When the arms of the city were resting, one could travel from Asia to Europe in twenty minutes; but when the southwest wind stirred up the waves and began to rock the ships that crossed back and forth between the Asian and European sides, the passengers on board and the tea glasses in the bars below deck would slide around. And from the ship's portholes it seemed as if the European bank rose up and crashed down with its houses, Byzantine walls, orthodox and Armenian churches, the Genoese Galata Tower, the Ottoman palaces, and mosques. On such days, when the turbulent seas tossed the ships to and fro, my father would return home from his trip saying that he would be rocking in his sleep that night. On such nights he always used to step out onto the balcony and gaze over toward Europe and say: "The sea has gone mad. I wonder if my shoes will see Europe tomorrow?"

Both banks of Istanbul remind me of a fairytale my mother told me as a child. Once upon a time in a distant country, a young man was searching for the beautiful bird called Zümrüt-ü Anka, which was to fly him to Mount Ararat. There he wanted to meet a holy man who knew the answers to the three questions that the Sultan had posed to the young man. On his way to find the bird, he entered the house of a giant. Inside sat the giant's mother, sharpening her teeth. Immediately the young man took hold of the breasts of the giant's mother and began to suckle them. The giant's mother said, "Child, child, I would have eaten you, but you have drunk my milk. Now my sons will come and eat you up. Here, take this mirror and make your escape. If my sons approach you, throw the mirror down behind you." When the giant's sons returned home, the mother concealed the young lad between her legs. The giant's sons said: "Mother, it smells of human flesh here." They drew air in through their nostrils and followed the trail that ended between their mother's legs. "Run! Be off with you," the giant's mother commanded the young lad. So off he ran, with the giants following him in hot pursuit. The young boy turned around and saw them drawing nearer. He threw the mirror down behind him, creating a vast sea on whose opposite bank the giant's sons remained.

This also happens in Istanbul. If you throw a mirror behind you a sea will form between you and your dwelling. You are on another bank, on another continent, in another life. You can throw a mirror behind you every day in Istanbul. The sea is always there. Europe is there, Asia is there. The lights of Europe can be seen from Asia, and the lights of Asia from Europe. One day my mother and her girlfriends traveled to the European side of Istanbul in order to buy European textiles imported from Europe "proper." *Avrupa mali* (European goods). In my youth I once sunbathed topless on one of the islands in Istanbul. I thought I was completely alone on the beach, when a boat with two couples suddenly motored past. One of the men stared at my breasts. His wife then said to him, "I am not speaking to you any more." He responded, "Why not? Today is a fine day for looking at European goods." He thought I was European.

My mother's powder tin from Paris was not thrown away after it became empty. It lay on the small table next to her bed, beside Dostoyevsky's book *The Idiot*. As a child I used to surreptitiously sniff at both the tin and Dostoyevsky's book. When one of my mother's girlfriends was having problems with her husband, my mother would always suggest a trip to the European side: "Let's go to Europe. There we will steal a day from the Angels of Fate and forget our troubles." Or: "Let's shake out our worms in Europe." The problems of the Asian side were transported to Europe in ships and deposited there. When these women traveled to the European side, they said, "Let's go up to Europe." And when they returned to the Asian side they said, "Let's go down to Asia."

My childhood neighbor, Madame Athena, an Istanbul Greek, once drew the folds of her aging cheeks back behind her ears and fastened them with adhesive tape. With the tape behind her ears, Madame Athena took me to the harbor. I was eight years old. She looked younger with her cheeks stretched back to behind her ears, so I walked quickly. She kept stumbling on the ground as she tried to keep up with me. She often said to me that she was neither Asian nor European, but Byzantine, and I accompanied her to the Hagia Sophia. I loved the Hagia Sophia. Its floor was uneven. And on the walls were frescos of Christ without the cross. And this Christ was a very handsome man. I tried to imitate the position of his fingers. The thumb lay across the little finger and the ring finger while the remaining two were stretched out. Madame Athena once told me a story about two mad men in Istanbul: one stood on the European bank and said, "From here Istanbul is mine"; the other stood on the Asian bank and shouted across to the European side, "From here Istanbul is mine." Once as Madame Athena and I were returning to the Asian part of the city from the European side, she pointed out to me a small tower in the sea. "The Byzantine Emperor built this Leander Tower out in the sea, just off the banks of the Asian side, as a place to hide his daughter, who, it had been prophesied, would be bitten and killed by a snake. When his daughter developed a craving for dates, the emperor sent someone to take her a basket of the fruits from the European side. She was bitten and killed by a snake that had concealed itself in the basket."

I grew up in Istanbul between the Asian and European part of the city. Over both skies I saw rainbows, the moon, snow, the stars, and thunder and lightening. One night, when the skies of both Europe and Asia were aglow with the flashes of lightening, I sat on board a ship that was taking me from the European side to the Asian side. The tea vendors were plying their trade, the loose change ringing in their pockets. When we went aboard ship on the European side the thunder and lightening ceased and the moon appeared to bathe the harbor in light. Wherever one touched the ship one also touched the moon. That night everyone held a piece of the moon in his hands. As the ship departed a couple sat down beside me. The young man said, "So you have given the key of your house to another. I am leaving. Goodbye." With that, he jumped from the ship's deck into the sea, reemerging in the moonlight. The ship was located exactly between Europe and Asia. All the other passengers hurried to the ship's railing, causing it to lurch to one side and the tea glasses, together with their saucers, to slide towards the railing. The tea vendors cried, "tea money, tea money!" The ship's crew threw two buoys overboard to the young man, but he didn't want one. The ship turned around and headed back toward the young man, toward Europe; and finally he was hauled from the sea in a lifeboat. The moon, which hung in the sky exactly between Asia and Europe, followed everything that happened. And after the young lad had been hauled back on board ship, his clothes and hair dripping wet, someone asked him, "Where were you fleeing to, brother?" "To Europe," he answered. To Europe, to Europe. The ship then turned around and headed back toward Asia, the tea vendors found their customers and collected their money, and the moon illuminated the empty tea glasses. Then the ship suddenly turned around again, heading back toward the European side in order to retrieve the buoys, which had been left in the sea and were also drifting toward Europe. To Europe, to Europe.

In both parts of Istanbul one often heard people discussing: Are we Europeans? Where does Europe begin? How European are we?

To become genuine Europeans we must eat all the bread from two hundred bakeries. We'll never belong to Europe. Where are we and where is Europe?

European cars never caused accidents. European dogs had all studied at European universities. And European women were all natural blondes.

An Istanbul artist who had studied in Paris once bought a nylon sex-doll for a friend, who also lived in Istanbul. When he returned home he gave it to his friend and said, "Here, your wife, from Paris." The friend stared at the genitals of the nylon doll and shouted, "You bastard! You've already slept with my Parisienne. The seams are all open, her organs will have to be sewn up again." Later when I lived in Europe — in Berlin, Munich, Paris, Vienna, Barcelona, Madrid, Amsterdam, Copenhagen, Florence, Venice, and Athens — the only friends I knew who, like the Turks of Istanbul, agonized over their European identity were those living in Barcelona under the Franco régime. At the time they often wondered: "Are we Europeans? Are our Pyrennees the backside of Europe or the frontside of Africa?"

During my youth in the '60s I become a member of the student opposition movement and traveled on the ships back and forth between the Asian and the European side of Istanbul, clutching books, among them Kafka, Büchner, Hölderlin, Böll, Joyce, Conrad, and Borchert. And just as in my childhood, it seemed from the ship's portholes as if the bank on the European side was rising up and crashing down, with its houses, Byzantine walls, orthodox and Armenian churches, the Genoese Galata Tower, Ottoman palaces, and mosques. As I read Büchner's *Woyzeck*, rain beating down against the ship's portholes, there appeared before me in the flashes of lightening the figure of a Turkish man who could have been Woyzeck. As a child my first European guests were dead people: Madame Bovary, Robinson Crusoe, Isadora Duncan, and Molière. As a young woman active within Istanbul's student opposition movement, I once again held the dead Europeans as books in my hands and in my heart as I traveled on board the ships between Asia and Europe. And on these nights the moon shone over Istanbul, illuminating the books. When I subsequently emigrated to Berlin to work in the theatre, I never felt as if I had emigrated to Europe. At the Bochum Theatre we staged Büchner's *Woyzeck*. I saw Woyzeck in the theatre, but no longer on the streets of Germany. Yet Woyzeck existed on streets of Turkey. There I saw men who touched your heart in the same way as Büchner's character. I was in Europe, among my dead friends. And they did not leave me alone. Prince von Homburg, Woyzeck, Hamlet, Heinrich Böll's *Acquainted with the Night*, Wolfgang Borchert's *Draußen vor der Tür*, Brecht, Kafka—all reside in Europe's sky, next to the moon, and touch the lives of people even if they are far away. The dead have created the European sky. I once sat in a Lufthansa airplane en route from Berlin to Istanbul. A Turkish woman rose suddenly from her seat, threw herself to the floor of the airplane and began to scream. Everyone jumped up: "What's happening?" The woman's children had all died in an accident in Istanbul and she was flying back for the funeral. Some of the passengers in the airplane held her hand. The woman cried, "Open the doors. I want to search for my children in heaven!" She kept looking out of the window, as if she might see her dead children in the sky. "Open the door!" Then she turned and glared at the passengers behind her, as if imploring them to scour the European sky for her dead Turkish children. As the woman peered into the sky many passengers followed suit and looked out of the window. After our arrival, the doves of Istanbul suddenly flew into the airport building and landed on the suitcases belonging to the many European and Turkish travelers.

— *Translated by John Raynor*

Geir Pollen

Is it not the destiny of the European novel to
see to it that such existential questions on the
dignity and potential of the individual human
being are constantly asked, even when they
are felt to be shocking and outrageous?
© Jo Michael

Geir Pollen

Norway

Born in 1953, Geir Pollen studied Scandinavian
languages and literature, Russian, and German. He taught
at a grammar school, held courses in creative writing, and
translated the works of Yves Bonnefoy and W. G. Sebald.
From 1989 until 1995 he was a member of the literary
council of the Norwegian Writers' Association and since
2001 he has been chairman of the Association. Geir
Pollen has published three poetry volumes and four
novels. His works have been translated into German,
Danish and Serbian. He lives and works in Oslo.

On the European Ingredient in the Text (with a Sidelong Glance at an Eel in a Bathtub)

Er det ikke den europeiske romanens bestemmelse å
sørge for at slike eksistensielle spørsmål om
enkeltmenneskets verdighet og livsmuligheter hele
tiden stilles, også når de oppleves som uhørte,
utillatelige; at de ikke får lov til å gå i glemmeboke.

On the occasion of the fiftieth anniversary of Knut Hamsun's death I delivered a lecture entitled "What Is a Norwegian Author?" in which I attempted to examine some of the ideas and expectations of the literary public and of writers themselves that constitute the concept of a "Norwegian author." I started with a concept of author as historically seen in Norway, one which is inextricably linked to great national projects—or the national project; for what it is actually concerned with is a continuous project covering more than 150 years and which, briefly, discusses the nature of the concept of "Norwegian," how Norway, so to speak, becomes Norwegian. For the fact is that Norway as an independent nation is one of the youngest in Europe, if we exclude those nations that have arisen or been resurrected since the fall of the Iron Curtain. For more than four-hundred years—that period in our history which Ibsen, filled with national indignation, calls the Night of Four Hundred Years— Norway was more or less continuously incorporated into other nations, especially Denmark, with Danish as the official written language. It is true that in 1814 Norway got its own constitution, though as the result of the Napoleonic wars and the Danish alliance with the defeated Napoleon the country at once entered an almost century-long union with Sweden, still with Danish as the official written language. The Swedish–Norwegian union lasted until 1905. In other words, Norway's history as an independent nation with its own independent written language has existed for less than a hundred years. That is not long. And from the first, when ideas about an independent Norway with its own Norwegian identity begin to appear as a result of the dissolving of the union with Denmark and the new constitution of 1814, writers played an important role, both practically and politically, as enlighteners of the people, agitators, and also symbolic figures—models of the nation that would sooner or later arise from the ashes of the unions. The concept of "author" and that of the "nation" or the "national" exist in close symbiosis in Norway, a symbiosis that survives right up to our own time, I respectfully maintain, as an integral part of the Norwegian writer's self-concept. Naturally this state of things is of decisive importance to the work produced by the Norwegian writer. Knut Hamsun is not only the first really modern Norwegian novelist, but also—and that is not by chance—the first Norwegian writer who fundamentally and irrevocably breaks with the specific idea of "the Norwegian writer." He does this in 1940, at a time when he, himself, was at the height of his fame and the Third Reich occupied Norway. Two years later, as the foremost successor to Ibsen and Bjørnson, he hailed Adolf Hitler as "a champion of the gospel of justice for all nations." Even today there are many Norwegians, particularly those of the older generation, who have not forgiven him for this.

Why do I allot so much time to this old story in a piece required to take as its leading title "Writing Europe" i.e., a text that will attempt to encircle both the Europe that I, a Norwegian writer, write in as well as the Europe that writes in my texts? Well, because I think this theme of "the European element" cannot be elucidated from a Norwegian point of view unless it begins right here: by demonstrating that it has traditionally been vital for Norwegian writers to be, and become, understood as precisely "Norwegian," and that viewed historically, "to be Norwegian" has meant to be not-Danish, not-Swedish, not-like-the-others. In short, we have stated definitively what we are and what we have as a negation of The Others and The Other. This self-understanding with a negative sign, so to speak, is still alive: on the two occasions when Norwegian governments applied for membership to the EU, in 1972 and 1994, a majority of the Norwegian people voted "NO" to union with the rest of

Europe, justifying this vote with varying references to our difference from Germany, France, Great Britain, the Benelux countries, Denmark, Sweden, Finland, and so on. Norway wants to be The Variant Country of Europe: Norwegian farmers are not like Danish farmers, Norwegian fishermen are not like Spanish fishermen, Norway's meager population is scanty in a different way than that of Luxembourg. It is symptomatic that when I told some of my acquaintances what the theme of this symposium would be, they reacted with the following spontaneous reply: "Ugh, that sounds like a typical EU affair!" Let me just interject that I am, of course, aware that the belief in one's own otherness is not a uniquely Norwegian phenomenon, though in its youthful arrogance Norway may shout louder and more excitedly about it than Europe's more senior, experienced nations. I name no names, to avoid offending anyone. Indeed, I am not unaware of the belief in one's own otherness as precisely a stamp of "Europeanness" itself: France, the nation of culture, is unwilling to resemble the great financial power Germany, and vice versa; the island kingdom of Great Britain wants to be different from continental Europe; ancient, orthodox Russia refuses to be like the materialistic, godless West, and so on. An American is only too eager to cry, "We are all Americans!" even though the American "WE" is still less homogeneous than the European one, while I find it hard to imagine a European leaping up on a podium to proclaim "We are all Europeans!" with particular conviction or enthusiasm.

But now let's allow these preliminary skirmishes to be what they are: a badly camouflaged attempt to get around the extremely complicated question this essay ought to be discussing: Is there anything I can dare to call a European signature, impression, or projection in what I write? To be honest, my first reaction to the question was: I don't know. For it is not the type of question a writer puts to himself as he is writing, and nothing seems so ancient, finished, and totally uninteresting as the books one has written and published oneself. I seldom read them—and never in bed! My second reaction was: Is there anything at all "European" in what I write? And if so, what might that be in the Europe of our time, when The Great Discussion in which all can join exists only as a huge, resounding silence or void; or a time when the European communities, including the Norwegian, most resemble a café during its busiest hour, when everyone talks in their loudest voice, where every table has its own conversation? What is the concept of "European" to mean when The Great Discussion is replaced by The Small Discussions? Moreover, the title and questions posed for this symposium indicate that not even the promoters themselves are sure whether there is any answer to the question outlined in their invitation. "Europeanness" probably has something in common with the medieval proof of God: only when human beings start doubting the existence of God does it become absolutely necessary to prove that He does. What is obvious needs no proof, no grounds for belief. My third reaction was: well, yes, you can find something "European" in my novels, but more as an invisible watermark than a visible signature. From the beginning my writing has been marked by Europe because I have consciously tried to distance myself from the time-honored, closed, self-reflecting, self-sufficient Norwegian; I have wanted to be just as consciously not-Norwegian as the Norwegians traditionally have wanted to be not-Danish, not-Swedish. Concretely this implies that I knew how I DID NOT want to write long before I had any clear idea of how I wanted to write. Moreover: my understanding of the very concept of *literature,* and of the *novel* in particular, has always been linked to Europe; the novel is no less than a European invention—this applies also to the American and Latin-American novels so popular in recent decades. To me this has been an extremely extant reality, not merely a fact of literary history.

What do I mean by "time-honored Norwegian"? In poetry: mainline lyrical poetry written in a romantically colored poetic language that is bound up with a strongly monologic subject, with Norwegian nature (mountains and fjords, snow and pine forests) in its role as a perpetually fresh source of reference and metaphor, and with a tangible, though unexpressed, affinity with the pre-urban and pre-modern. In prose: The psychological-realistic novel with roots in the nineteenth century, usually with moral, political, or religious undertones. As a young, immature poet, I embarked whole-heartedly on writing selfless metapoems in an objective, I could almost say gray, laconic tone, inspired by such widely varying, but un-Norwegian, spirits as the French poets Mallarmé and Ponge, or the Germans Brecht and Celan. At that time my pet statements on literature were, for instance, Mallarmé's famous: "Poems are not written with ideas but with words," and Flaubert's somewhat less well-known warning to young budding poets against, as he says, "using one's own heart as a trampoline."

I also had a great regard for Flaubert's often-quoted declaration: "Madame Bovary, c'est moi." Concurrently, as I absorbed myself in those writers I did my best to read and understand French, German, and Russian theorists who wrote at the intersection between philosophy and literature. I think for instance of Roland Barthes and Walter Benjamin. There is no doubt that my basic attitude to writing was formed at that time, and the first uncertain deposits of what I now think of as a European signature on my own writing were laid down then. In his first crucial work on literary theory, *The Zero-Point of Literature,* Barthes makes his well-known assertion that "from Flaubert up to our own time, the whole of literature has been a complex problem of language," which also implies that the wide scope of the novel demands the same fastidious care as the narrow scope of the poem. That is a fundamental demand for me. The novel is not first and foremost a mirror of man's interior and exterior world, a way of reproducing a psychological course of development or an actual reality, but an arena in which research into existence is carried out by means of ambiguous, fluctuating writing.

I have always foreseen the novel I wanted to write as a kind of architecture or topography of writing, a work that unfolds in space rather than in time, which can be more easily described in terms of a relation, for instance, rather than as a chronology. The novel as a linear narrative or description, if I disregard children's reading, never really managed to grab me, and as a novelist I regard myself as almost the opposite of a writer of epics or a historian, and not in the least as a psychologist. It's true that all my novels have easily recognizable elements of narrative; but the narratives do not complete themselves, they are moved along by other narratives that comment, fill out, reflect, interrupt. I should like to say that this is

the European element in my novels: the leisurely, elaborate
thought, the leisurely, elaborate sentence, searching, full of guard-
edness, always aware that life is never seized, but must always be
seized; the notion that one writes to think through what one
doesn't understand, doesn't know enough about, that which keeps
one awake or pesters one's dreams; that one writes in an attempt to
surmount an interior resistance, or to resist an exterior one, and
not necessarily because one has something spectacular to say. One
of my favorite aphorisms about the novel, which also summarizes
what I would like to identify as the novel's "European signature," is
this one by Milan Kundera: "The novel is not about reality, but
life." If there is any European signature to be found in my novels it
can be recognized in the unfinished, the untested. Europeanness
always signals more questions than answers.

My first novel, *Eel,* can usefully stand as a model. It deals with
both a respectable teacher of German, who bears this name, and a
very greatest puzzle posed by the fish genus, *anguilla* in Latin,
which is a prized food item here in Germany as well, as far as I
know. Why does my thoroughly level-headed German teacher feel
such an irresistible, erotic attraction for his sweet, young, immature female German pupil, to the point that he can hardly think of
anything except her? And why does the peerless eel roam all the
way from the distant Sargasso Sea, where it is born, right up to our
northern waters and then ten years later swim back to the Sargasso
Sea to spawn and die? Why does it do this? Why couldn't it stay in
the Sargasso Sea and be content with that? It is worth noting in
parenthesis that as I was writing this I read, to my great joy, in a
Norwegian newspaper the following lovely little article. It might
not have any connection with the matter in hand, so please forgive
me for devoting time and space to it here; but I'll take a chance, for
something inside me says that it does belong here after all, within
the context of this discussion on, or around, the European element
in the text. In all its prosaic beauty the newspaper piece tells us: "A
German family has kept a live eel in its bath since 1969. Into the
bargain they have taught the eel to move into a bucket when someone wants to take a bath. 'He is one of the family,' says Hannelore
Richter of Bochum. Her husband caught the eel on a fishing trip in

1969 and took it home for dinner. 'But the children fell for the eel
and refused to allow it to be killed and cooked, and ever since then
it has lived in the bath. It even moved with us to a new house.'" I
only ask: may one not write a novel about such a fish? And may
one not deeply regret that this story was unknown in 1989, when
Eel was written, and therefore could not have its rightful place in
the novel?

My third novel, *Hutchinson's Successors,* published by Suhr-
kamp Verlag in autumn 2001, deals, among other things, with a
Scottish timber merchant Robert Dalton Hutchinson, who closes
down the very profitable timber business he runs with his brother
in order to spend all his time and all his talents on such a totally
useless, and in many ways absolutely ridiculous, passion as fly
fishing, i.e., the art of catching a fish with a strange creation of hair
and feathers wound round a small, sharp metal hook, which the
unsuspecting fish believes to be a real insect. This man came to
Norway at the beginning of the nineteenth century, a year or two
after the dissolution of the union with Denmark, and published the
first known textbook in Norwegian about the noble art of fly fishing, the self-important title of which is *On the Use of Fly Fishing in
Norway.* However, *Hutchinson's Successors* is also about a woman,
Solveig Fjellberg, who nourishes at least as great and strange a
passion as the old Scot, which is to make and dress herself in exact
copies of the royal gala dresses of Queen Maud, the first queen of
independent Norway. And finally it is about a man, a solitary, intense antiquarian bookseller, who is passionately fascinated by the
passions of Robert Dalton Hutchinson and Solveig Fjellberg—and
passionately tries to understand them by telling a story about them,
that is to say, devoting all his time and all his abilities to something
so totally futile, and more often than not financially unprofitable,
as writing, writing, writing.

Both *Eel* and *Hutchinson's Successors,* and for that matter my
most recent novel, *When the Golden Sun Burns,* which, incidentally, is to be published in German in the not-too-distant future, in
their modest way pose questions about life and human motives.
They offer no answer, they do not pretend to be psychological narratives able to illuminate the darkest labyrinths of the human mind,

they do not set up any moral rules, they make no suggestions; but they ask, they wonder, they keep disquiet alive: why are we as we are, why do we act as we do? Why all those incomprehensible, often self-destructive, inappropriate, absurd, pathetic, not seldom incredibly cruel, but also not seldom incomprehensibly good, moving, beautiful things that humans actually do? That humans actually are? These perpetual, fundamentally unanswerable, questions—not some political or pedagogic project—form, to my way of thinking, the "European element" in my novels. A long list of great European novelists—Kafka, Mann, Musil, Broch, Beckett, Celine, Hamsun, Bernhard, etc.—have asked them before; but that doesn't matter, for they have no final answer and will never go out of use. At present I have actually finished reading, though not marveling at, the autobiographical novel written by the winner of the Nobel Prize for Literature, Imre Kertész. *Fateless* relates the experiences and happenings that the author lived through as a young lad in German concentration camps, including Auschwitz. These are depicted not as a unique manifestation of irrational wickedness, an alien tumor in the body of rational Europe, but as something completely possible, almost normal in its unheard-of way. "The uttermost truth about human degradation in modern life," as we read on the cover of the Norwegian edition of the book. What other medium than the novel would have the courage and ability to hold up the image of the Nazi extermination camps—itself the symbol of annihilation of all we are accustomed to attach to Europe and "the European"—in such a manner, as a matter of fact, objectively, without moral indignation or metaphysical protest. This objectivity renders the camps even more terrifying, challenging, and inaccessible to the reader because Auschwitz becomes, so to speak, one of several other existing and real rooms in the European house that we all live in; and the community, the history, the culture that surrounds us? And I think: is it not the destiny of the European novel to see to it that such existential questions on the dignity and potential of the individual human being are constantly asked, even when they are felt to be shocking and outrageous? To see that they are not allowed to be forgotten, these questions with which neither the sciences, nor technology, nor the market, nor politics, nor the media occupy themselves to any tangible degree, partly because science, technology, the market, and politics, etc., force people into cubicles, into sectors—into the mine shafts of specialization—while the novel presents the individual in concrete situations, in the world of senses, emotions, experiences, memories, dreams, hopes of the future, and so on, which in every age make up the world of our life. And thereby the novel does its bit to put spokes in the wheels of the powers that want to degrade, reduce, place the individual in parenthesis?

If it were not that it sounds so intolerably pompous, I should like to have concluded by saying that certainly, I feel more like a European than a Norwegian—and this is not concealed agitation for Norwegian EU membership; on the contrary, I think of the sum of impulses that has made me write the novels I have written. For to the extent I am able to say anything about my literary talent and its origins, I consider that it has not sprung from any Norwegian nature or Norwegian national feeling, as the romantics like to imagine, but purely and simply from the texts and ideas I have met with and have grabbed my attention, which have overwhelmingly been written and thought out by European writers. I recall a definition of Europeans: "Those who cherish a nostalgic longing for Europe." In other words, the European is a person who longs for something that once existed, but is no longer there. The word *nostalgia* derives from Greek *nostos* (homecoming) and *algos* (pain). Thus, the European literally longs painfully to return to a Europe that is no longer to be found. And the "European signature" that can be seen like a watermark in my novels must, if this definition is correct, be a signature placed there by a dead hand, a ghostly hand quite simply—or a hand that in some mysterious way has kept itself alive from the past, somehow immortalized by time itself?

Yes, fine by me; as far as I can see the present-day European hand is more occupied in setting its signature to other things than literary texts—to modern media and information technology, market economy, sports events, and the entertainment industry, for example. No, the heroes of our time are definitely not writers, but entertainers, sports stars, and the *nouveau riche* real estate agents.

To be honest, I find it difficult to see any new, modern European signature in the novels written in this part of the world today; the European signature that I see inscribed into my own and others' texts is a creation born somewhere else, in another time. But against all odds it has survived until today, like the eel in the bath. Even if it is far from its source and will never be able to get home, it moves as if nothing had happened, it still keeps its secrets, still won't allow itself to be completely understood.

— *Translated by Anne Borne*

Jean Rouaud

Poetry is what once was called grace and what the
Romantics called the expression of genius, where we
contemptuously reject inspiration, that which we no
longer dare to name, but feel as an imperial need to sing.
© Holger-Andre.de

Jean Rouaud
France

Born in Campbon (near Nantes) in 1952, Jean Rouaud
studied literature before becoming a seller of newspapers
at a newspaper stand. *Les champs d'honneur*, his first
novel, appeared in 1990. He became famous overnight
and was awarded the Prix Goncourt. Jean Rouaud lives
and writes in Brittany.

Further Reading:
Fields of Glory. Arcade Books, 1993.
Of Illustrious Men. Harvill Press, 1995.
World More or Less. Arcade Books, 1998.

In Memory of Ernst Wiechert

*La poésie est ce que jadis on appelait la grâce, et ce
que les romantiques appelaient l'expression du génie,
elle est aujourd'hui, depuis que nous rejetons avec
mépris l'inspiration, ce que nous n'osons plus appeler,
mais que nous ressentons comme un impérieux besoin
de chanter.*

First of all, I would like to make use of this gathering to confess my debt of gratitude toward a German writer. He is not one of the big literary names of this country, his work has practically fallen into oblivion. When I happened to refer to him here, people were surprised to find me interested in an author who is usually ranked in the highly dangerous category of regional writers preoccupied with earth and blood. He is just a little shy of being considered a propagandist of the Third Reich, all the worse for a man who, in his capacity as university professor, denounced the conquering spirit of the Hitler régime, an act for which he was forced to suffer internment in Nazi concentration camps long before the beginning of the war. The camp experience provides the catharsis of his ultimate novel *Missa sine nomine*. I have chosen to honor the memory of Ernst Wiechert because my reading of his books at the age of fifteen marked my first encounter with literature, that is with the rosy-fingered Dawn, with tales that are not limited to the sum of incidents that keep you in suspense. I see clearly now that my interest did not arise from the rare poetry of the text alone. It was the result of an encounter passing through time, space, and the border between two languages. In *Die kleine Passion*, which tells the story of Hans, a fatherless child living in this marshy and wooded part of East Prussia, where invasive religion presses with all Heaven's weight on the consciences and behavior of its inhabitants, someone whispered something about an almost-me into my ear for the first time. Today I can see that I was not then aware of these similarities. That universe was readily familiar to me, requiring no big effort on my part to imagine it. A humid country, a rural society that can no longer claim autonomy, ignorance of the city lights and deafness to the rumble of the world (in *Jedermann*, the sequel of *Die kleine Passion*, the same young people find themselves on the front lines of the first slaughter of the century), the imprint of religion leaving such a narrow scope for individual action that destiny appears to be all traced out. Between this universe and mine there lay not those thousands of kilometers that separate Lutheran East Prussia from Catholic Brittany, tempted by Jansenism for a time and deeply marked by the severe prescriptions of the Counter Reformation. Without feeling the necessity to express it in words, it appeared to me immediately that Wiechert's fictional characters and I belonged to the same geographical and mental region.

There have been other, more esteemed, readings since this first literary fascination and I have felt flattered when, in the context of my work, Proust or Claude Simon were mentioned, to whom I could add those who have been essential to me—Chateaubriand and Flaubert, as well as Malcolm Lowry and Kerouac; but to tell the truth, as far as the basic elements of my literary endeavors are concerned, I would not really have needed them: I had already encountered everything in the work of Wiechert. Yet, beyond personal reminiscences, the one thing in his books that seduced me above all, that was important to me, that enticed me toward this high idea of literature, was the biblical tone of his writing, which one understood to carry a higher mission than just simply telling a story. What it said, in sentences interspersing the text like gold veins and sounding as if they had been borrowed from Psalms or the proverbs of Solomon, I remember vividly, like this one, for instance, which I still cite now and then: one only humiliates oneself is what it said in this lyrical, conjuring language, which did not allow any word to be careless at the risk of becoming sententious and that all history expressed in quasi-liturgical language would inevitably tell the story of a chosen people, whichever, wherever it may come from and however humble it may be. The writing was the poetic tongue-of-fire of the Day of Pentecost, lowering onto the characters of the text and transforming them into universal advocates of the human condition. The writing was this act of choosing. And every book was a small piece of the great book of the world, like a shadow, transferred through the centuries, of the novel of the Hebrew people, where this man of divine descent came to announce the death of death. And we all know how deeply the spreading of this good news has influenced our vision of the world. We practically owe everything to it. Therefore, through the grace of the writing, it became possible to make a lost corner of northwestern France a promised land.

This biblical, prophetic, evangelic tone accompanied me during my entire childhood. I heard it every Sunday in mass, uttered from the top of this small space capsule symbolizing the Ascension and the celebrant's intermediate position between God and his flock, this powerful sentence constantly recurring like a leitmotif—and at that moment it was as if a piece of Heaven had settled down upon the believers assembled in church: verily, I tell you. And since it was the self-proclaimed Son of God who spoke, it was quite impossible to doubt his words, for it was clearly affirmed at the beginning of St John's Gospel that this Man born of a woman was the word come flesh. Out of which followed that the word, the body, and the truth were one. All this was Him.

One can well imagine what operations were necessary in order to get fictional characters to go on their way unhindered and spreading their small pieces of truth, a truth no longer absolute, but temporary, occasional, transitory, human. The sum of the truths bound to the firm desire to persevere when the victory over death is no longer certain at all. The last one to believe in texts literally was this poor old fool Don Quixote, who is a fool first of all for thinking the romance of chivalry to be the word of Gospel and that it would be sufficient to rely on it to create the character of a knight errant, a *miles Christi* as he was called in the twelfth century. The first hero abandoned by God. The rupture between fiction and the real, that is between Heaven and Earth, is accomplished from the beginning of the novel through the charge against the windmills. Therefore, fiction is just a machine to mill the winds. The word becomes *flatus vocis* again. He is crazy who believes in what is written. And off with the formidable semantic gymnastics of the Council of Nicaea, which resolved the old dispute about the divinity of Christ by imposing this idea of double nature, to be imagined as opposing forces inside an atomic nucleus, all God, that is word, and all man, that is the suffering, demanding, aging, dying body. As doubt was rising and man began to recognize himself in the human part of the Savior, in the decaying temple of his corpse and not in his glory, rejection was spreading, leading finally to the inevitable separation. The word regained Heaven and the body was left to itself to satisfy its desires as its only means of resisting unavoidable death. The late invention of the realistic novel, in this part of the world that had awaited the end of time with terror and hope, was made at this price. At the price of this disincarnation. The lights of reason having replaced those of the Spirit, the illumination they brought into the world showed it in its crudeness and cruelty, Pascal's vision of men in chains who were to be liberated by all means available. The hero of the novel, last representative of the knight errant for whom the romance of chivalry, or the novel, had been invented, telling him that by saving the humiliated he would obtain his salvation, with nothing to rely on other than his own resources, who had nothing to expect from Heaven any more, he undertook it to save himself without assistance. He intrigued—sometimes that passed, sometimes not. In this one discovered that intrigue, if methodical, implacable, is something of a physio-chemical experiment reproduced in a laboratory. Thus Zola had only to get inspired by the theories of biologist Claude Bernard and literature would not wait to claim scientific status. Which Roland Barthes was determined to prove in displaying all the seductions of his sparkling intelligence before retracing his steps during his last years and admitting the vanity of his project, confessing that, until then, he had merely been producing attempts, "rugged form where analysis contests with romance and method with phantasm."

For poetry, this repressed part of the realistic novel, the divine part of the double nature—fiction and representation of the real—which the latter often eliminated within itself to radiograph the colloquial of humanity, cannot be reduced to science. It is what once was called grace and what the Romantics called the expression of genius, where we contemptuously reject inspiration, that which we no longer dare to name, but feel as an imperial need to sing. It is this restrained, broken song, this irrepressible song coming from an earthly and, at the same time, heavenly body like a fossil wave, which I heard with pleasure coming up from Ernst Wiechert's pages. It is for catching his echo that I place my sentences to the listening post.

— Translated by Dagmar Rohde

Robert Schindel

Today Central Europe has, however, become
an illusion: its culture was lost forever when
the European Jewry was eliminated.
© gezett.de

Robert Schindel
Austria

The poet, author, and editor Robert Schindel was born the child of Austrian communists of Jewish descent at Bad Hall in 1944. His father was murdered at Dachau concentration camp in 1945, while his mother survived Auschwitz and Ravensbrück. After studying law and philosophy, Schindel became politically active as the spokesperson of the Vienna Commune and then moved in Maoist circles until 1978. Meanwhile he began working in the field of film, television, and radio. Robert Schindel has received numerous awards, including the Austrian Literature Prize Award in 1992 and the Erich Fried Prize for language and literature in 1993.

Further Reading:
Born-Where. Studies. Translated by Michael Roloff. Ariadne Press, 1995.

"We're All Right."
Europe's Influence on My Writing

Aber mein Schreiben hat seine Muttermale leider nicht im Reformeuropa, sondern in jenem europäischen Gulag. Je mehr dieser in der Geschichte zum Erdreich geht, desto mehr mögen künftige Texte zivilisatorischen Fortschritten Rechnung tragen.

1

The train had reached its destination and stopped. A woman, who was almost thirty-two years old, looked at the station sign. She became aware of the word *Auschwitz* for the first time in her life. A friend sitting next to her said that he too had never heard of the place. The date was the first of November, 1944. Both were under Gestapo detention orders. The man and the woman got out together, were separated, and would never see each other again.

The woman is already familiar to those who have read my essays. She was Gerty Schindel. Her friend was René Hajek, my father. Both were well dressed. They had got out of France fourteen months earlier because the exiled Austrian Communist Party had instructed them to organize a resistance group in Linz, a city on the Danube that is the main city of the northeastern, or Upper Austrian, province. Members of the group were given forged French identification papers, making them citizens of Alsace to account for their German accents. Gerty or rather Annette, as she was known in the resistance, became Suzanne Soël. My father's new name was Pierre Lutz. Moving from Paris to Linz inside my mother's belly, I listened to the changed tone of speech. Gerty, an active member of the illegal Communist Party in Vienna, had been arrested before the war and sentenced to five years inside. Now it was essential that she carried out her tasks in a place where she was known neither to the citizens nor to the authorities.

The Alsatian group had volunteered to become registered as foreign workers in Austria, or Ostmark, as the Nazis called it. They lived in a skiing village near Linz. Gerty was the dark-haired French woman working as a maid in the Maischberger Inn. Then I came into the world. Four months later their cover was blown. She was recognized in the street by Mottl S., a young Jew in hiding. One wheel of my stroller had come off and rolled in front of his feet.

"Gerty, what are you doing here?"

My mother replied in French, but it did not help. When they got hold of Mottl he told his torturers everything he knew. Before they had finally worn him out my parents were already on the train to Vienna. They had been exposed as Viennese communists and Jews. I was in another train taking me to a safe hiding-place in Vienna. A nursery nurse had swiftly removed me from the scene.

My parents stayed for eight weeks at the Gestapo's Austrian headquarters at Morzinplatz in Vienna, courtesy of the assassin Johann Sanitzer. They traveled on to Auschwitz, where they were to wait until tried for high treason. Traveling with them were their documents, stamped RU for *Rückkehr unerwünscht*, i.e., "Return not recommended."

They arrived into a European community packed into the smallest of spaces. Hardly a nation was missing from the list of inmates. In harmonious unison, they fed together from the same tin basins, though the harmony was broken when they were shouted at. Then the Italians, the Poles, the Germans, the Greek, the Czechs, the Slovaks, the French and the Dutch all trotted off work in their wooden clogs, at the double — *faster you lousy swine, one-two, one-two*. The same kind of thing went on in the women's camp. Harmoniously everyone shared the common latrines, typhus and dysentery clearing out people's insides until no life was left, until they were no longer able to get up or were already in the death-house, gasping out their inter-European last sighs.

Auschwitz? It was the European answer to the Gulag Archipelago, a finely-meshed spider's web holding thousands of flies, a city of death serving so many places: from Natzweiler to Majdanek, from Neuengamme to Saloniki and back to Stutthof, from Drancy, Strutthof and Westerbork to Jasenovac. This was United Europe of the slaves, and the victims and the killed. It was organized by a mastermind, who with its skilled helpers had woven the net—by Germany and its collaborators.

When that Nazi Germany was at last laid waste, it left behind an ancient continent devoured, desolate, petrified. Then the moment passed—"Life flowered in the ruins," as the saying goes—and the spring of forty-five turned out to be enchantingly warm and lovely—or so they say.

2

I emerged from under all that rubble, overshadowed by the huge, overheated political machine in the East. I had been tucked away inside a crèche run by the National Socialist People's Welfare Organization. It was right in the middle of Glasscherben Island, as it was then known. Before the war the Viennese called it Matzoth Island because there were so many Jews living there—in my Leopoldstadt.

Post-war children in Vienna: we grew up as best we could, playing football with stones or tennis-balls or rubber balls. I was given a leather ball, so I became the prince of the Jesuitenwiese. Angrily, we watched as they cleared one ruined site after another, all great places for playing, let's say, the French against the Vietminh. Dull municipal housing rose on cleared sites, and from the windows grouchy grown-ups were snarling at us. People in this city loved dogs, not children.

The Russians were there. If you asked the children, they would have nothing but good to say about the Soviet soldiers. They swung us high in the air and we breathed in the strange odors from the mouths of tow-haired, laughing Seryoshas and Alyoshas. The Yanks were chewing their gum in the classier parts of town. As for the French and the British, no child in Vienna can recall anything about them.

Odd things happened. The teacher, who had been a Nazi, would be very quiet for whole lessons on end. Occasionally someone would mention his service as a low altitude pilot in the Wehrmacht (the German army). But for us children, Europe had vanished. Only the United States and the Soviet Union existed.

I was a Young Pioneer, a Petrel as we were called in Vienna, when I started writing. The Petrels was an organization for children run by the Communist Party. We children were anyway quite taken by the idea of the Soviet Union, not because we figured it was nice to kids, but because it was socialism incarnate. We sang "The East is red" (China is young) too. Socialism was pushed at us in terms of a splendid future, a glowing alternative to exploitation by US capitalists, who were slowly taking over Europe too.

First Fragments of Childhood

Murder strode on the stage of my childhood,
they strangled my father there, well and good.
When the labor camp released my mother.
She found me, and loved me, but I was another

A tramp of the passions, forever restless;
I messed about and did not give a toss.
But the tumbling walls of school and fortress
Stirred up winds of rebellion and waves of loss

A child at play in a world they had made,

still deep in my dreams colored
socialist red,
as comrades' slogan-filled mouths kissed my own

Childhood behind me, and future in the shade
of Marxist–Leninist trees, I was stilled, I bred
long-nosed kids, stones on my father's tombstone.

The European Coal and Steel Union was of no interest to those who thought like me. To us the whole idea of Europe seemed rightwing, reactionary—the large corporations wanted to create supranational conglomerates and dressed it up as "European Integration." Adenauer was a suspect figure as far as I was concerned. Those who acknowledged him as a "great European" had not the slightest idea of what a "Great European" was supposed to be like.

After August 13 in 1961, we sang "Auf der Mauer, auf det Mauer, sitzt der Konrad Adenauer" (On the Wall, hour after hour, sits Herr Konrad Adenauer). We pinned all the blame for Germany's division on the West. We fought the revisionists and the exiles, who presented a view of history — and probably still do — that was based on systematically redistributing guilt over time. For these people 1945 was the zero-hour when all the wrong-doing began. Take the way the "German people" looked on approvingly, while the Nazis were behaving like utter barbarians in Sudetenland and Schlesien, setting precedents for the later expulsions — actually, no, it didn't happen. It took time before it dawned on us activists that two wrongs do not make a right.

By then my writing was branded by their denial of guilt and their vociferous accusations against their former victims, all of which also seemed increasingly to characterize Stalinism. I was too young to join in the hymns to Stalin and later on, I became a Maoist but was driven mainly by opportunism. Given my previous experiences, I could not face starting to sing songs of praise this time round.

To a young man, who had been socialized as a member of the Left and always carried the knowledge of an exterminated family at the back of his mind, the European idea was devoid of any attraction. What did it really stand for?

3

It looked like standing for an orchestrated activity, an aligned society, a catalogue of values aimed at masking the old German glory-dreams with democratic maxims, while criminalizing all left-wing activity. The trail of democracy led back to the once-so hostile Western allies and the careful Euro-builders tunneled into prehistory, pushing all memories of cracking selfhood and buried corpses out of sight. The turncoats were lining up, respected politicians now: regional First Ministers, Ministers of Transport, of Trade and Industry, Federal Presidents — all present and correct.

In Austria the value system was similar, though the dishonesty had taken one more turn for the worse. As is well known, our crafty Austrian politicians sold the world the story of our fate as the

first victim of Nazi Germany. Stepping smartly back from the edge
of the mass graves, piled high with shot Jews, Russians, partisans
and police and well inside the auditorium of post-war Austria, they
could report back on another performance they had seen, though
of course not participated in. Others were up to all sorts—these
partisans, these Asiatic Ivans, and so forth. Jews, now? No Jews
anywhere to be seen, tough but was only home on leave at the
time. Easily ten thousand Austrian soldiers must have joined in
"scorched-earth" raids, yet no one seems to have noticed a single
crime committed by the Wehrmacht. Or, had there been something
to be seen, they knew how to keep their mouths shut. That entire
generation was a marvel: although part of the fighting machine,
they walked through massacres, as a man as totally innocent as a
bunch of Sir Galahads. They had carried out their duty, that's all.

This was certainly more true of the second generation of senior
politicians than the first. As well as the middle and lower ranks of
the two main political parties, they were avowedly just spectators
of—OK, unfortunate events. The third force to reckon with, the
"Independents," was a far from insignificant group of ex-
collaborators. Their former convictions were tempered now, in the
sense of being reduced to the "good" aspects of National Socialism:
"Hitler was ein böser Mann, docht baute er die Autobahn" (Though
Hitler was as bad as they say, it's true he built a fine motorway).
That Jewish business was a bad mistake, as was the anti-
clericalism. Generally, it had been a bad idea to fight angels and
devils at the same time. In this mental morass every brown flower
that grew looked blue thanks to the widespread Austrian disorder
of colorblindness.

We were presented with the European concept as constructed by
this lot. It became entrenched, at first supported and later taken
over by the country's conservatives. Certainly, one of the core ideas
was that Hitler had already envisaged a united Europe and actually
got his way; remember the "European Archipelago"? The conservatives turned their backs on this version of the unification idea
and found up-to-date replacements: United Europe as an economic
barricade to keep the heathen communists at bay, and as a liberating force for our East European brothers and sisters. In order to set

up this Europe, it was first necessary to break it into two parts and also, whenever speaking about "Europe" to align it with the West.

As we all know, the waves of rebellion in '68 were directed towards this value-system.

Gradually, very gradually this West-oriented system started to change as it agreed negotiated settlements with the Eastern block. Its national economies were crumbling, as our mercantile rulers' democratic deficits became obvious, and—finally—as Gorbachev's *perestroika* arrived on the scene. The previous, baffling generation went down the tube and with it went quite a few of the old glorious ideas.

The events of 1989 finally led to socialism as we knew it being dumped, but by that time a new idea of Europe had already emerged. It had more in common both with the old central Europe and with the pan-European movement than with the image of Europe cherished by so many on the right.

4

Years ago, the writer Milo Dor asked: "What kind of Central Europe will we have if we accept English as our means of communication?" Dor was born in Budapest, grew up in Belgrade and lived in Vienna after the war. Today his Central Europe has become an illusion: its culture was lost forever when the European Jewry was eliminated.

Still, inside me the old times still are alive and breathing. I find them again in Milo Dor's writing and the works of Aleksandar Tišma, Ivo Andric, Robert Musil, Joseph Roth and many others. In that sense the old place has meant and still means much to me.

WORDS GOING ON A JOURNEY I
(In the middle of the karst landscape)

1

Surrounded by crags and corpses on the karst limestone
here and there puddles of blood woodland under the pale sky,
a lake with rippling water in the midst of the stone landscape
its southeastern history is huddled up,
words piled up close, ears like waving reeds, eyes like objective
        lenses.

Crouching in a hollow high up in the karst
they stay watching the farmstead being shot to pieces

Nearby, bent over tightly to keep still but rising traveling
what a driving force her wings lend her
fluttering then flying into the distance
away from the silent seas of blood that infect all with stillness,
flying away from the valleys of misery from the armor-clad hilltops
gaining height and width in her flight to leave
the shadows over the landscape, to slide into our senses

   2
I am reporting this. Was he pissed? I saw it,
I refer to my own eyes rolling popping from their sockets the girl in
       front
there next to an old man Srebrenica my lost love
bending finally together your gebihatschter and his goratsch
Ah don't geddit! Report comprehensibly the facts of the atrocity
for our files we take an interest in how them over there
fucked some place Srebrenica what's that with the knife
in the gob of someone or other is it true, really is it

   3
Passing high above the Alps the words separate
leaving the cavalcade scattering disappearing in downward flight
coming through the computer screen as images,
reeds are bending over to mined ground, massacred bodies
words are pushing their way from ear to back of tongue and there
new words join them and the entire continent is chattering.
There is the landscape to which farmers and doctors
former children and soldiers once quietly devoted so much.

During the last century just this region has been torn apart and its
flags soaked in blood. During the '90s it turned back into itself, hid
in its smallest space, threatening at first to become the cause of
Europe once more splitting into nation-states.
   In Austrian Klagenfurt, close to the Croatian border, during the

Bachmann literary awards in 1992, the shooting was heard as close
as if it were inside the room.

WORDS GOING ON A JOURNEY II
(Killer-Serbia)

While sleep is overwhelming me I'm thinking vaguely
of voices after the fading echoes of the southern Slav turmoil
and in my almost-sleep I see
as if I were there how the Ustaše flags are brought
by men riding into the farms of Krajina, I hear the ceaseless shoot-
        ing
by the Slavonians from the east, the army at
Vokovar, the dead,
the filmmaker Niki Vogel shot down,
the fine airport in Ljubljana, a northern city

Clinging to love the butterfly dances round the reading-lamp
Bosnians in Srebrenica have been shot and dumped long since
and Chechnyan people mumble about their right to self-
        determination
Like the Serbs and Muslims in Krajina,
German people of South Tyrol, what so special about Erdberg?
Watching the World channel my eyelids swell with blood
looking at Mr Ignorant and Mr Grumbler,
observing the bombardment of the white city it is as if
to die for Serbia meant that every shot went to pot
try breathing with your belly.

Those I watch here on my own make me laugh
in sleepy Vienna folk are beating up H, the poet, and driving him
from their editorial offices and their pubs because he is in mourn-
        ing
for the federal state, because he wants fair reporting
of the terrible facts of the matter,
before I can close my eyes Mr Joseph Roth or someone so like him
comes staggering across my belly, so I whisper to him

should not really Franz Joseph live
rather than Tuđjman and Milošević?

I turn the cover falls off one leg
I push my behind towards the south-east lay both hands
on my cheek, now I had better sleep for
in the morning I must write about a character
in my novel who is not guilty
'cause it is not too late for writing stuff.
Down in the street the snow-clearing machines rattle
as if they were tanks waiting then finally my dreams carry me
        away.

Once more, the one-sided media coverage proved — if proof were needed — how swiftly nationalistic rabble-rousing can develop. The Serbian and Croatian variants of nationalism certainly share the guilt for the wars in the Balkans, but old notions of the Killer-Serbs led to Serbia being fingered as the sole responsible state.

When Peter Handke denounced this one-sidedness, the German and Austrian media responded by practically declaring him an enemy of peace and democracy. Given this media campaign, it is understandable that Handke himself kept his protective stance towards the Serbian policy rather too single-mindedly, over-reaching himself in a way which in the end failed to clarify matters.

But even during this crisis the new Europe grew in stature, slowly but steadily.

5

I feel quite good about the European Union, and was pleased that we Austrians were not outside it during the Haider years. It would have been most uncomfortable to be left alone in the company of Haider and his cunning Austrian henchmen during a period of growth in populist politics.

Now, the enlargement of the Union to include East European states means that the EU must develop social policies. Battles about social conditions will also be fought in the context of the purely economic union. Such battles, fought as new class confrontations and not as conflicts between nation states, should lead to improved social provisions. In this way the Left, with its insistence that the international validity of the opposition between labor and capital, will also become involved into the shaping of Europe.

That's all right by me. I must admit, though, that it is not from the Europe of reform that I get the native tongue in which I write, but from the old European Gulag. The further that historical period descends into the underworld, the more should it be taken into account for future inquiries into the progress of civilization.

It is in 1945. The train stops. The doors are pulled open. Men, wearing uniforms no one has seen before, throw sacks full of straw into the carriages. My mother, who is thirty-two years old and weighs all of thirty-two kilograms, turns to one of the uniformed men.

"Why these sacks of straw all of a sudden?"

The man, a member of the military police, finds nothing to say. The prisoners are silent too. They come from an assortment of concentration camps. Then the man speaks up.

"It's the ninth of May. They agreed about peace today."

He glanced at the skeletons standing and lying everywhere in the carriage.

"You're all right, see."

— *Translated by Anna Paterson*

Ivan Štrpka

Today I wouldn't describe Europe as a continent,
more as a form-creating context. It is an open context
in the midst of other contexts. It is writing itself.
© Maxim Segienko/PHOTOMAX

Ivan Štrpka

Slovakia

Born in Hlhovec in 1944, Ivan Štrpka is a writer, author, and translator. In 1963 he co-founded—with Ivan Laučík and Peter Repka—the writers' group *Lone Runners*. After studying Slavic languages and literature and Romance languages and literature in Bratislava, Štrpka became an editor for the democratic weekly *Kultúrny život (Cultural Life)*, which was banned after the 1968 invasion. From 1970 he worked for Slovak television as a dramatist and editor of children's programs. He translated into Slovak works by Cervantes, Borges, and Pessoa and also published successful records with the musician Dežo Ursiny. Štrpka heads the literary newspaper *Romboid*; he lives and works in Bratislava.

Oh, Children Smeared with Honey and with Blood

Nenazval by som dnes Európu kontinentom, skôr
formulujúcim sa kontextom. Otvoreným kontextom
uprostred iných kontextov. Píšucim sa.

I speak to you from an unknown place, I broadcast a smoke signal from the middle of the youngest and least visible of the summits of the great literary tradition of this multicolored, rich, and ancient continent. I declare myself precisely from a place of action, perhaps precisely from a small literary black hole, undiscovered and slightly exotic, right in the geographically phantasmagoric center of Central Europe. We are at home with myths. "I remember Paris and I've never been there," as one of our most spirited comics sings, thus indiscreetly revealing our tradition of brooding and melancholic frustration stemming from historical isolation and a lack of self-criticism and free movement. There is also a widespread opinion that life in the midst of such a phantasmagoria must be a great source of energy, creativity, penetration into space-time, a true gate into a new reality.

Let's be brief: I speak to you as a Slovak poet from the Slovak Republic. This means, as my friend, the poet Ivan Laučík, has so rightly admitted, "I write to you ... from an uncertain place on the map."

Precisely this uncertainty of place, this unanchoredness in firmly closed coordinates of forms and empty stereotypes, this uncertain place opposed to definitiveness, a place developing inside itself and at the same time within you, this infirm, moveable place of ceaseless change and tilting, moveable identity of which the only support and acceptable framework is plural—this move-

able ground of a fertile wilderness beneath our feet (to which nobody belongs *a priori*), this ahistorical, enduring unrest of place,
which ceaselessly pumps a living tradition from a floating archae-
ology of the uninterrupted consciousness of connections, of the
movement of intuition, empathy and directly from the air of culture, creating a fragile shell of protective atmosphere for the matur-
ing of life opposed to the impatient rolling of history (as noted by
Nietzsche) — this moveable place of a poem, this uncertain living
place of our current change, this changeable place that today I can
point to without embarrassment as the fundamental point of my
trials in life and in my writing. From the beginning I have unconsciously felt in my fingers a living nomadicity of writing as my
ancient wandering, uninterrupted thread. Yes, this unrest of place,
this visible and proven nomadicity, is placed somewhere deep
within me as a mark of identity. It is a pact of European identity. It
is a fundamental paradox of life, inevitable for life and its growth.
The paradise of writing is moveable, its hell is immobility. Communication within this code is more a permanent purgation of our
perceptions and their own words. With this game or personal religion it is not only a matter of truth or the lie of the mere suggestion
of words.

At the very outset the question of value stands before me. These
are the values of a poem and the values of the individual, specific
human life. There is also a nagging feeling that there can even be
some relationship determined by destiny. This ceaseless tension
directed towards the sheer value of meaning seeks its own solution
and fulfillment — it wishes to break and evoke form in a radical
way: style decides. Isn't this still a theme of European culture?

I remember that I first encountered the word *Europe* as a small
boy exactly in connection with value and style. From my father's
account: in the first days of peace at the end of the war that produced the most casualties of all, the soldiers of the victorious Red
Army were reconstructing a temporary bridge over the river Vah.
They were in a hurry, harsh orders rapped out, often beams and
construction workers fell into the river. They drowned. "Russia is
wealthy! We are many! Go on! Don't hold things up, we haven't got

time!"—the commanding officer waved his arms when this happened. Before the eyes of our own shocked people he didn't allow anybody to rescue them. "Barbarians, human life doesn't mean anything to them," my mother called out in distress. This bridge was a metaphor for our future and for Communism in practice. Individual life lost its value completely. They were a new people, the new liberators of Europe. They came to free us, too, from the values of our own lives. In this revolutionary practice they became exemplars for us in the name of their great idea.

I was a child and I understood as a child. I knew then nothing of Stalin and Hitler, of Communism and Fascism, of war, of concentration camps and gulags, of the holocaust, of the uninterrupted thread of blood that leads directly to us. I knew nothing of Christianity, or even of Hölderlin or the Knights of the Round Table, of the atom bomb, or the search for the Holy Grail. But then with my mother and father I sat on the lovely firm bank of civilized Europe, or perhaps more precisely, on the fertile bank of the childish word *Europe*. I didn't intend to leave with regard for the opposition of destiny, human stupidity, and greed, the devastation of nature and permanent stink of history that lives on human blood and human indifference to others. This still flows in that same river within me into which they fall again, but no longer step—and floating there are the victims and the fishing floats of our interests. The mere value of an individual human life is still there as is this life in which all of us so cheerfully and anxiously surmount inscrutable waves of despair and euphoria.

Without pathos and without cheap irony this is the foundation stone, the ideal changes with growing shadows of reality. Nothing more. When I speak about Europe today I think mainly of an image. I will confess to a childhood illusion: I somehow feel an unconscious inner flash of honor and the holy glory of knights on pilgrimage, yet I feel an aversion to all forms of crusade. I think of a net of communicating images. For me the West is this. Reality and its ceaseless research. The Mind. Chiefly this is what lies behind reality and the West, too. This stands behind it as dream and value. Let's consider this together—live together in our different parallel experience for the last half century that we have survived, face to face, as specific hostages of an abstract powerful enmity that produced fear. Let's speak about this in our own unique language, as individuals—this can't be appropriated or stolen by any power.

Perhaps our—Eastern and Western—common, stimulating theme is not so much lack of freedom, but mostly an experience with freedom, different and various antagonists placing layer upon layer of attempted implementations and usages of freedom to extremes. In fact, what about freedom today? It is precisely with its consequences and borders that we must now take the greatest care.

From the beginning the size of internal freedom has carried us against the totalitarian stream, in spite of it and over it, as a spontaneous and free culture. Power ruled the masses and the unreconciled individual retired deep within either the masses or deep within him or herself. And existed. Sometimes the individual survived. Today it's only of use as a gloomy European fairy tale from the folklore of the last century. This was another Europe, but it was in Europe because the routes of my country within the hermetic seal of a forcibly implemented phantasmagoria continue to sever Europe. It was the responsibility of Europe. Yet—who is Europe?

I began to read seriously and write a little less seriously in the famed 60's, in the era of a palpable relaxation and general rise in hope. Perhaps I began with a bit of provocative and quixotic gesturing. A young person should kick out of his or her path all the crap, stink, and necrophilia of collective assent—and all this should be done with his first declaration aimed at clearing his or her own space. Yet seriously, "perhaps everybody who is born serious shouldn't become Don Quixote—he has something better to do than be awkward with some imagined realities," as Nietzsche observed. Truly, this applied to the whole exterior unimaginable reality of our lives in the midst of an absurdly caged society that was no good at all for anybody. It applied to its change—that is to say, from within. Nothing less. Oh, children smeared with honey and with blood, they want everything and wish to lose nothing! Precisely and to the point: with my friends of mind and heart—one, Ivan Laučík, the other, Peter Repka—as a nineteen-year-old in 1963, I founded a group of poets, The Solitary Runners. Its first declared step was, of course, to produce a manifesto with the innocent title "Return of the Angels" (in the midst of vehement Communism). Of course, it was stopped by proactive censorship. The highest echelons had acted and a circus was begun. The prohibition of "Return of the Angels" lasted for twenty-five years.

Of course, this didn't apply only to literature—it applied to life and to the world in which we were sentenced to live. What was fundamental, wholly determining, stimulating, and overriding for us was the radical, unreconciled conflict between sequestration and openness. This was within ourselves, in our inner lives, in our thoughts, in our relationships, in our society, in our reading and writing, in our morals, and chiefly in our actions that crown the work called human life in this world. No assiduous literariness, no poems for their own sake, permitted by the state and exhibited passively to the consumer, no aesthetic objects closed within themselves, no masks of a prescriptive and emptily gesturing culture poisoned by ideology. No forbidden words and forbidden fruits, no diktats, no "apparent realities." It applied to a guaranteed and consciously responsible freedom for us, it applied to ceaseless co-creation, to a real free and imaginative movement from our own energy on our own paths. This movement can be undertaken solely by oneself—and solitary in the midst of a devastated and sequestrated world, in the midst of an unheeding mob, split into the silence of a slavish lethargy and passivity that secretes an unbreathable herd-like smog into the midst of an illegally manipulated people, sentenced by power to a lie, to a half-truth, to hypocrisy, to dissimulation, collaboration, and wholesale immobility. It applied to us—á la Camus—in the glory of living freely and the virtue of freedom created by our own energy. We talked about ethics, about the ethics of poetry, and we thought continually about the ethics of openness. We thought of human spontaneity and intimacy. We thought of the free space in human heads, about these parallel words. We thought about cultivating perception and sensibility. We invoked strong experiences, sincerity, authenticity, also irony, an open derangement. We talked absolutely down-to-earth that we come from the pure countries of our childhood—and not from a filthy history that they liked to call revolutionary practice. Above all we arrived to—addressing again the fundamental questions touching identity and meaning, and their conditions—the space for the individual, the individuality, and solidarity of the individual as opposed to the perverse, forced self-identification of the masses with power. We sought clear meanings and we didn't wish to be tempted by words to which we weren't even attached. We said that Communism and war were equally absurd. We said that we were committed to the "Return of the Angels" into human hearts and heads. In the age of ideological interpretation, the role of these words—to be committed and to be angels—were absolutely incompatible in their connotations. And they acted as a blasting-charge hidden in the paper corridors and the well-masked chasms and fossils of spiritual life. We said we wished to live and incarnate in our poems in a way that had a chance to have a creative impact on our mental life. This was in order that the poem should pass the test of a lived experience outside its own language. It would be open and function in unique intimate communication. We said that the poem is a message of meaning and we quoted Ginsberg to that effect. At the very end of the text there appeared, with a virtual tender smile as a message, "let not the sun go down upon your wrath," which is a clear quotation from the letters of the Apostle Paul. Humph!

"Solitaries of all countries unite!" Peter Repka cheerfully parodied the sacred ritual chant of Communism, which bared its teeth in all corners of a flattened world. This phrase of theirs had only one side. Its own mental movement was blocked to all intents and purposes. This was in spite of the fact that at the time we expressed our fundamental feeling for life, the feeling of the solitary runner. On the horizon of sequestration to orthodox immobility its own movement is experienced through openness. Running itself is a lack of fixedness, indefiniteness, a continuity of meaning, and the rediscovery of place. It is a living open space of creativity simply continuing and stripping meanings—intense life in the present, in direct action. Simply: it is the ideal place for the poem.

And solitude? It is a separation and exclusion from the queue. A rejection. It is choice and expulsion. Let's say it is a person himself or herself, the extreme stage of a person within his or her confronted and self-reflecting nakedness and sensibility. It is an intimately radical state of a person searching within the concealment of his current context. It is like the open poem. It is like solitary running—the supreme act of the present in the present, an always moving open form that endures until it runs on. It is like openness to communication that endures while direction and connection endure. This radical style of writing and mental existence has always remained with us. Openness and sequestration meet herein a conflict of creating alternatives of one's experience in a moveable and unpredictable talking space of individual utterance.

The poem, in fact, is an unpredictable nomad in the midst of a firmly settled world. It is an ancient mixing of the correct borders of things and the unceasing mixing of languages and styles of poems, all in a continual mutual influence; and rejection uncovers for me behind the word Europe, an exciting, varied, always blossoming nomadic tradition of poetry and its living *fata morganas* that time immemorial impinge forcefully upon a complacent reality and our blunted sensibilities.

It was precisely in this tradition that we began to write in the midst of a sequestrated reality, patiently, our vision eagerly directed, full of our own inspiration. We moved at our own pace in this network of changing, living, breathing context. What we cling to is an openness to contact, mutual reading of one another, empathy, which on the nomad's path always finds a fresh print.

I take risks, though I don't like laboratory experiments. I prefer to try things at the sharp end. In this way you know what it can withstand, what is valid, what works within its reality in the midst of a wider reality beyond words.

Writing for me has always had an analogy with running. It is action. It leaves behind itself a design, a possibility, an unclosed solitary pact—not product. It leaves, literally behind one's heels. From the first step, which is infirm, unstable, in fact continuously perishing only able to project itself, it grows into a mobile network of meanings.

Simply, a step perishes, the action lasts. You can continue to try.

It is open. What lasts without a firm place is writing. Within it every fixed point perishes. Within it we gain an unusual plasmatic form of movement that creates space by itself, continuing the world in which it exists. It has no objective. In fact, it is this "has no." Thus it could also be with this pure "is."

There is still fire behind a runner's heels. And writing. This is why he continually hurries ahead into the unknown. To put out the fire or burn? In any event the ground here is hot. The only fixed point of meaning is the place where the reader stops. Such running and such reading are the most profoundly active solitude and revelation. What we are directed toward is a ceaseless renewal of the beginning. I perceive it in this way—in the midst of a self-renewing instability. I would prefer another, calmer explanation. But from what should I strike off?

Of course there is an obligatory written text, though it's character I have not precisely indicated. Before us is something like a pure act. Or it is a pact of instability, renewing itself in a directly stable way. "I write to you from a future void / wedged already into this moment and from an uncertain / place on the maps" wrote Ivan Laučík, traveling with concentration by pen over the map he is creating in just such a manner. "Three thousand years more," adds Peter Repka, "and the birds will stop fearing us." Writing is a ceaseless stepping of an uncertain existence from itself. It is a Slovak tradition. Writing is perhaps something like the persistent forgetfulness in the shyness of birds, which at first sight has no connection at all with our uncertainty or even our adherence to the air. A proximity is offered. The possibility here is the naked sign.

Without any mysticism or illusion: something that does not exist writes within you to somebody within you who is not yet here. It is as if he or she originates involuntarily word by word.

From time immemorial this has been our Slovak existential motif: we write to demonstrate that we actually exist. But for me there's an inevitable and slight tinge of an eternally ironic anarchy that demolishes in advance what is definitive and gives as form, as a mission, or destiny. We create ourselves. There's something in this that frees me. It allows me to laugh at any social fetishism and all the substitute roles of writing. Simply said: poems are written to be tried out, to become their own reality—and we, too, together.

My poetics are defined by process "the open poem!" An exploding, continuing, and achieved conflict of sequestration and openness. It is a current meaning-creating conflict directed towards resolution. A hermetically sequestered fullness and a hermetically sequestered emptiness has harmed my life and my writing. It is a lie of the pure, sequestered, institutionalized form. It is the dark power of sequestration and control by the System. It is the empty power of form, a mere institutional lie.

"Poverty protected me from believing that everything under the sun and in history is good. The sun taught me that history is not everything," said Albert Camus. This is not just a proud resistance of poverty and light-leading writing. An unimpeded knowledge of possibility shines at us from the wealth of every pure page. In this connection I don't dare to talk about truth. But here is sensibility, rebellion, refusal, and acceptance, depth, joy, and anxiety, a moment of identification, perhaps ecstasy, that allows us to live in reality and profoundly—to extend our depths, create our own word without considering history, or in spite of history.

Long ago (four years before the occupation by the fraternal armies of the Warsaw Pact that came to definitively free us from ourselves), one Spring day in 1964, eager for life, sequestered in the Phantasmagoric empire in the midst of Central Europe, I sat on the banks of the Danube in Bratislava with Allen Ginsberg, whose presence among us was something almost unreal. He had landed like a living Martian, like a vision. With excitement we pointed at the clear, empty air of a seemingly impenetrable Iron Curtain on the river bank in front of us. Our daily border that he had passed through miraculously was so near that we could almost press our noses against its unbreakable glass. Only the sky flowed freely and indifferently on all sides. Allen sadly shook his head: he sensed the absurdity, he sensed the border of borders that divided the world and which on our side was a prison. How was it from the outside, from the other side? Was it a projecting screen for illusions, for contempt, for enmity, for indifference, for hope, or for their own fears and anxiety?

We debated the borders of the world, smoked grass, and drank wine while sitting under a tree by a forgotten grave at the end of an old cemetery. The end of Allen's poem "At the Grave of Apollinaire" circled importunately in my head: "I am buried here sitting under the tree of my own grave." It was so pertinent that I had to say it out loud. Allen (who was thinking of Paris) smiled at these words and nodded in understanding. "Yes, I feel the same again just now—and it's a happy feeling." We laughed; and suddenly I understood. At that moment it was unambiguously my own excited feeling. At the same time I was above it—I had within me a majestic-deranged image of strange images completely under control. The broadcast was functioning. This time it worked along an ancient route: without writing and without paper. The border silently opened in my head.

This was a living moment of crossing the border. Our identities are connected daily to the world of the past that has already been completed. It's history as well: the graves repeat. And what is repeated are graves. We, here in another new world, continue along in our lives, directed toward hopes of uncertainty and toward our own ideas. We continue along with traumas and scars as well, with graves and the hovering feeling that history now stands firmly again on the side of the living. The graves are asleep and within them the unrest of their experience. It is like after the war. Our common heritage is a future Europe as fact and idea, as good will— a living broadcast. Growth has precedence. This the experience of graves will not be able to disintegrate.

Our own history, even the hysteria of history, has not yet been permitted to kill our future—as used to be the case in a kind of eternally repeated vendetta. Evil is specific, and the struggle with a living evil requires tough action. It mustn't be covered by the shadows of a substituted victim, our expedient fanaticism, and puritanical ideological darkness.

Let the dead bury their dead and the living both of them. Thus the alchemy of the present bubbles. What is alive today is for the benefit of the living and let it live with us. Let the rest fruitfully decay in gold-bearing flashes of dreams, putrefaction, and mercy—not abandoning the world of human memory. The mysterious interior judge in us always raises a finger and points at us: are you a mere close "I" or are you another—an opened responsive "you" responsible for both?

With regard to poets, I'm a mild optimist: they are often the destroyers of stereotypes, petrified canons, and gravestones; but also living respecters of graves. They live from the air of the future that now fills our days to the brim. Our tradition leaves us to drink in peace, to smoke, and debate by the graves of a completely living avant-garde and post-avant-garde poets. This Ginsberg feeling endures within us. Something substantial speaks in this—this happy feeling, that voluntary living chain that passes over borders and graves and ourselves, holding us alive, face to face with a future that desires to swallow us and fulfill us. We still call this culture.

Our strength is in consciousness, a full present in the presence of culture. Yes, a still enchanting culture calls somewhere on the horizon, but the lure of "the unbearable lightness of being" smiles more greedily at us, close from all sides. After long decades of unending demoralization, life as human virtue and creative thought is easily lost. And what about the demoralization of the poor? What about the burning necessity of the frustrated desire of many Europeans for a single, unified *Shopping-Center Europe* filled with goods affordable to everybody? It is important not to exchange mechanical-involuntary dogmas for the old silence. Of course even the highest, globally achievable consumer standard doesn't flow into paradise without history. We know this just as well in the East as in the West: that to sell oneself for things may be a new dominion, but it is certainly an old serfdom. It acts today as programmed dreaming, as the joyful, definitely nearly simple victory of an ideology of hedonism for the masses—and in this there is a devil. Perhaps a new Phantasmagoria is singing that the whole of victory lies outside before us. Culture brings an open appeal of value—style decides. It contains within itself the criteria of value—"making a poem is the measure (Dicten ist messen)," held Heidegger and placed emphasis on the words "making a poem." The solution is

within—it intensely indicates culture, eye to eye with its extended civilization. Which elegantly builds sophisticated traps for itself.
Now the whole of Europe is under our feet—not as a territory—as a fundamental word that is a fundamental experience, and its value, and growth.

Today I wouldn't describe Europe as a continent, more as a form-creating context. It is an open context in the midst of other contexts. It is writing itself. It is as open as the sea and it continues to open itself, bridgeable, overlayered with contexts, dissolving the firm borders of stereotypes and writing. It opens other floating borders and coordinates of perception. This breathing, this ceaseless change, uncovering and concealing, the ceaseless flowing of information and influences, the skirmishes of imagination and influxes of thought, this wondering listening, this new attention to others, and the free standpoint for one's original style, this ceaseless mutual reading of one another in my eyes is an open chance for us and for everybody.

Energy concentrates. The thunder and lightning in the arsenals are under control. Xenophobia is fading, nationalism is deaf and blind. Skepticism scowls severely. Irony keeps an elastic watch. An eagerness is growing. The seeds of a sensibility as yet unknown are germinating, different new crops are growing in different gardens. In the midst of this the golden worm of new questions, while old doubts continue to gnaw away. Because writing—in the name of its meaning—is a ceaseless doubt about writing. Doubt itself is an old European virtue.

Here is a living sketch of the interior borders of these processes: it creates a sharp "no," declared by the individual who rebels, face to face, against any closed System that minimizes and destroys the space of an individual's sensibility so that he can't react with human dignity and communicate in a particular culture. It doesn't matter whether it's the unlimited power of money, the consumer, the media, dumbed-down entertainment, or the sheer, uncontrolled power of anything. Its border exists in me too. This open and threatened crossroads of conflict, this moveable border of values is actually myself.

It is I. The responsibility for the values of my life are the single thing that I have at this moment, whatever else counts as wealth. I think that today this is very European—and it is right that I don't want this to be taken away any more. I know: children smeared with honey and with blood want everything and wish to lose nothing. Does Europe write? I know the great temptation of a new beginning and a clean page. On this all revolutions wish to write. Only take care: from the necessity of purity the temptation of purity easily comes and from this often the temptation of the torch. Don't put the chance for change to the flames—it is right here with us—in the midst of clear thought it dances in its first letters. Perhaps it is better not to give up a childlike face and accept maturity. The revolution has been sketched. Now Europe is a charm for children.

The nomadic tribe of poets and solitary runners—minorities still searching for a mysterious common language of individual speech—have, from time immemorial, restlessly and impatiently crossed our great homeland. We write essence at home in uncertainty, in an uncertain place. We are writing ourselves. We are writing Europe. On a clean page? Or on a new palimpsest?

— *Translated by James Sutherland Smith*

Richard Swartz

I am bored despite the fact that until the end of our lives light is something we can never take for granted as we keep pondering the nature of Justice and Truth and the possibility that we might have been happier with some kind of light that was different from that closest at hand.

Richard Swartz

Sweden

Born in Stockholm in 1945, Richard Swartz studied
history and Slavic languages and literature at the
University of Stockholm and wrote his doctoral thesis as
an exchange student in Prague between 1970 and 1972.
Since 1976 he has been East European correspondent
for *Svenska Dagbladet*. He lives in Stockholm, Vienna,
and Sovinjak (Istria) and writes for several international
newspapers, including *Frankfurter Allgemeine Zeitung*.
With his reports and analyses, he rapidly became an
important voice in Eastern Europe and was declared
persona non grata by various communist states. Swartz
has received various journalistic awards for his work. In
December 1996, *Room Service* was chosen by the
Darmstadt Academy for Language and Literature as book
of the month.

Further Reading:
Room Service: Reports from Eastern Europe. Translated
by Linda Haverty Rugg. New Press, 1998.
A House in Istria. Translated by Anna Paterson. New
Directions Publishing, 2002.

The Light Falls on Me

*Och ändå är just ljus något vi ideligen tvekar om, ibland
in i det sista, om vilket som är det rätta eller sanna, och
om vi ändå inte hade blivit lyckligare med något annat
än det ljus som råkade stå just oss till buds.*

Europe's light is distinct from light elsewhere in the world. The light in Africa and Asia is positively fiery in comparison, and in the Americas too, the light is different and more intense, as I myself have observed in North America, where a burning light can set the whole sky aflame, that American sky, which people there take so much more seriously than we do our European sky nowadays — or at least, take more seriously than what might be on the ground below it.

Rather like the effect of our cooking fires, light with that burning quality changes the world it falls on, from first thing in the morning when it starts raising the temperature of landscapes to boiling point, until everything simmers and all firm outlines begin to vanish, initially becoming indistinct and soon afterwards starting to dissolve, so that by midday the flames of this not-European light have already cooked all it has fallen on.

Those who are used to such light protect themselves as best they can. They keep still, well out of its way and dress in sheets of fabric rather than clothes. Newcomers soon succumb, first falling ill and later perhaps going mad.

In Europe light of such fieriness is rare. Once only did I experience such light for more than a week, although "experience" is not actually the right word to describe what happened that summer in Istria. The light almost drove me crazy. Comatose, I was lying on top of my bed behind closed shutters, not so much to keep out the light but to exclude the burning sky, which made staying awake as impossible as sleeping. Outside, the powerful light set about bleaching the world in a grand laundering session using light instead of water. The world crumbled, dissolved by a light that made my head ache. I had visions rather like dreams at night, which replaced what had once been the real world. Still, I could not escape because I was too exhausted.

Then the rain came, a cloudburst that brought back the world. While all that water was pouring down from above, everything was returning to its old shape and I felt better almost at once. It meant that I returned to Europe, although it might be more true to say that Europe returned to me.

Away from Europe you usually know where the light is coming from, which means that you can avoid looking at just that area of the sky. A not-European sky allows itself to be observed only through half-closed, narrowed eyes. The mercy that there could be worth pleading for, is would be less — not more — light. Outside Europe it is precisely this light that dominates everything. Landscapes and people, mountains, trees and houses all seem to be where they are simply to serve as the light's pretext for showing off and setting fire to the world at will. When you are in these parts of the world the sky above you is nothing but the light's own estate, as if it were a great prince demanding that everyone and everything submit to him. In the sky the light sprawls as it pleases, without being confined by any walls.

Here, where we live, it can be quite difficult to find the source of the light. Our European light often reaches us in roundabout ways. At times we come across it just by chance. Then it reaches us as a reflection or an afterglow, maybe falling on the wall of a house or in the narrow band across a floor. Without this indirect light there probably would be no Europe as we know it.

For perfectly natural reasons a light such as this seems to lack warmth, evoking ideas and feelings in our minds rather than warming our bodies. It easily lets us free, though. At times it seems to illuminate the sky above Europe from a point somewhere below the horizon, leaving the impression that it is there only on loan for a while, a little like the way European cities in the past used to have—actually, still did during my childhood—brightly colored posters, stuck up on walls and wooden fences, advertising something that would soon be over and done with again. Light of this kind does not last. It soon fades and dies away, just as it usually did not take long for the posters to become ragged and for new ones to be pasted on top.

Our European light is not very strong. In no way does it measure up to the sheer power of light in Africa or Asia or South America, and it hardly ever burns. The European light, weak and hesitant, somehow seems to look cautiously over its shoulder, exploring its surroundings. This light, which only in southern Europe occasionally behaves as if it were capable of filling the entire sky and dissolving the world, never really succeeds and is anyway far more closely linked to the earth than to the sky. This is a decisive difference. One consequence is that this light illuminates the foreground more than the background.

Painters are of course much more dependent on light than writers. In European visual art is it is always possible to find something in the foreground that has attracted the artist's attention, while the background is often left shrouded in shadows, painted in dark, dull colors, or reduced to a few brushstrokes. European museums are packed with just such foreground-pictures, which—had it not been for their very varying motifs—might have truly claimed to be nothing except images of our European light.

Outside Europe the opposite is the case. Who would there take an interest in the foreground? How could it even be possible? The light is shining over the background; it is not the front of the stage alone that is illuminated, but the backdrop. Outside Europe the source of the light is, of course, that great blowtorch right above in the sky and so the light wipes out the foreground and exposes the background, more often than not making people who live in places other than Europe turn inwards rather than focus on the world outside.

Here in Europe, the light makes us see what is under our noses. Only the foreground is invested with meaning. What is close by, that is to say, what is comfortable and familiar (or things that should be so) become more important than the greater context in which we find no such familiarity or comfort. We have a tight world nearby, easy to investigate with the senses. It is this very closeness that allows us to see how even these familiar things become brittle, how every day new cracks appear where none should be. This superficial fracturing gets to interest us more than what is held in place below the surface coating and keeps it intact despite its narrow, almost invisible, cracks.

Meanwhile the most appalling events take place in our European background. Back there the ashes are stirred yet again, new graves are dug, but our light is too feeble to reach all these murky goings-on. It fails to shine on things we don't want to know about and which are on their way into obscurity or already hidden in darkness.

Here in Europe there is simply too little light. To prove to myself that I am right about this, I need only open my kitchen window: on a winter's day, such as today, the light is etching fragile, yet severe, patterns, an effect aided by the snow in the yard, patches of white that from the fourth floor look like pieces of a torn sheet. The frail light picks out reflections and shadows in just a few shades, or so it seems at first, but closer inspection reveals an endlessly shifting range of many of the main colors that belong to European foregrounds—black, brown, gray and off-white.

Though there is nothing special to be discovered, I can easily sit for hours at my kitchen window and look out over this yard.

Particularly during the winter I find myself longing for a kind of light and warmth that is different from what is on offer in Europe. But at these times it is normally enough to pull out from my shelves a South American novel and start leafing through it; white-hot light flows from the core story of these books, blinding me and wiping out what is presumably argued on the pages—light which turns most things into background features. Under such intense illumination, the family becomes more important than its individual members, instinct more important than rational thought, fate more important than freedom, tradition more important than psychology, blood more important than snow and the sun, always at the same place in the sky, determines the shape and perspective of everything and all colors fuse, disappearing into this white, glowing, all-consuming furnace.

But all this is alien to me. I hardly find it even interesting. Worse still, I find it boring (this, I imagine, is the most European of my responses). I am bored despite the fact that until the end of our lives light is something we can never take for granted. And still light is constantly preoccupying us, as we are never sure if we got the best or enough of it, something which makes us wonder if we would not have been happier with some other kind of light different from that at hand.

"Mehr Licht" — "More light" — is, regardless of rumors to the contrary, what Goethe did not say on his deathbed. Besides, he died sitting in an armchair. Someone must have figured that all truly famous people have a phrase ready when the moment comes. But, in this case at least, it is an invention. Even so, this desire for more light has taken on a life of its own, surviving him who never asked for it in the first place.

What might be the idea behind this fable? Are we to imagine that Goethe asked for more light in order to disperse the darkness gathering around him? Or that the old poet, who at that point in time was already looking into another world, had become full of wonder at how much more light there was compared with the world he was about to leave?

Or is it that Goethe is asking not so much for light, but for what cannot easily be had in isolation from it? The heat from the flame in the hope that it will keep the chill of death at bay?

As for me, I think he was cold. Goethe had seen enough light; his entire life's work had been created in just that European light, which is caught in all he wrote to such a degree that it is impossible to get away from it.

The same European light, weak and pale as it might be, is falling over my writing too.

— *Translated by Anna Paterson*

Nikos Themelis

If insistence upon the multicultural identity of
Europe, and hence the need to safeguard national
cultural identity in every society, remain priorities,
then it will also remain difficult to identify European
elements in a national literature.

Nikos Themelis

Greece

Born in Athens in 1947, Nikos Themelis studied law in Thessaloniki and in Cologne, where he received his PhD. He worked as a lawyer for the Greek Ministry of Economy and then as an advisor to the European Union in Brussels. Subsequently, he joined a team of advisors to the Greek prime minister, whom he continues to advise today. The novel *The Subversion*, which tells the story of the author's grandfather, has been a Greek bestseller for the past three years. In 2001 Themelis was awarded the Greek State Prize for his second novel *The Search*, published in 2000. With *Glimmer of Light*, published in 2003, the author has completed his historical trilogy.

Looking for a Widened Self-Awareness

*Αν διατηρηθεί σε προτεραιότητα η εμμονή στην
πολυπολιτισμική ταυτότητα της Ευρώπης και κατ' επέκταση
η ανάγκη της κατοχύρωσης της εθνικής πολιτισμικής
ταυτότητας κάθε κοινωνίας, τότε θα εξακολουθήσει να 'ναι
δύσκολη η ανίχνευση του ευρωπαϊκού στοιχείου στην
εθνική λογοτεχνία. Ακόμη πιο δύσκολη η παραδοχή της σε
οποιεσδήποτε προσπάθειες αυτογνωσίας.*

The Symposium *Europa schreibt. Was ist das Europäische an den Literaturen Europas?* (Writing Europe: What is European about the Literatures of Europe?) comes at a critical moment for the future of Europe. Our times are seen by some as a challenge, by others as a matter of deep disquiet.

I propose to approach our theme from a distinctive viewpoint, from that of the political and constitutional expression of "Europe." The European Union is now at the crossroads of enlargement, with ten to thirteen prospective new members, most of which belonged to the Eastern bloc until some ten years ago. At the same time a great debate has opened, not only among economists and politicians, but also within society at large. Over the next two years important issues will be settled on the evolution and transformation of the European Union. Key questions include "more or less European unification?" and "more or less of a 'social' Europe?" Opinions on all issues diverge.

Bewilderment pervades our societies with regard to the phenomenon of "globalization" and its ramifications. This bewilderment breeds both avid support and entrenched antagonism. Social problems, such as unemployment, social integration, and exclusion—both aspects of our multicultural societies—the relationship between growth and the environment, the cultural models engendered by the electronic media industry, the content and aims of education, issues of freedom and equality, solidarity and social justice, even issues of democracy, all require urgent, and often novel, solutions.

For some people—and this is, *itself*, the worst problem—*no* solutions are called for. Market ideology constantly aims, and often manages, to escape the sphere of economic activity where it belongs, permeating into the realms of society, politics, and culture. Whenever this takes place, those realms are diminished, their nature distorted.

I have the feeling that those values and principles that formed the ideological backbone and the cultural foundations of postwar Europe, and which were distilled in European thought over the course of centuries, are becoming marginalized. I am convinced that citizens are increasingly being presented with oversimplified dilemmas while their problems are becoming increasingly complex. I feel that our society is progressively being subjected to processes leading to the depreciation of issues and ideas that used to occupy an important place in our collective conscience. And even if nobody dares to challenge these values and principles formally, in practice they cease to be priorities in the value system of a large part of society.

Alongside these great issues I would also place those of individual and collective self-knowledge that emerge frequently and forcefully. To be more precise, the need to bring to the fore common cultural values and principles as determining elements of our behavior and way of life. If we sincerely felt this need and succeeded in placing it again at the center of public discussion, if we succeeded in opening up the discussion to society at large, above and beyond the familiar boundaries of the so-called world of intellectuals, then it would be easier for us to find answers to the major issues that trouble European societies. We may also be able to achieve wider mobilization, a wider consensus on decisions, which could lead to a better and more tolerable *modus vivendi* and *modus operandi* in our societies. Confronted with this reality, literature certainly does not have the first say. Nevertheless, as part of the intellectual production of culture, what position does literature take?

I would like to make my position clear from the outset in order to avoid misunderstanding. I do not believe that cultural creativity, in our case literature, should follow rules in order to serve goals pertaining to extraneous spheres, such as the political, the social, or the economic. Nevertheless, by drawing stimuli and material from within its own context, by weaving this material into an original creation, e.g., into the fictional core shaped by the author, literature very often, or even inevitably, provides answers, transmits messages, adopts or dismisses opinions, and thus exerts an influence on the reader. This is how I believe that the value load of an ideology, in this case that of European thought, may find its way into literature, as an integral part of the writing process, assisting or influencing the process of self-knowledge and self-consciousness and not as a goal in itself.

With your permission, I would like to cite my own work as an example. Let me start by giving some necessary historical context: during the period of rule of the Ottoman Empire, Hellenism, as a broad notion, underwent an important process of development, not only within that Empire, but also in major Russian centers and in all the territories later controlled by the Austro-Hungarian Empire. Greeks, citizens of the one or the other empire, engaged in increasingly intense economic activities, mainly in commerce, shipping, and banking. In the Balkans, Greek emerged as the dominant language of commerce and financial affairs. Small communities were thus born, notably characterized by prosperity, a cosmopolitan spirit, and high levels of education. These groups constituted the first web of the Greek bourgeoisie, composed thus of small communities a long distance from the present-day frontiers of Greece. To mention only the most important communities: Trieste, Vienna, Belgrade, Braşov, Bucharest, all the major cities of the Danubian principalities, Odessa, the cities of the Black Sea coast, Constantinople, Smyrna, and Alexandria.

This microcosm, all the time a part of Hellenism, was the first to adopt the ideas of the Enlightenment, of freedom and equality, to embrace modernity, and to become adaptable, self-confident, creative; it also was the conscious promoter of the goals of the 1821 Greek revolution against Ottoman rule. Since then an enduring conflict has unfolded in the territories that were later to compose the Greek nation-state. This was a conflict between, on the one hand, a western European ideology that had at its heart the principles of the Enlightenment and, on the other, an ideology emanating from the Greek Orthodox Church, which, along the way, had incorporated other national, popular, and folk elements. Put simply, this conflict could be described as a conflict of East versus West. Apart from a narrow circle of historians, little light has been shed on this aspect of the history of Hellenism. In the same way, Greek literature, as far as I know, has not felt the need to draw on the material it provides.

My two novels unfold as two parallel stories taking place in the late-nineteenth and early twentieth centuries. Two different views have been advanced regarding the genre of these novels. According to the first view, they are primarily historical novels, and only secondarily *Bildungsromane*. The other view sees them the other way around. Europe is present in both novels. I will refer only to the first, which has been translated into German as *Jenseits von Epirus* (Beyond Epirus), as well as into Turkish and Italian.

European ideology and reality enter this novel via two routes. The first concerns my effort to bring to life the historical context of the period as accurately as I could and to shed light on particular aspects of it. Such aspects are the fragmentary and belated formation and rise of the bourgeoisie and the mobility of ideas in society and in economic life that characterized this era in southeastern Europe. At the same time I aimed to present the difficulties faced by the ideas of the Enlightenment and of Humanism in their confrontation on two fronts, on the one with the old world, and on the other with the nation state and nationalism in general, an ideology increasingly prevalent in the territories under Ottoman rule during that period.

The second route is the choice to create a character who would be a "carrier" of these ideas; a positive *persona* who pursues, and in the end realizes, his lifelong aspirations. Moreover, someone who, through the narratives of those describing his life, matures into a character not only appreciated as successful, but who is also elevated to the status of a mythical prototype in the society in which he lives. This is the story of an adolescent, the son of a successful bourgeois merchant, who after his father's disappearance and his family's subsequent financial ruin attempts to rebuild his life by pursuing his fortune in the East, in Smyrna, the major commercial center of Anatolia.

The social context of *Jenseits von Epirus* is a world that has experienced neither the Renaissance nor the Enlightenment, a world cut off from the developments it now seeks to catch up with after decades, if not centuries, of delay. A world dominated by false beliefs, superstition, by the absolute hegemony over the Christian population of the Eastern Orthodox Church, which approached the issues of the day in a simplistic way on the behalf of people of low or non-existent education. Under the Eastern despotic regime the sense of equality, of the rule of law, and of freedom are all absent, with all the negative consequences and distortions this absence produces. At the same time, however, and up to the early years of the twentieth century, there is concurrently a wider social consensus for peaceful coexistence within the framework of a multicultural society.

This complex reality comes gradually into contact with the ideas of the Enlightenment and with ideas coming from the West in general, such as the free development of the personality, individual initiative, entrepreneurship, and a positive attitude towards the modern era and the challenges it brings, as for example the "invasion" of the steam engine in Anatolia. Nikoles, the central character, tries to stand on his own two feet, to provide answers to life's dilemmas great and small, to acquire more knowledge, to adopt innovations, to become self-sufficient, and to succeed as an independent entrepreneur, attaining, as his father had before him, the status of an *efendi*, best translated as a benevolent boss with an important position in society.

Throughout the course of his life, up to the moment of his sudden death, Nikoles reasons, makes decisions, and acts according to the ideas instilled in him by his father, ideas that, in general, we would characterize as those of the Enlightenment.

To give a few examples: Nikoles always remembers his father's most important piece of advice—to adopt a critical stance in any situation. The quest for truth and of its interpretations is achieved through adoption of a critical point of view in which rationality, *Vernuft*, is the main tool.

During the course of his life he tries incessantly to define and adopt an ethical stance that is distinct from the theocratic ethics of both Muslim and Christian dogma. He aspires to express a lay morality, permeated by ideas that have come to him from the West, albeit in a vague and uncertain form, without reference to any Christian dogma.

Knowledge, scientific proof, and the pursuit of a wider education provide him with a driving force. His perspective is most clearly defined in his animated dialogue with the teacher, in which they discuss the issue that is most central to the Hellenism of the period: the *Megali Idea*, the Great Idea. At the time, the *Megali Idea* was the dominant irredentist dogma, aimed at the realization of Greek nationhood. It was supported to different degrees by the overwhelming majority of those inhabiting the territories of the free Greek state. In simple terms, *Megali Idea* aimed at the expansion of that state to embrace the entire Byzantine Empire! When his friend, the teacher, passionately defends this idea, Nikoles responds by putting forward his own *Megali Idea*: Education.

"Not only reading, writing, and learning, but also education that opens minds and enlightens them. The kind of education we find if we look at what Koraes, and those who thought like him, talked about. The education which can unite people, whether they live here or at the other end of the Aegean, and even further away, in the Balkans, or the West. The kind of education that can, little by little, provide everyone with the freedom he seeks, that can teach him tolerance towards those who believe in another god and respect for that which is different. The kind of education that is able to create a great new society that will embrace us and empower us, a society where our progress will not depend on the arbitrary whims or the decisions of the few."

I could refer to other examples in which European elements, not only ideology, are woven into the fabric of the novel. For instance, the cosmopolitan and multicultural character of late nineteenth-century Smyrna, where the European West met the East in a magical way. In Smyrna all faiths and nationalities coexist in an environment of a previously unthinkable respect and tolerance of diversity. However, we should be clear that fiction remains fiction. It is the adventure of a life, a web of human relationships, of dependence and subordination, but also of freedom, love and friendship, of the dilemmas, decisions, and confrontations of the central character with people and situations.

As we now know, that attempt to infuse European thought into the societies that constituted the Ottoman Empire had only limited success. It fared slightly better in the Greek territories. Various expressions of nationalism, religious dogmatism, deeply-rooted traditions and world-views, coupled with a general distrust of the intentions of Western European diplomacy stretching over long decades, prevented these ideas from prevailing and becoming an integral part of the local identity. Even in the Greece of today, where public opinion polls indicate that an even greater majority of the population favors the country's European orientation than do the populations of other member states of the EU, remnants of the opposing world view are still evident in broad sections of society. The most important objective for contemporary Greek society is the fulfillment of its ongoing project to modernize and rationalize itself.

Over the past decade the younger generation of writers has increasingly provided examples of work extending the boundaries of creative freedom. Their work is in dialogue with the contemporary social milieu, where frontiers with the rest of Europe fell long ago. This dialogue takes many forms. As a rule it is silent, latent, and undeclared; for example, we find common themes, dealing with current social conditions, such as the solitude and isolation of life in big cities. Also on the increase is the shared recourse to common literary genres, such as the crime novel, or the very personal use of everyday modes of expression. This dialogue is highlighted when, for instance, literary texts deal with the communication problems experienced by people from different traditions.

Nevertheless, the multiple elements of European identity are fused in Greek literature, becoming integrated to the extent that they are adopted and perceived by the wider public consciousness as authentically national. In the prevailing climate of globalization and its inherent dangers, culture is perceived as the final bastion. If insistence upon the multicultural identity of Europe, and hence the need to safeguard national cultural identity in every society, remain priorities, then it will also remain difficult to identify European elements in a national literature. It will be even more difficult to acknowledge its contribution to any attempt at self-awareness.

— *Translated by Dr. Victoria Solomonidis*

Emil Tode

Apparently it is hoped that the development of a European identity will impede the progress of an aggressive nationalism. I fear the opposite might occur. It would be best if Europe stopped being so self-analytical.

Emil Tode
Estonia

Born in Tallinn in 1962, Emil Tode studied biology and
taught at a village school. He is a translator of
contemporary literature into Estonian. He completed
Borderland, his first volume of prose, during a stay in
Paris in 1993–94. Critics praised the work, and the
author has since been awarded several prizes, including
the Estonian National Prize for Prose.

Further Reading:
Border State. Translated by Madli Puhvel. Northwestern
University Press, 2000.

Europe, a Blot of Ink

*Loodetakse nähtavasti, et euroopa identiteedi
arendamine võtab agressiivsel natsionalismil tuule
tiibadest. Mina aga kardan hoopis vastupidist.*

Ten years ago, in the late autumn of 1992, I spent a month on a
farm in the south of France, in the *Département* of the Ardèche. As
it turned out it was an important time for me. For the first time in
my life I came in contact with those beings commonly called Europeans and had the opportunity of meeting them on their home
ground. Up to that point I only knew of them from legends and
fleeting encounters on my travels abroad. But to be able to stay
with real people in their own house is a different story. It gave me
the opportunity of detailed anthropological studies.

My hosts — let's call them Françoise and Gérard — were a delight-
ful elderly couple. They were lawyers and had retired to a farm
belonging to the wife. There was a large house, and they took in
visitors as paying guests. Officially they farmed, which meant that
a neighbor planted a small field in springtime and in the autumn he
harvested the crops. This way they avoided paying taxes and managed to earn just enough to live on. I was working for them as an
unpaid laborer, and they gave me free board and lodging in return.
This enabled me to stay in France and learn some French, which
up to that point had only been a book language for me. I chopped
wood and did general farm work. At mealtimes I joined my hosts at
the long table in the large, cold kitchen and partook of their rata-
touille, quiche, and roast lamb. Employing me on the farm seemed
to be more an act of charity for them than a worthwhile invest-
ment. Perhaps it was also an interesting way of passing the time;

for like me, they had the opportunity of conducting their anthropological studies, with a native of the former Soviet Union as their subject. The tourist season was over and there was a profound stillness everywhere. The most exciting, and in actual fact only, event during the course of the day was the arrival of the mail van, a small, yellow Renault that approached the farm on a dirt road leading through a small stand of oaks. Apart from that, the only other person that came along the road was a tiny, wizened old man with luminous eyes who passed through the woods with his herd of goats. He lived in a small cottage in the valley below, and each morning at precisely the same time smoke issued from the chimney on the roof. As Françoise explained to me, these people had refused kindly but firmly to allow progress into their lives. After a lot of urging they had agreed to have electricity brought to their house, but they never used it apart from operating one small light bulb with it. They cooked their meals over an open fire and the man sawed and chopped the wood for the fireplace himself. Sometimes you could hear the saw going down below. They made small, hard cheeses from the milk of the goats, which my hostess occasionally brought from them, though she was not very enthusiastic about it. Frequently the old woman, even smaller and more wizened than her husband, accompanied the goats. Both seemed to have formed a symbiosis with the animals. The most stunning thing for me was the luminous smiles on the creased, weatherbeaten faces of these old people. I always felt that they were sincerely delighted, overjoyed even, to see and greet me, a complete stranger, in their parts. In Europe, and—as the European spirit spreads further afield—also in our part of the world, particularly in the cities, where most Europeans nowadays live, you come across laughing faces as soon as you enter into a commercial relationship with someone, or at least express your intention to do so. Often, when the open indifference or downright hostility of these smiles saddens me, I try to recollect the enigmatically joyous faces of those two old people. Are they still alive, herding their goats, I wonder? For me they were the last happy people on this continent.

At the time I did not know that the area where I spent those late autumn days was part of the "desert français," the French wasteland, a term used for more or less all the country outside the sprawling urban district of Paris. It is an arid plane where chestnuts, wine, olives, and wheat used to be cultivated. Today the only industry that yields an income is the tourist trade, for the area is picturesque and rich in testimony of the past: medieval villages with fortifications, Romanesque churches, and suchlike. My hostess praised the German tourists above all others: they were never choosy about their food, and whatever the fare was, they said, "Bon, bon!" The French, according to her, were far more difficult in that respect.

Françoise's frank and lively opinions about all questions of morality and politics were generally charming, if occasionally questionable. She blamed the disastrous situation of the French farmers, for example, on East European cattle farmers "who had no idea how much a cow cost." This subject came up repeatedly, at dinner or when watching television (although these two activities generally coincided) or when one of their children came down from university to visit. At the time France was preparing for the referendum on the Maastricht Agreement. Some of you may remember that the vote was practically a tie, with a majority of only one or two percent in favor. Anyway, there was heated debate and the differences of opinion divided the family. Gérard, the more quiet, and reticent, and conservative partner (he came from Normandy) was determined to cast a "no" vote. Françoise, on the other hand, was undecided, oscillating between the two positions. On the one hand she rejected the idea of the European Union; on the other hand she feared the consequences should the agreement be rejected by the majority of the French. I remember her lively tone of voice when she summed up the situation with the words, "C'est la guerre en Europe!"

C'est la guerre! — "There will be war." This sounded unbelievable to my ears, quite fantastical even. But I realized she was serious. Her fear was real and I thought about what she had said. Up to that point I was of the opinion that war could only arise in the context of Eastern Europe, in Russia, or in the Balkans, whereas for Germany or France war was a thing connected to the past. As I thought about this, I understood that Françoise and Gérard had lived through the last war between Germany and France and that this experience was with them at all times. One evening, when we were watching the news and some minister was asked about the question of unemployment, she said in the same unequivocal tone of voice, "They are frightened of having a revolution on their hands!" I don't know which one she meant—the student unrest of 1968 that held unpleasant memories for her or the French Revolution of 1789 and the subsequent wave of terror, during which the village priest was hidden in the cellar of their farm house.

Looking back I am beginning to understand. At the time Françoise's remarks about war and revolution were a complete mystery to me. But if something is puzzling it stays in your mind, whereas if it is clear and comprehensible, you soon forget it. No doubt we all remember grown-ups saying things that we failed to understand when we were little and that never became any clearer because we could not summon the courage to ask for an explanation.

Only ten years ago Europe was the embodiment of our dreams. Dreams of a good, and safe, and happy life. And all those people opposed to the European Union seemed to me to be reactionaries spoiled by a comfortable life or dreamers who, for lack of better things to do, had constructed an enemy for themselves that they could fight against without jeopardizing their own lives. For Europe appeared to be a fundamentally peaceful, democratic, flourishing place—the place of all things good and admirable, as those living in the vale of tears that the rest of the world constitutes saw it. In my country, Estonia, politicians and literati never tired to emphasize that, in actual fact, we had always been part of Europe and that by becoming a member of the European Union a historical injustice would finally be redeemed. However, this claim is not entirely sincere. Of course we are part of Europe—where else would we belong? Yet there are equally sound reasons—more sound today than ever before—for disputing this claim to membership. I am no longer certain which side I agree more with, just as I am not certain anymore that Europe really is "good" to the core.

The Europe that we are dealing with is a political reality that has emerged as a product of wars and conquests. Today Europe is dominated by the European Union and by an ideology viewing Europe as an indisputably positive and benevolent construction based on shared values (which is an accurate description as far as the currency is concerned). According to this ideology, those opposed to Europe are no more than an assemblage of narrow-minded and selfish nationalists, an objectionable crowd that it is best to shun. In a way there is no alternative than to be in favor of Europe.

Interestingly the main argument in favor of the European Union is — fear. In Estonia it is the fear of Russia and of poverty (those two notions somehow being identical). Of course Europe is also something to be feared, because joining the European Union somehow means giving in, surrendering to a system of politics and legislature that was developed without our having had a share in it, entailing a voluntary submergence into a system where the old members are in charge. But the fear of Europe is far smaller than that of Non-Europe, just as Françoise feared "war" (Germany) and "revolution" more than the conditions of the Maastricht Agreement.

I know it sounds strange, but to me it seems that right from the beginning fear has been the driving force holding Europe together. In the past it was the fear of Stalin's Eastern bloc, the fear of famine (the impetus for a common agricultural policy), and the fear of losing the position of world supremacy that Europe had gained for itself in the course of centuries. There is a world of difference between the Europe of today and the grand Europe of the nineteenth century, with its empires, which in fierce competition with one another, ruled over large parts of the planet and exploited it mercilessly through construction of a neofeudal economic order that continues to operate on a global scale. It is an economic order in which the population of the rich industrial nations consumes, not unlike the feudal lords of the Middle Ages, all the gifts of the earth, while the population of the Third World is forced to perform physical labor of the lowliest kind and, like the peasantry of the Middle Ages, lives at the very edge of subsistence.

Europe can look back on an incredible story of success. Viewed objectively Europe is no more than an insignificant peninsula of the Eurasian landmass that had the audacity and the entrepreneurial spirit to oppose the rest of the world. In Soviet times the maps we had in our geography lessons showed all of Eurasia; even the maps of Europe showed a Europe that extended as far as the Ural Mountains. On both kinds of map countries like France, and Germany, and Great Britain looked like miniature states somewhere on the edge of the world It seemed strange that the disputes between these dwarfs determined, to a large extent, what "world history" was all about. In the meantime I have become acquainted with a very different cartographic practice according to which a map of Europe frequently does not even show all of the former Holy Roman Empire of German Nations, but instead ends just north of the border between Germany and Denmark so that the city of Hamburg has moved to a place on the periphery. On those maps places like Italy, France, and Germany appear to be enormous and their shares in the Euro-universe of vaguely equal size.

The biggest fear in Europe today seems to be of the possible consequences that this incredible success story might bear. Europe has spread its civilization across the globe and set in motion a process that is now called globalization, though it is increasingly unable to control this process. Of the new fears the biggest is that of America, which, looked at from a historical perspective, is nothing more than an extension of the old Europe. The absolute cultural supremacy that America can claim for itself in today's world is another historical achievement brought about by Europe. In my view the attempt to create a common cultural identity in Europe ("European literature," "European music," "European film") aims at constructing a counterweight to this dominant power, constituting a nostalgic reminiscence of one's own lost supremacy. A European identity will have to constitute the cultural equivalent to the euro, the currency now in competition with the dollar. But even a superficial comparison of the bank notes shows that these two identities—the American and the European—cannot be compared or, to be more precise, that there is no such thing as a European identity. Below the famous and, seen from the outside, dubious motto "In God We Trust," the dollar notes bear portraits of America's founding fathers, just as, before the euro was introduced, the bank notes of the various European countries depicted images of famous people from their individual states and representatives of their individual national identities. On the euro notes, however, there is nothing but emptiness: bridges with empty arches, empty doorways, and empty windows. Possibly this is meant to symbolize openness and freedom; but an identity meant to integrate societies cannot be founded on purely abstract ideas—it requires real people and meaningful symbols.

The problem here is that great writers, even though they may be considered to be part of a European literature (and why should Whitman, Marquez, and Mishima, not to mention Tolstoy and Dostoevsky, not be seen as standing in the same tradition as Goethe and Camus), still belong to the cultural heritage of the nation of their origin. As long as there is no common European language, a European literature as the creative force behind a common identity is unlikely to develop (and literature doubtlessly played an important part in the emergence of national identities in the eighteenth, nineteenth, and twentieth centuries).

To my mind, the search for a European identity has simply been taken too far, or rather, the demands made upon it cannot be fulfilled. After all, thanks to the success story described above, Europeanism is not confined to Europe and certainly not to the European Union, not even in its extended form. It is therefore impossible to compare the idea of a European identity to that of a national identity or even to consider it as the sum of the individual national identities. From a historical perspective Europeanism is of an imperialist and cosmopolitan nature. If it were to confine itself to its original home ground it would fall into a rapid decline proceeding as inexorably as its earlier expansion (whether one considers this to be a good or a bad thing is another question). In the context of the European Union, the question of European identity should, in my view, be avoided altogether, for I believe that the search for identity is based on yet another one of the European fears—the fear of nationalism. Apparently it is hoped that the development of a European identity will impede the progress of an aggressive nationalism. I fear the opposite might occur. In the last few years of its existence the Soviet Union strove towards a common Soviet identity based on the essentially cosmopolitan idea of socialism to create Soviet man—just as now in Europe the European, as such, is to be created on the essentially cosmopolitan notion of Europeanism. Far from achieving its proclaimed aim in the Soviet Union, these efforts resulted in a strengthening of nationalist thinking in its darkest and most aggressive aspects. After all, one who acts out of fear frequently ends up bringing about precisely that which was feared. It seems to me that the fear of growing nationalism and American influence leads to activities that, paradoxically, end up strengthening both. In order to counteract American influences a "European America" is created; and in order to combat nationalism the concept of supernationalism is introduced. Inherent to the idea of a European identity is the preconception that to be European is somehow better than being Chinese or American.

It would be best if Europe stopped being so self-analytical. After all, why should a conglomerate that evolved out of a coal and steel union have a cultural identity of its own? Why does the cooperation between states necessarily involve the creation of a common culture, especially in view of the fact that this culture already exists and has grown beyond the borders of a geographical Europe?

The two old people with their goats in the Ardèche, who refused to admit progress into their lives, or were at least indifferent to it, and whom I described as the last two happy people on our continent must surely be dead by now. Had anybody told them they lived in Europe they would probably have reacted with surprise. For Françoise and Gérard, two educated adults who lived through World War II, the question of Europe was a complex moral one. For their children Europe is probably an irrevocable reality, with its contours clearly marked in their school textbooks. As if Europe was an Island. Whereas it is hardly more than a peninsula, the westernmost edge of an enormous continent that has spread like a ink on blotting paper and colored the whole continent. And this is precisely the reason why Europe fails to find itself—there is nowhere that is not Europe.

— *Translated by Susanne Höbel*

Colm Toíbín

What is Europe then? It is not a culture and not an identity. It is a word we should set about undermining further as time goes on.
© Jerry Bauer

Colm Toíbín

Ireland

Born in 1955, Colm Toíbín is today one of Ireland's best-known writers. For many years he edited cultural and political journals and published *In Dublin*. Then he wrote several non-fiction works on contemporary political and cultural matters. He published his first novel, *The South* in 1990, while his fourth and most recent novel, *The Blackwater Lightship*, appeared in German translation in 2001. Colm Toíbín's works have won several awards, including the Encore Award (1992) and the E. M. Forster Award (1995).

Further Reading:
The South. Penguin USA, 1992.
The Heather Blazing. Penguin USA, 1994.
The Story of the Night: A Novel. Henry Holt & Company, Inc., 1998.
The Blackwater Lightship: A Novel. Scribner, 2001.
Love in a Dark Time: And Other Explorations of Gay Lives and Literature. Scribner, 2002.

The Future of Europe

Europe is a word whose meaning is loose, whose connotations are diverse and various. No one is sure where it begins or ends.

It is very difficult to make generalizations about Europe and the European heritage. There are too many differences in our historical experiences: the Renaissance occurred mostly in Italy; the Reformation took place in some areas and not in others; the Inquisition happened in Spain but not elsewhere; the Enlightenment had a distinct influence on public and private life in some countries but not in others; the Industrial Revolution did not occur in certain part of Europe; some counties plundered their colonies, others not so much; some were deeply influenced and greatly enriched by their own colonies, others not so much; some parts of Europe were changed by the rise of nationalism and the rise of fascism and the rise of communism, but each in a different way.

Europe is as diverse as European languages are different. There is no such thing as a set of European values; there is no such thing as a common European identity.

I cannot talk about the future of Europe, since I do not know what Europe is. Neither can I speak about its past, since its past is various and many aspects of its past are beyond my understanding.

In the European countries now, I believe, we possess two identities. One is bound up with memory, family, community, and personal experience. We may call it home if we like, but some people are in exile from it. The second identity centers on a nation, a state, an imagined community larger than neighbors and friends and family. This can have single name with no complex or gnarled heritage; or it can come with many hyphens and uncertainties. Thus we may feel French in France with no uncertainty; or Lithuanian in Lithuania; or we may feel British in Northern Ireland with a great deal of uncertainty; or Russian in Estonia; or Turkish in Germany; or Jamaican in England.

None of us, is, however, capable of developing a third super-identity as European and feeling this with the same emotional strength. The other two identities are too strong, too essential, no matter how strange and complex they have become. I believe that Europe is too large a term to mean much to most Europeans.

I feel easier when the word Europe is replaced by the two words — European Community. I know what that is. I have views on its future. My views on its future, however, are inevitably bound up with my views on the discrete and undefinable nature of the European experience and the increasingly complex heritage of people who live in Europe which I have briefly outlined above.

I was born in the Republic of Ireland in 1955; thus I was eighteen when Ireland joined what was then called the Common Market. In the decade or so before joining, Ireland must have seemed a very backward place to those who came from the more developed European mainland. All our secondary schools were fee-paying and run by the churches, for example, until 1967, when the fee-paying part was abolished; there was draconian censorship of books until 1966; the death penalty for capital offences was still on the statute books when we joined the Common Market; there was no divorce; contraceptives were illegal; abortion was (and still is) illegal; women did not sit on juries; homosexual acts between men were illegal. Ireland was an agricultural country, Catholic and conservative, repressive, with a very basic infrastructure. And its constitution had a bellicose claim against some of the territory of its nearest neighbor. That is, without any recognition in international law, it claimed jurisdiction over Northern Ireland.

The slow liberalization of Ireland between then and now came from many directions, from the spirit of the time perhaps more than anything. But a number of momentous changes to the society came directly from its membership of the Common Market.

In 1973, the same year as we joined, we elected a new government, and this government was unusual, certainly the best educated, most liberal, most forward looking government we have ever had. Very quickly they were faced with a crisis. Women in state jobs had always been paid less than men, and had been forced to retire on marriage. Brussels ordered the Irish government to change this. The Irish cabinet, despite all its liberalism, did everything it could to avoid making the change, claiming poverty. Brussels insisted. The change was made. Thus ideas of equality began to take root in Ireland.

In 1979, to take another example, a Dublin academic, David Norris, appealed to have the Victorian laws against homosexuality, which had remained on the Irish statute books, declared unconstitutional. He lost in the Irish High Court and then also in the Irish Supreme Court. His lawyer Mary Robinson took the case to the European Court of Human Rights, which in 1988 instructed the Irish government to change the law. The government did not do so. It was instructed again in 1989. And again in 1990 (the year Mary Robinson was elected President). Again in 1991. Again in 1992. Although the Court is not a function of the European Union, the Irish government, involved in serious negotiation over structural funding with Brussels, felt embarrassed enough to change the law in 1993. They emptied the chambers of parliament, and passed the legislation without a debate. Even the most liberal politicians did not wish to speak on these matters. It is fair to say that without the ruling of the Court of Human Rights it would have taken them another twenty or thirty years to change the law on homosexuality.

These are merely two examples of how being a member of the European Community has served the interests of liberalization and modernization in Ireland. The relaxation of the interstate customs controls in 1992 also eased tension between north and south in Ireland by removing the customs posts from the border. I could offer many other examples, including directives on the environment and on other forms of equality. I do not believe, however, that this influence has made Irish people, even the most liberal, feel more European, merely that the institution known as the European

Community has come to serve our interests, and thus the institution is viewed with sporadic affection and loyalty. But this could easily change should it no longer serve our interests.

Over the past few months, both in Ireland and in the wider European Union, there has been a debate on enlargement, and this debate has been haunted by a specter, and this specter is called Turkey. The opposition to Turkey's entry has offered many reasons: its underdevelopment; its large population; the readiness of its workers to migrate; its record on human rights; the fact that most of it is not even in Europe; its natural hinterland in Asia; its dangerous neighbors; its fragile democracy; its attitude to Cyprus; its relationship to Greece.

Some of these arguments could have been used against Ireland in 1973. It, too, was underdeveloped. It, too, had a fractious relationship to its nearest neighbor. Its workforce, on each economic downturn, left for Britain and the United States. It, too, had a political culture which was not based on the principles of the Enlightenment.

Some of those who argue against Turkish entry are prepared to spell out another reason why the Turkish application has been viewed with little enthusiasm; others merely hint at it. Turkey is not a Christian country. That, for many people in Europe, both in the political elite and among ordinary voters, is the issue. Turkey equals Islam; Europe has stood as a bastion against Islam since the Crusades, the argument goes. Europe had a Renaissance, a Reformation, a Counter-Reformation, an Enlightenment, an Industrial Revolution. Islam's development has been slower and stranger. Islam will always be dangerous and alien.

The counterargument is easy to make. While Christianity gave us the great Romanesque and Gothic churches and the religious paintings, it also gave us the cruelty of the Inquisition, the cruelties of colonization, and, in our last century, it gave us the basis for murdering almost the entire Jewish population of Europe. What cruelties has Islam inflicted compared to these cruelties?

I think, however, that these arguments miss the point of what has been happening in Europe over the past fifty years in which the European Union has been an essential tool. First of all, it is hard to describe Europe as having a Christian heritage at all, because the word Christian here covers so much and took on so many different guises and had so many different impacts in European countries. I do not mean simply that the Protestant and Catholic divisions in Europe make it difficult to talk about a single Christian heritage. I mean that each place in Europe seemed to allow its religious spirit to develop as a mirror image of the place's own needs or qualities. Local conditions shaped the tone and tenor of Christianity. Thus Slovenian Catholicism differed from that of Croatia; thus Scottish Presbyterianism differed from the Church of England; thus Lithuanian Catholicism differed from that of Poland; thus Catalan Catholicism differed from that of Andalusia.

There was no single heritage; there was diversity. Progress often came from dissent rather than from doctrine. And there is as much dissent and humanist debate in contemporary Turkey as there was in Ireland in 1973. Islam also has many mansions. And over the past thirty years the European Union has been a great secular, and secularizing institution, so that to talk now about excluding Turkey from the Union because it is not a Christian country is to miss the point of what has happened in Europe, and will go on happening, and is to couch what might be base racial prejudice in terms that are lofty and meaningless.

To talk about Christianity as the governing factor in our political identity is to ignore how much difference the thinking and writing in Europe which opposed or ignored Christianity has made to that identity; it is to ignore the contribution to our heritage of both the Islamic and the Jewish population; it is also to ignore the vast population living and working in our countries who are not, neither in their faith nor their heritage, Christian.

Europe, then, like Christianity itself, is a word whose meaning is loose, whose connotations are diverse and various. No one is sure where it begins or ends. Its culture cannot be endangered because it does not have a culture. Any time in the past it set out to define itself in terms of single and definable racial, cultural, or religious origins and aims, it caused havoc.

What is Europe then? It is a name for a set of interests, organized into the European Union. It is a word open to interpretation, full of associations, floating freely. It is not a culture and not an identity. It is a word we should set about undermining further as time goes on.

Jean-Philippe Toussaint

I am, then, as much in my life as in my books, a pluralist
and nomadic European, taking playful delight in the variety
of languages and cultures proper to Europe, at home
everywhere on the continent—or nowhere, which amounts
to the same thing.

Jean-Philippe Toussaint
Belgium

Born in Brussels in 1957, the author, scriptwriter, and
editor Jean-Philippe Toussaint studied political science
and history in Paris. In 1989 he made a film version of his
novel *Monsieur*, in 1992 he made a film version of his
novel *L'appareil-photo* entitled *La Sévillane*. In the
following year, he was invited by DAAD to spend a year in
Berlin, where he completed the film *Berlin 10:46"*. In
1997 he wrote the screenplay and directed the film *The
Ice Rink* (with Bruce Campbell, Tom Novembre, Dolorès
Chaplin). Jean-Philippe Toussaint's books are translated in
twenty languages, his films have played in numerous
countries. He is the author of literary texts published by
prestigious magazines and newspapers world-wide. Jean-
Philippe Toussaint lives in Brussels and Corsica.

Further Reading:
The Bathroom: A Novel. Translated by Paul De Angelis.
Obelisk, 1990.
Monsieur: A Novel. Translated by John Lambert. Marion
Boyars Publishers, Ltd., 1991.
Making Love: A Novel. Translated by Linda Coverdale.
New Press, 2004.

You Are Leaving the American Sector

Je suis donc, aussi bien dans ma vie que dans mes livres, un Européen pluriel et nomade, qui joue avec délice de cette variété de langues et de cultures propre à l'Europe, et se sent partout chez soi en Europe–ou nulle part, ce qui revient au même–, aussi bien à Brux-elles qu'à Paris, à Londres ou à Venise, à Madrid ou à Berlin.

From a visual point of view I would rather that my text not be translated into English.[1] I would rather, from a simply aesthetic point of view, neither as protest nor as polemic, that my text be the only one not translated into English, but into an Oriental language (Chinese, for example, for a better understanding by all). In fact, even before it is put together, I imagine with trepidation this volume on the European specificity of European writers translated entirely into English, and I cannot stop from thinking that my few pages in Chinese, insinuating their ideograms into this pudding, could possibly throw an ironic light on the situation of languages in Europe, and the domination of the language spoken ... in America. To be sure, it might seem a very insignificant detail to ask which languages the text I am now writing will appear in, but it is never-theless a question of language (which is no trifling matter for a writer).

In fact it is not by chance that I would like my text translated into Chinese, because, in order to achieve the distance necessary for grasping the possible European specificity of my books, I intend to take a detour through Asia. I take the idea of a detour, roaming and carefree, with its seductive Tristram-Shandyesque flavor, from the French philosopher François Jullien. A Hellenic scholar, he ex-plains that his methodological choice of passing through China is a way of stepping back from the history of European philosophy, suggesting even that he "went through China to better read Greek." Paradox aside, the idea of a detour should be taken seriously, like a necessary distance, an indispensable retreat to interrogate a reality that has become too familiar. By means of this detour through Chinese thought, things that might seem banal or be taken for granted again become remarkable and problematic. So rather than simply ask myself what is specifically European about my look at reality, I would like to put the question another way: how, for a Chinese reader, am I a European author?

First of all, the places inhabited by the characters of my books are as European as they come. The apartments they live in are European and the hotels they stay in are European. Of course Paris, my city (I am Belgian, but I went to secondary school and university in Paris), is at the heart of my books, and one could almost say that the narrators of all my books are Parisians, they live and work in Paris (if you can call that working), which they leave only for brief trips abroad, to Venice or Milan. Then, leaving France but not yet Europe (one must wait for my last novel, *Faire l'amour*, for the first trip to Asia), my narrators settle here and there about the continent, in a village on the Mediterranean (*La Reticence*) or Berlin (*La Télévision*). This diversity of European cities present in my books, sometimes simply a decorative element (Paris or Venice in *La Salle de bain*), but sometimes also an essential part of the story like Berlin in *La Télévision* or Sasuelo in *La Réticence*, gives my novels a European flavor that must seem all the more vivid when seen from afar, from Shanghai or Peking. I am, then, as much in my life as in my books, a pluralist and nomadic European, taking playful delight in the variety of languages and cultures proper to Europe, at home everywhere on the continent—or nowhere, which amounts to the same thing—as much in Brussels as in Paris, in London as in Venice, in Madrid as in Berlin.

I was born in Brussels (Belgium) in 1957, I went to primary school in Belgium and secondary school and university in Paris (France). Afterwards, I lived in Madrid (Spain), Berlin (Germany), Corsica (France), and again in Brussels (Belgium). A native and resident of

the city that symbolizes, better than any other, Europe and its institutions, I am myself a reasonably good synthesis of the European
spirit, a meeting of Latin and Germanic characters, to which, like a
pinch of salt, one could even add an ounce of East-European flair
due to my distant Lithuanian origins. For personal, cultural, or
familial-touristic reasons (a trip to Lithuania, my grandfather's
homeland), or to accompany the translation of this or that book in
this or that country, I have been to most countries in Europe. I
speak French (very well), English (rather well), German (rather
badly), I can get by (badly) in Italian and (very badly) in Spanish. I
can read the newspaper in German, English, Spanish, Italian, and
French. My books have been translated into the principle European
languages: English, German, Italian, Spanish, Dutch, Swedish,
Danish, Finnish, Norwegian, Greek, Portuguese, Catalan, Czech,
Hungarian, Bulgarian, Bosnian, Romanian, and Polish. I am, then,
in all respects a European writer, and like the Austrian writers who
write in German or the Irish writers who write in English, I come
from a small country and I write in a big language.

On closer inspection one will not find political or economic motifs
in my books, no social tableau of the contemporary world. Yet my
novels are intensely contemporary. My first book, *La Salle de bain*,
was innovative as much in terms of its form and fragmentary structure as in its very everyday themes. The recurrence of places (or
non-places) representative of the contemporary world, bathroom,
waiting room, supermarket, phone booth, airport, etc., gives my
books, I believe, an a-geographic, universal dimension, to the point
that a Chinese reader will find his way as well as a European reader
by superimposing his own impersonal spaces on my descriptions.
In the same way, the philosophic or metaphysical motifs present in
my books are not particularly rooted in European culture. There is
no organized, referenced, cultivated philosophical discourse, but
rather a practical philosophy traced out in the most common in-
stants of everyday life, in its lulls and downtimes, in elevators, in
the street, the bathroom. So just like the European reader the Chinese reader would be familiar with the principle themes evoked in
my books and savor the inquiries on the meaning of life, the imper-

ceptible variations on the symbolism of water, and reflections on the passage of time.

Some time ago a literary review asked me to name the ten best literary works in human history. Without giving it much thought, I chose only works by European authors. I named Pascal and Montaigne, I could have added Goethe and Shakespeare, I could have recalled Dante and Cervantes; but I cited mostly twentieth-century authors, Proust and Beckett, Musil and Kafka. It all happened as if in my own personal pantheon there were simply no great South American, African, Indian, or Chinese authors, or any North American authors either, and, of course, no Oceanic authors (they don't write there, they surf). No, for me, without even thinking about it, all the great writers, all those who had influenced me, who had made up my culture and nourished my own pursuits from my schooldays to my last books, came from Europe. Without really thinking about it—although it must be obvious to a Chinese reader—I very naturally situated myself within the European, and even French, literary tradition that starts with Flaubert and continues to the *nouveau roman*, with its constant attention to style and form.

In December 2001, riding a night train in south China between Canton and Changsha, I looked at my Chinese editor's wife lying in front of me on her couchette reading *La Reprise* by Robbe-Grillet, in Chinese. Watching her read I wondered, fascinated, what exactly she got from Robbe-Grillet's book. I myself had read it several weeks earlier, and it seemed to me that its coded universe, in which style takes on such importance, would not be easily accessible to a Chinese reader. Of course I had often wondered what Asian readers were reading when they read European books in translation. And every time someone tried to persuade me that they lost enormously in translation, my response, paradoxically, was that most European readers, when they read a book in their own language, also lose much with respect to the author's intentions, and that, in the end, each reader, European or Oriental, cultivated or ignorant, was just at a different point on the scale of how much was lost between the author's intentions and what the reader could still discern, and that, in the end, a cultivated and sensitive Chinese reader could get more from a book translated from a European language than a European reader ignorant of the finesses of style in his own language. Because literature, beyond continents and frontiers, is an intimate exchange between two human beings.

— *Translated by John Lambert*

1 The presentation note to Europa Schreibt states that "all essays will be translated into German and English."

Dubravka Ugrešić

To the question of what is European in European literatures,
I have only one answer, the shortest variant of which would be:
Mr. Bhattacharaya, an Indian who lives in America
© gezett.de

Dubravka Ugrešić

Croatia

Born in Kutina, Croatia in 1949, the author, translator, and literary theorist Dubravka Ugrešić studied comparative literature and Russian language and literature at the University of Zagreb. She is co-publisher of a ten-volume encyclopedia on the avant-garde in Russia. She was the first woman to be awarded Yugoslavia's main prize for literature, the NIN. In 2000 she received the Heinrich Mann Prize for her work as a writer. In 1993, after a series of public attacks, Dubravka Ugrešić left her home country, moving to Amsterdam where she lives as a writer.

Further Reading:
Fording the Stream of Consciousness. Translated by Michael Henry Heim. Northwestern University Press, 1993.
In the Jaws of Life. Translated by Celia Hawkesworth and Michael Henry Heim. Northwestern University Press, 1993.
Have a Nice Day: From the Balkan War to the American Dream. Translated by Celia Hawkesworth. Viking Press, 1995.
The Culture of Lies: Antipolitical Essays. Translated by Celia Hawkesworth. Pennsylvania State University Press, 1998.
The Museum of Unconditional Surrender. Translated by Celia Hawkesworth. New Directions Publishing, 2002.
Thank You for Not Reading: Essays on Literary Trivia. Translated by Celia Hawkesworth. Dalkey Archive Press, 2003.

European Literature
as a Eurovision Song Contest

Na pitanje što je danas evropsko u evropskim
književnostima imam samo jedan odgovor čija bi
najkraća varijanta bila: to je Mister Bhattacharya, Indijac
koji živi u Americi.

The concept of European literatures—as it is generally used by EU politicians, cultural managers, publishers, old-fashioned university departments, and often by writers themselves—is not very different from the concept of the European competition for the best European song.

Let us recall, the Eurovision Song Contest is the favorite annual TV entertainment of many Europeans, and the hottest point of mental unification of Europe. The Eurovision Song Contest is a grandiose (grandiose European-style) presentation of European pop-music kitsch. But nevertheless, there is greater enjoyment to be had from things other than the pop music itself, ranging from costumes *(this year the Cypriots were the best!)* to spectacular performance *(this year the Irish used so much smoke on stage that they nearly started a fire!)*. Enjoyment is to be had in the method of voting *(Croatia, ten points! Belgium, two points!)*; picture postcards of various countries, linking up with studios in Tallinn and Dublin; then "politics" and its transparency *(everyone knows that the Croats gave the Slovenes the most points, and vice versa)*; the participation of new European representatives *(Hey, this year we've got Bosnians!)*; the absence of all non-participants *(The Serbs will never sing in Europe, not in a million years!)*. And as far as the actual music is concerned, one expects the Turks to bring something of their oriental musical kitsch, the Swedes to defend the colors of West European musical kitsch. The greatest European TV show also has an educational function *(viewers learn the names of new states: Lithuania, Estonia, Latvia!)*, a political-ideological function *(OK, we've taken in the Estonians, but we won't have the Turks, singing with us is quite enough for them!)*; and, incidentally, of course, it makes a financial profit. There are sometimes excesses, such as the Diva *(Viva la Diva!)*, the Israeli transvestite, but excesses within the framework of the mainstream are always welcome.

European literary life, with its literary representatives, whose names are always (always!) backed by the name of a state, frequently does not differ greatly from the show described above. It's true that there is less of the spectacular. However, TV broadcasts of the annual Booker Prize ceremony increasingly confirm that literature too is a spectacle. The winners leap onto the stage *(Canada, ten points!)* and pronounce words of gratitude in the manner of pop-singers. It is true that the judges' speeches are more eloquent, which is understandable—after all words, and not musical notes, are the writer's craft. If we take into account the commercial effect of the Booker performance, and also the principle of exclusivity (the Booker is awarded only to books in English), then all of that combined supports our initial comparison, however unjustified, malicious, and inaccurate as it may seem to some.

The Participation of G. Drubnik in the Whole Thing

Some thirty years ago, in 1971, an issue of *The New York Times* published a spoof article about Gregor G. Drubnik, a Bulgarian writer who had ostensibly been awarded the Nobel Prize for Literature that year. The article was full of discriminatory epithets, such as *the remarkably stupefying quality* of Drubnik's works, and it was supposed to be highly amusing. The very idea that some Bulgarian could ever win the Nobel Prize for Literature brought a smile to everyone's lips.

Had I come across that article at the time it was published, I too would have laughed. At that time I was studying comparative literature, and I was full of myself. I read European and American writers, wrote student essays on Proust and Joyce. I read well-known and less well-known Russian writers, I studied literary theoretical schools at a time when, it seems, literary theory was at its height. I was convinced that I was in tune with the great literary world. It was also a time of a great publishing boom in the former Yugoslavia, a lot was being translated, and I followed every accessible foreign literary innovation. When in 1982 I found myself in America for the first time, the choice of translated literature in the bookshops seemed to me modest. Of course I could not admit that to anyone. No one would have believed me, and besides, only a few years later, the picture of American bookshops, as far as translations are concerned, changed radically for the better. And my conviction that big things happen only in big places remained unshaken.

At the beginning of the 1990s the situation was to change: both Zagreb and Belgrade bookshops would become terribly empty, in terms of both local and translated literature. At that time my books began to set off into the world, and somewhat later I myself followed them. In my conviction that I was communicating masterfully with the big literary world, whatever that meant, I forgot the possibility that this world was not communicating with me nor was it unduly interested in communication.

When my novel was published in England in 1991 one critic ended his review with the question: *But, still, is this what we need?* It was only later that I realized what the critic's sentence meant. As I traveled I did not notice that I was dragging with me the label *Made in the Balkans.* And if someone comes from the Balkans, he or she is not expected to perform cultural mastery in front of us, but to conform to the stereotype which WE have about THEM, the Balkans or about the places *where all of THEM come from.*

I had, therefore, forgotten where I came from and where I had landed, or in other words, I had overlooked the established codes between the cultural center and the periphery. I was expected to confirm stereotypes about the periphery, not destroy them. As far as my literary mastery was concerned, I could have chucked it in the bin since it appeared simply to irritate my foreign literary surroundings.

It turned out that Drubnik's cold-war phantom shadow had not quite disappeared during those thirty or so years. With time the number of labels that others stuck on me and my books only increased. In addition to the label *Made in the Balkans*, there were new ones: the collapse of Yugoslavia, the fall of communism, war, nationalism, new states and new identities. My texts communicated with the foreign reader weighed down with voluminous baggage. I often seemed to myself like a traveler dragging several suitcases in each hand and trying at the same time to retain a certain elegance. Unlike me, my West European colleagues traveled without luggage, and all that the reader saw was them and what they wrote. While in my case the luggage buried both me and what I wrote. The situation changed radically in my local literary landscape as well. There too labels appeared, there too it suddenly became crucial for an understanding of my writing to know whether I was by nationality a Croat or a Serb and what my mom and dad were.

Some ten years ago I had an elegant Yugoslav passport with a soft, flexible, dark red cover. I was a *Yugoslav* writer. Then the war came and—without asking me—the Croats thrust into my hand a blue Croatian passport (it had resolutely rejected red, the Communist color, but the hardness of its cover reminded one of the old Soviet pass for the Lenin Library). The new Croatian authorities expected from their citizens a prompt transformation of identity, as though the passport itself was a magic pill. Since in my case it did not work very well, they excluded me from their literary, and other, ranks. With my Croatian passport I abandoned my newly acquired "homeland" and set off into the world. Out there, with the gaiety of Eurovision Song Contest fans, I was immediately identified as a *Croatian* writer. I became the literary representative of a milieu that did not want me any more and which I did not want any more either. But still the label *Croatian writer* remained with me, like a permanent tattoo.

At this moment I possess a passport with a red cover, Dutch. I continue to wear the label of the literary representative of a country to which I am not connected even by a passport. Will my new passport make me a *Dutch* writer? I doubt it. Will my Dutch passport ever make it possible for me to reintegrate in Croatian literary ranks? I doubt it.

What is actually my problem? Am I ashamed of the label *Croatian writer*? No. Would I feel better with a *Gucci* or *Armani* label? No. So what do I want?

If by the will of some criminals, and then by the ostensible majority will of the people, I lost the label *Yugoslav*, why now—again not by my own will—should I wear the label *Croatian*? What's more, if the Croatian cultural criminals angrily stripped the *Croatian* label from me (because I publicly snarled at a time when, according to them, I should have kept quiet), why do others, people who are in any case completely indifferent, continue assiduously to stick this label on me?

And why am I so sensitive to labels? Because in practice it turns out that identifying baggage weighs down a literary text. Because it continues to be the case that an identity tag alters the essence of a literary text and its meaning. Because an identity tag is a shorthand interpretation of the text, and regularly wrong. Because an identity tag opens the way to reading into a text something that is not there. And finally because it is discriminatory, discriminatory for the literary text itself. Because I come from the periphery. An American writer, I imagine, does not have this problem.

Why do some of my colleagues, unlike me, find it important to retain their identity tag? Because identifying writers according to their nationality, according to the country to which they belong, is implanted in literary and also in commercial communication. Because that is the easiest way to travel from the periphery to the center. Because for many people an identity tag is, at the same time, the only way to communicate, not only locally, but also globally, to be accepted and recognized as a *Bosnian* writer, as a *Slovene* writer, as a *Bulgarian* writer. Because a label is the fundamental assumption of every market, including, therefore, the literary market as well. Because identity and trafficking in identity is a well-tried market formula that has enabled many writers from the periphery to move, justifiably or not, into the global literary market.

Europe As Far As India

Having learned from the American commercial and ideological example, and then from the international success of Indian, Caribbean, Japanese, African, or Chinese writers who live in Great Britain, the cultural bureaucrats of the European Union, and all those who are concerned with culture, "culture buffs" in other words, all endeavor to adapt to the situation.

The culture of the EU is, on the one hand, worried about globalization, which is another name for American cultural imperialism. And while the Americans themselves use the term *imperialism* without much embellishment, the Europeans beat about the bush. They are afraid of being accused of excessive anti-Americanism, like the French, who become animated every few years over the protection of their cultural products, but equally over what has been taken from them, over their lost cultural primacy. It turns out that anti-Americanism is not culturally, or politically, or strategically, or financially profitable: besides, in the American cultural industry, it is not only American sellers who earn good money, but also European buyers.

European "cultural identity," whatever that means, is "threatened," on the one hand by the omnipresent American cultural industry and, on the other hand, by the East Europeans, who are waiting to enter, carrying their cultural bundles in their hands; and then also—and this is the most painful point of the European cultural subconscious—by émigrés from the non-European cultural circle, whose number is growing dangerously with every passing second. And where, really, do these numerous Moroccans and Algerians, all these Chinese and Arabs belong? How should they be classified? According to their passports? According to the language they use? According to the cultural circle to which they belong?

Proud of its ideology and practice of multiculturalism, for the time being the cultural bureaucracy of the EU perpetuates its well-tried formula—*Me Tarzan, you Jane*—that is, the formula of recognizing different cultural identities, stressing regional and other variations, and, of course, integration, although no one knows what that is supposed to mean. To everyone, therefore, his place of worship, to everyone her *burka*. And as long as the Moroccans lay out on their counter something *Moroccan*, whatever that means, and we display something of ours, something *European*, whatever that means, everything is all right. That is, on the whole, how cultural products are exchanged, that is how the global market works, that is the established mechanism driving the dynamics of cultural life.

And everything would be all right if there were not non-mainstream individuals, dysfunctions in the system, which subvert canonized concepts regarding culture, about what it is, and what it ought to be. These individuals outstrip the conceptual apparatus of cultural promoters, managers, and the cultural bureaucracy of the EU. These individuals outstrip the conceptual apparatus of critics and interpreters, university departments, teachers, and readers. No one knows what to do with them and where to place them.

And really, what are the Dutch to do with Moses Isegawa, an African writer who lives in Holland and writes in English? What are the Dutch to do with me? I live in Amsterdam, but do not write in Dutch. What are the Croats to do with me? I do write in Croatian, but I don't live there. What are the Serbs and Bosnians to do with me? The language I write in is BCS (Bosnian-Croatian-Serbian, the neat abbreviation dreamed up by translators at the Hague Tribunal). What are the Dutch to do with a Moroccan writer, who, instead of writing profitable prose about the cultural differences between the Moroccans and the Dutch, which everyone would understand, has undertaken to recreate the beauty of the Dutch language of the nineteenth century, which present-day Dutch writers have forgotten. What are the French to do with an Arab who aspires to be the new Marcel Proust, and what are the Germans to do with a Turk who aspires to be the new Thomas Mann? There are similar examples, the only problem is that their number is growing.

Among the dysfunctions in the existing literary system I have my favorite example, my hero. I met him at a book fair in Budapest. Joydeep Roy Bhattacharaya was born in Calcutta. He left Calcutta when he was twenty and took a degree in philosophy in America. He lives in New York and teaches at one of the neighboring universities. Joydeep has written a novel that attracted a fair number of positive reviews. The subject of his novel is Hungary and a circle of Hungarian intellectuals in the nineteen-sixties. The Hungarians promptly translated his book. One Hungarian writer, an intellectual, complained to me, that, *er*, the novel was indeed concerned with Hungary, but in an *Indian* way. *It would be better if he wrote about India,* was his brief comment.

Joydeep is a young and attractive man. And very photogenic. His American publisher brought out his novel in the secret hope that Joydeep would have second thoughts and write something about India. Something like *The God of Small Things*, only from a male perspective. My mother, to whom I showed Joydeep's book with his photograph on the back cover, instinctively took the American publisher's side. *Why doesn't he write about India,* she sighed, *he's better-looking than Sandokan.*

As I talked to Joydeep I was astonished at his knowledge and passion for the former Eastern Europe. "It wouldn't occur to me to change my mind," he told me. "What do you mean?" I asked him. "The novel I am writing is set in Dresden, in the nineteen-fifties. After that I've got a novel about the battle for Stalingrad, written from a female perspective," he added.

As I said, Joydeep is my hero among my writer colleagues. In a world in which an identity kit is something like a toothbrush — that is, something one cannot do without — he has chosen the most difficult path. He has thrown his identity kit into the garbage, in the name of freedom of literary choice, in the name of literary freedom. Joydeep is absolutely conscious of the consequences of his symbolic suicide. "At home," in India, I presume, they don't like him, and it is debatable whether they have ever heard of him. People in the places he writes about complain because they are firmly convinced that only they can write about themselves, that only they have the copyright to their subject matter. American and British publishers tolerate Joydeep's Eastern European "virus," because they look forward to his recovery, to the moment when Joydeep will return thematically to the place he belongs, India.

To the question of what is European in European literatures, I have only one answer, the shortest variant of which would be: Mr. Bhattacharaya, an Indian who lives in America.

— *Translated by Celia Hawkesworth*

Dragan Velikić

Each writer carries within himself his own parts of the globe, regardless whether
it is Macondo or Buenos Aires, Alexandria or Dublin, Trieste or Berlin. Writing is exactly
the ability to convert the content of a map into a system of signs.

Dragan Velikić
Serbia

Born in Belgrade in 1953, the author Dragan Velikić grew
up in Pula, Istria and studied literature in Belgrade, where
he lived until 1999. He is a representative of the 'other
Serbia' and a member of the *Group 99*, a pressure group
formed in response to the war by authors from Slovenia,
Croatia, Bosnia, Serbia, and Kosovo. As a journalist,
Velikić wrote, until going into exile, for opposition
newspapers and was editor in chief of the independent
Radio B-92 in Belgrade. Dragan Velikić currently lives in
Belgrade.

Further Reading:
"The Boat for Rushdie." In *The Rushdie Letters*,
Nebraska Press, 1992.
"Astrakhan." Extract. In *Balkan Blues: Writing Out of
Yugoslavia*. Edited by Joanna Labon. Northwestern
University Press, 1995.
"A Woman from a Catalogue." In *The Prince of Fire. An
Anthology of Contemporary Serbian Short Stories*.
Edited by Radmilla J. Gorup and Nadezda Obradović.
Univ of Pittsburgh Press, 1998.
"Belgrade." In *Balkan Perspective–Writing across
borders*. Hungarian National Committee–Europian
Cultural Foundation, 1999.
"Which Way and Back." In *In Defence of the Future*. Folio
Verlag, 2000.

B-Europe

Svaki pisac nosi u sebi deo globusa, svejedno da li je to Makondo ili Buenos Aires, Aleksandrija ili Dablin, Trst ili Berlin. Pisanje i jeste veština pretvaranja unutrašnje mape u sistem znakova.

1

We don't think of Moldavia, Bosnia, or Serbia when we say "Europe." Geography is not enough by itself to get you on the floor. The floor is the European Union. And outside of the walls surrounding the Schengen area are the expanding balconies on which countries at the edge of Europe wait to one day descend to the promised floor. When it comes to Serbia, actually Yugoslavia, the reason for an almost ten-year-long expulsion even from the balconies are the Balkan wars of the past decade. At the very moment when the war happened, this country stopped being European.

"Europe" is not a norm being reduced exclusively to comfortable trains that always run on time. However, trains are part of Europe as well. And not at all by chance, trains that travel from European balconies to the European floor — whether it is the Hungarian "Bela Bartok," Croatian "Mimara," Serbian "Avala," or Polish "Warsaw Express" — judging by appearances, comfort, and punctuality they do meet European standards. I assume that Eastern European countries will become a part of the European Union, but only after using for domestic traffic the same kind of trains that connect them to Europe. Great Britain's example proves my point.

Yugoslavia's expulsion from Europe began with trains. Belgrade disappeared overnight from the European railroad timetables. You would not see it listed on any airport schedule. And that's not all.

Because of sanctions by the European Union against Yugoslavia, it was impossible to send a package heavier than twenty grams out of any European city to Yugoslavia, which had become a house without a street address. A strict visa policy had quarantined Yugoslavia. The once most-wanted passport on the black market (since Yugoslavians were able to travel to West and East without a visa) was reduced in this way to a useless piece of paper with which you could travel only to a handful of bordering countries. Such isolation leads to a bunker-mentality that becomes contagious. Recent political changes in Serbia have put this country back on the balconies, looking ahead to a long and tiring journey, the final destination of which is certainly the European floor.

The term "Europe" seems to be free of any negative connotation. Europe is a place where a high standard of living has been achieved. It is a place of peace and order. The poor cousins on the outskirts of Europe certainly see it this way. For years they have prepared to enter a unified Europe. And Europe imagines the outskirts gazing at it with a certain look in their eyes. And it wants the outskirts to confirm this look as their own. Strictly speaking, it often demands a regular supply of stereotypes rather than authentic art pieces. These stereotypes became the official version of culture for the countries on the outskirts during this time. And here is where we should look most closely to find the reasons why some of the movies, theater performances, and books that skillfully filter all that refuses to fit the ready-made cliché were so successful. Here we reach a paradox: according to certain artworks, there exists a reality in the countries on the outskirts (meaning Eastern Europe) that does not actually exist except in terms of Europe's opinion.

In these days of globalization, extraordinary computer programs, fashion, supermarkets, and shopping centers, it is possible to go to wildly different regions to buy the same product, from Greek pickles and Bulgarian yogurt to Danish butter and Italian pasta, French perfume and Portuguese shoes to Swedish furniture and Swiss watches. One day we all will be able to choose from the same products, and it will be possible to buy everything everywhere. As a consequence of a globalization, all places will be stuck in the horror of sameness. Traveling will become superfluous too. Since it is not possible to travel to the same.

However, up until now the same only appears to be the same. Licenses are getting better, and originals will soon become superfluous. Still, there is a noticeable difference between a Milka chocolate and Nestle coffee produced in Switzerland or Germany from those made through Hungarian or Czech licenses. A whole industry of the "same" was installed on the European outskirts. Now licenses, let's call them B-licenses, supply B-Europe in order to satisfy the needs of the inhabitants of this region. I don't mean pirate products of dubious origin, of course. And there is nothing wrong with that, because this is a reality. Besides, Serbian Coca-Cola is, in many ways, better than that from France. However, product programs of multinational corporations are turning the whole world into one place.

2

In the last couple of years only one movie from the Balkans was celebrated in the West. It is, of course, Emir Kusturica's movie, *Underground*. Even though the artistic qualities of this movie are undeniable, I am convinced that they are not the reason for its fame. The reason rather lies in its content, the picture of the Balkans that it offered to the West. Let me remind you: in this movie the Balkans are pictured as an orgiastic place, a place of pure insanity, as a place where people eat, drink, sing, make love, and kill all the time; thus, it is an almost mythical place, a wild place where all is allowed. There is nothing paradoxical about the fact that exactly this picture of the Balkans pleased the eye of the West: it confirmed, I tend to think, its tacit, phantasmagoric public assumption about those others, the people from the Balkans, the ones so different from them, entirely different from those in the West, while reinforcing its belief in Western unity and inaccessibility. This assumption about the Balkans led to a satisfied gaze from the West because it offered it exactly what it wished to see as a picture of itself, as a confirmation of its own perfection.

When it comes to literature, the West likes to see the kind of literature from the Balkans that focuses on the absence of democracy, that expresses a thirst for the kind of democracy that always considers the West as a norm. In other words, it responds to a literature that presents an image of the West as its thematic center. In this literature the Western gaze can again be satisfied by persuading itself that it is deeply desirable, able to confirm to itself that it is on the right track. In this literature the West experiences a narcissistic joy, seeing itself as the inaccessible object of the others' dreams. The West remains closed, as far as I can tell, to a different kind of literature that also exists in the Balkans, one that uses styles and themes that are not the result of "political" or ideological conditions, a literature that cannot be reduced to the witnessing of a hard life on the European outskirts, a literature I would like to call "pure literature," a literature, so to speak, facing itself and questioning the literary abilities of language. Western culture keeps for itself any expectations regarding artistic experimentation that come with such literature, hording the mandate to challenge and transform literary praxis. This too is very easy to explain: it is the only way for the West to "protect" its own domination, to confirm its own ideal picture of a territory in which sophisticated intellectual "interventions" are being achieved, and to continue with its own narcissistic satisfaction.

3

There is no form of electrolysis that can deconstruct a literary world into its constituent parts. Books you read in childhood form your image of the world; they are a writer's third parent. Books are the name of the ship's home carved into the bow. And of course it is possible to be a writer form a certain region without ever having lived there, just as a Swiss-built ship that flies the flag of its home country might never sail into a Swiss port.

Writing is a means of considering the possibility of living other lives. I. B. Singer is right to say that a writer is one who remembers, but one who creates his own memories. We can create our own and "others'" memories (of characters) if we feel a longing to add a chapter to life. Not because we are not satisfied with our own lives, but because every writer lives through his books the many shades of the one and only reality.

The invention of my memories started one day in November 1958, when the train from Belgrade stopped at the shore of Pula, where the tracks looked as if they ran into the sea. The next scene is lit by a bulb on the bottom of a large enameled lampshade: a room in the Hotel Central that long ago, back when Pula, the city of my childhood, used to be Italian, was called the Milan. And during the Austro-Hungarian Empire, at the beginning of the last century, when the Irish writer James Joyce spent a couple of months in Pula, this hotel went by the name Europe.

I believe that every writer possesses a modest number of tones, scenes, sounds, and fragrances that are acquired in childhood, during the "ahistorical" period of life, that is, during one's own myth-making. These are settings that he uses repeatedly each time he begins a new book. He builds a world by inventing that which is infinite; namely: combinations. Each writer carries within himself his own parts of the globe, regardless whether it is Macondo or Buenos Aires, Alexandria or Dublin, Trieste or Berlin. Writing is exactly the ability to convert the content of a map into a system of signs. Heinrich Schliemann, while looking for Troy, used maps found in Homer. In spite of the amateurism of his archeological technique, he understood the messages hidden in the verses of the *Iliad*. And the Irish writer James Joyce constructed an entire city by carefully studying Ulysses' journey. He dreamed of Dublin in Trieste, Pula, Zurich, Paris. He transplanted many streets from old Trieste to Dublin, just as he recalled names from the phone book with his keen ear and gave them to his characters. On the "street furniture" of Dublin he recognized the indestructible layer.

This durability is also destruction, decay. The act of preservation implies hay and cotton, essential oils, acid, and at least a pair of glass eyes instead of real ones. However, these glass eyes can see deeper than decrepit, gelatinous gazers; these eyes can hear tones, words, a sound that bears an unknown heritage. There is a code layered deeply in language that is graphic and acoustic, and in all our stupidity we will name the little meanings that drip out onto the surface like a sandblast, a coincidence, destiny.

A literary workshop is a warehouse. The creation comes from a search through this warehouse. The sediment out of which every writer builds his literary world is unique and unrepeatable like a fingerprint. I believe in hidden, parallel universes that surround; we only occasionally notice the blinks. Actually, the writer is searching for vibrations. Like a spider, the writer is weaving a web out of himself, out of his own sediment. Like the circulatory system in a human body, the world of reality and the world of literature pulsate in the same way. My tower, which I have inhabited since reading through all of Karl May's novels, is built from Cervantes' humor, Italo Svevo's tensions, James Joyce's circular routes, Danilo Kiš' Pannonian remembrances, from Herman Broch's sleepwalking. Strings that connect me to other literary worlds are just as invisible as a "colonial style."

There is no identity for a writer other than the one in literature. Or should this identification be in my passport? Or even in my birth certificate? In my case it is simply a fact that I was born a Serb in Belgrade and that I grew up in the Croatian city of Pula on the Mediterranean coast. These facts exist as no more than a way of entering literature, first as a reader, ultimately as a writer. They embody a uniqueness produced simply by our being born and growing up surrounded by a certain environment. Later, facts from the biographies of favorite writers and the residue of their books add to this uniqueness. Spaces are being layered by which we pass only on late-night trains, just like the words of an unknown language.

As a child I often took walks through the Monte Ghiro Cemetery in Pula. In the old section of the cemetery, between pine trees, there are, even today, worn ledgers that list the names of Danish, Dutch, and Swedish officers and engineers who built the harbor and arsenal in Pula in the middle of the nineteenth century. I also used to find Hungarian, Slavic, Jewish, Italian, Germanic names. Everything is connected, Milos Crnjanski, the classic author of Serbian literature used to say. In his writings I recognize the rustle of Dante's terzines, just the way I assume Gogol's absurd situations appear in Nabokov's stories. Just like the dense air of Bruno Schulz's interiors evaporates in Kiš's family-cycle stories.

"The perpetual mobile" of literary structure is a neurotransmitter that transports notes to the "sensitive" ones.

A friend of mine, who lived in Rome for a long time, told me about the red dust that used to cover cars on the streets on windy days. Once he asked a passenger where this dust came from; the answer was: "This is sand from Africa."

— *Translated by Sladja Blazan*

Tomas Venclova

As a writer, and primarily as an essayist, I consider it one of my main tasks to contribute to the dissolving of nationalist myths, especially these concerning "the dangerous Other" and "unique ethnic spirit perennially threatened by one's neighbors."

Tomas Venclova
Lithuania

Born in Klaipeda in 1937, Tomas Venclova is an author, writer, journalist, and translator. He studied philology at the University of Vilnius and during the 1970s became involved in the Lithuanian human rights movement. In 1977 he was able, following the mediation of Czeslaw Milosz, to leave Lithuania and assume a teaching post at the University of California-Berkeley. Having stripped of his Soviet citizenship by the Soviet authorities, he was granted political asylum by the United States. Since 1980 he has taught Russian literature at Yale University, and since 1993 he has been a professor of Slavic languages and literature. He has translated texts by A. Akhmatova, B. Pasternak, J. Brodsky, T. S. Eliot, O. Mandelstam, D. Thomas, and A. Jarry. Tomas Venclova has been awarded leading literary prizes in eastern and central Europe, including the Lithuanian National Prize for Literature in 2000.

Further Reading:
Aleksander Wat: Life and Art of an Iconoclast. Yale University Press, 1996.
Winter Dialogue. Translated by Diana Senechal. Northwestern University Press, 1999.
Form of Hope: Essays. Sheep Meadow Pr, 2003.

What Can Lithuania Give to Present-Day Europe

I would like to think that both duties—the duty of the poet and the duty of the essayist—are complementary. Both might be of some use for the future Europe that attempts to put simultaneously into life two mutually exclusive principles—unity and individuality.

In December of 1978, at that time a dissident and political émigré, I visited Berlin for the first time. That is, I visited West Berlin, which was separated from East Berlin by the Wall. Now I reread pages of my journal devoted to this trip as something pertaining to ancient history. Having been divested of my Soviet citizenship and passport, I could not enter the then DDR—but I still traveled under East Berlin on the subway and got a glimpse of Unter den Linden from the watchtower specially installed for tourists at the Brandenburger Tor. I wrote the following in my journal: "On the other side of the wall and booths with guards, lies, quite simply, the zone of death, collapse, naught. A void at the very heart of the continent. *Finis Europae.* The point of mutual annihilation of East and West." My native country, Lithuania, which I'd left pretty recently, was lost somewhere deep in the void: for a Western European it practically didn't exist. In the fall of 1990, having found myself once again in Berlin, I walked from Tiergarten to Unter den Linden, not even noticing where the Wall had stood until recently. I'll quote from my journal once again: "The ancient concept of evil as nothingness, nonbeing, lacuna has been confirmed. It vanished into thin air, leaving no traces, but the smell of sulfur and mould." That is at least how it seemed to me at the time. Europe expanded unexpectedly: around ten forgotten countries entered it, and more had gotten in line to do the same. Lithuania had already declared its independence, but was still in fact a part of the Soviet Union. It definitively entered world society during the following year, 1991.

Like many dissidents dreaming of the crash of totalitarianism in Eastern Europe, I still thought with fear about the time when it would start to fall apart: it seemed to me that this would lead to worse bloodshed than at the time of the October Revolution and Civil War. My inner eye pictured a sort of gigantic Chechnya, extending over decades. To my great relief, this didn't happen: the anachronistic system dissipated like a piece of wood rotten to the core. Like the majority of Lithuanians, I am proud of the fact that my native country was one of the principal catalysts in this process. In 1990–91, it acquired a status comparable to that of Greece in the early nineteenth century, or of Ireland in the early twentieth century—it became one of the timeless symbols of the fight for freedom. Although major bloodshed was avoided, there still were victims in this fight—the people who perished in the defense of Vilnius television against the Soviet army. They will never be forgotten.

Nowadays Lithuania, like its neighbors, is quickly transforming itself into a regular democratic country and, apparently, will soon enter the European Union. Its international situation is incomparably better now than at any other time during the twentieth century: I would say that it hasn't been so favorable since the fifteenth century, when the Grand Duchy of Lithuania played a significant political role in its own region and the rest of Europe, and was gradually becoming a developed, cultured, and tolerant state. We don't have territorial problems and claims or any serious disputes with our neighbors; the country is urbanized, boasts a decent infrastructure, and as for culture, we have several good universities, brilliant theater, four thousand new books published each year (all of this with a population barely over 3 million). True: the economic changes, like everywhere else in Eastern Europe, lead to difficulties and unnecessary social polarization. True: the mentality that reigned in the era of totalitarianism still hinders one from breathing freely—there still remains a greater amount of intolerance, fear, and simple ignorance than one would like to see. Rather than a holiday, freedom and independence turned out to be heavy labor.

Part of this heavy labor is the attempt to define our place within Europe. We often like to claim that Lithuania, strictly speaking, is the center of Europe: just outside of Vilnius there is a park called "Center of Europe"—quite popular with tourists—where one can see works by many contemporary sculptors from different parts of Europe. Geographically, this is indeed so: if one drew lines from the Northern Urals to Portugal and from the North Cape to Greece, they would intersect approximately on the territory of this park. But, of course, its very existence is proof of a certain psychological complex. Only a province can insist on being a center. When a country ceases to be a province, this question loses its relevance.

On the other hand, what is and isn't Europe? For ages it was customary for almost every European country to think that countries to its East are inferior in some sense, insufficiently civilized, resisting it just as chaos resists cosmos, or the subconscious resists the conscious. In France this myth applied to Germany, in Germany it applied to Poland. Poland, in turn, considered itself a European state, which had to civilize Lithuania, wooded and barbarian, though attractive in its mystery and antiquity. This mentality is very noticeable in classical Polish literature, beginning with Adam Mickiewicz (who, by the way, considered himself Lithuanian, as does our contemporary, Czeslaw Milosz). And those who wrote in Lithuanian pushed the border of Europe still farther: Belorussia and Russia turned out to be the realm of chaos, the subconscious, and the elements, while Lithuania stood guard at the border. Such thinking is popular in Lithuania to this day: worse still, one can encounter it among Western politicians and NATO military staff. It is important for us to understand that both ideas—the idea of the "center of Europe" as well as the idea of the "periphery resisting the non-West, the dangerous Other"— are colored to the same extent by myth. Fortunately, the young generation of Lithuanians is beginning to comprehend this.

What can Lithuania give to contemporary Europe? In my country one often hears voices claiming that Western Europe has lost the sense of ethnic national values, while the Lithuanians, like the other Balts, have preserved them—and preserved them in the course of a hard struggle against Soviet internationalism. Therefore, we can set an example for other peoples that have crossed over to universal, uniform, mass culture. This idea, alas, is connected to some deplorable traditions of European thinking and with right-wing conservatism. In my opinion, this only shows that Lithuania is crossing over (or, rather, has already crossed over) from nationalist romanticism, connected to the struggle for independence — and apparently useful in this struggle — to a more contemporary and rational, global thinking. The Baltic countries have always been very attracted to Herder's theory of the "national spirit," which postulates the equivalence of national culture to the ethnos and its folklore (strictly speaking, Herder lived in the Baltic region and came up with his theory based on his observations of our peoples). It is well known what the absolutization of "national spirit" can lead to (even if moderate Herderism is not necessarily a perilous route). Apropos, those who clamor most of all about nation and ethnos turn out, more often than others, to be collaborators: such were the supporters of Vichy in France as well as the numerous Lithuanian intellectuals who found a common language with Soviet Communism. These intellectuals are still active nowadays, but, in my opinion, they no longer control people's minds.

Still, Herder is not totally wrong. Each culture has its own unique face, and Lithuanian culture undoubtedly has such a face. We have a contribution to make to the "concert of humankind," as Guiseppe Mazzini at one point defined the interaction among cultures. The Lithuanian language is remarkable in and of itself — archaic and rich, with particularly sculpted verb forms, close in many ways to the languages of antiquity. It was on the verge of extinction for several centuries, just like, say, the Celtic languages, but unlike the Celts, we managed to keep it alive and ever evolving. As many linguists have pointed out, language is mysteriously connected to the particularities of one's worldview. Our writers — as well as the writers of other peoples — talk about a specifically Lithuanian Weltanschauung, reflected in folklore and mythology (the Lithuanians have preserved both their folklore and ancient mythology better than the majority of European peoples—even sometimes no worse than the peoples of the distant continents). Add to this the complex and unique history of the country, in which there is room for the romantic Middle Ages as well as for the no less romantic rebellions against tyrants. The history of Lithuania reminds one of the history of Poland (to which Lithuania has been closely connected), but, if you like, it surpasses Poland's by virtue of its exotic quality. Folklore and history were and continue to be, at least in part, the underpinnings of Lithuanian literature. But important as they are for us, they are perhaps too idiosyncratic to arouse serious interest in the West. And then it's hardly appropriate to insist on being a sanctuary of the past in the contemporary world. More important, I think, are other characteristics of Lithuanian culture, pertaining to its frontier situation, the intersection of different European zones within Lithuania, and our city life.

The originality of Lithuanian cities is immediately apparent in their architecture. It's a combination of Gothicism (hardly inferior to the Gothicism of Paris, Köln, or Ulm, but on a smaller scale and perhaps even more exquisite), Baroque (reminiscent of Rome, Prague, Augsburg, but singular in nature thanks to its integrity and taste), and, also, Classicism (which reflects both ancient Athens and the Enlightenment). But there is also the architecture of Orthodox churches, the synagogues, the oriental mosques, and, finally, the functionalism of the twentieth, already past, century. This architecture combines with the particular style, particular experience of a polyethnic, multicultural city life, marked by both coexistence and tragedy. Many people would perhaps understand this better if I drew a parallel to the style and experience of Danzig (Gdansk), which Günter Grass attempts to present in his novels. Nowadays this is the experience of a small country, having made the transition from totalitarianism to freedom—an experience characterized in part by some comic and grotesque aspects. It is precisely this fact that may be interesting to a wider group of people. I think that contemporary Lithuanian literature is beginning to assimilate these new possibilities—to create books that reflect adequately the complexity of our spatial and temporal situation on the frontier.

The majority of Lithuanians wish to join the European Union and are getting ready for it, but in some circles—especially among intellectuals and publicists—there is a fear of losing our newly gained sovereignty, of exchanging subservience to Moscow for subservience to Brussels (or, as they also put it, of going from the yoke of Communism to the yoke of international capital). One could reply to all these concerns that a sovereignty of the nineteenth- and twentieth-century type is the equivalent of a candle in the age of electricity and a horse-drawn carriage in the age of automobiles and airplanes. What's taking shape at present, though not without difficulty, is the idea not only of a unified Europe, but also of unified humankind, an idea that was preached by Diogenes Laertios and the Christian Church Fathers, as well as Erasmus of Rotterdam and Kant. It's not superfluous, however, to also remember that the sense of ethnic and national identity, as well as the fear of losing it, is a legitimate emotion. Even if this emotion is not always civilized.

One is always more rooted in a certain place, which produces a feeling of being "on one's own turf." One is always rooted in one's own language as well. This is precisely why Marx's nationalist nihilism and, even more so, Soviet "internationalism" (which in reality meant obedience to the Soviet Union and even to Russia) were not realistic ideologies. But this doesn't mean at all that it's appropriate to prefer the interests of one's own country or ethnos always and everywhere, to blow up national egoism and territorial disputes in the manner in which this, alas, happened in the Balkans. The name of the Baltic region starts with the same letter "B" as the Balkans; the ethnic map of the Baltic region is almost as complex, and the mutual unsettled scores throughout history are not much simpler. In our countries—and those of our neighbors—there also were and are politicians (to say nothing of literary figures) ready to manipulate these authentic or fictitious unsettled scores and contradictions for their own profit. I am proud that we have managed and still manage to put a stop to this and come to civilized decisions.

We, the Lithuanians, of course, are not going to be the leaders of united Europe, but it will grant us greater stability and self-confidence, and will diminish (though not totally do away with) the danger of extremist dispositions. We will learn flexibility and self-criticism from the West, and will adopt the Western tendency towards self-reformation and experimentation. I have no doubt that in the final account all this will affect favorably both art and literature. And, by the way, national and traditional values won't perish, but will only continue to exist in the united world; they will collapse in the backward, isolated countries.

The concept of identity in this united world will also undergo changes. I don't think there will ever be an absolutely unified and centralized world—or, for that matter, even European republic. Part of the beauty and diversity of the world lies in its borders—to the extent that they don't become insurmountable. The cult of the national state will disappear, but the sense of Heimat and love of a certain region will, I think, always remain. Every region of this kind is a point of intersection of several cultures, and our identity will be precisely of such nature: mosaic-like, made up of segments, each of which is necessary for the overall completeness of this identity. We will not so much inherit as create it ourselves. Although one will always have one's principal language, multilingualism will become the norm. It's precisely writers, I think, who will become the pioneers of this future world.

As a writer, and primarily as an essayist, I consider it one of my main tasks to contribute to the dissolving of nationalist myths, especially these concerning "the dangerous Other" and "unique ethnic spirit perennially threatened by one's neighbors." One of the sons of the polyethnic Vilnius, I try to continue the tradition of its founders and it best citizens, that is, the tradition of crossing over the cultural borders. Still, poetry is a different matter. It is language mirrored in itself and reflecting upon itself: its phonetics, rhythm and intonation, the peculiarities and quirks of its grammar and syntax, the multi-layered vocabulary where archaisms and borrowings coexist with words one may invent or resurrect—all this remains particular and inimitable. In a sense, poetry preserves these cultural borders that make our life colorful and worth living, and transforms the crossing of them into a joyful adventure. I would like to think that both duties—the duty of the poet and the duty of the essayist—are complementary. Both might be of some use for the future Europe that aims at an unattainable yet precious goal and attempts to put simultaneously into life two mutually exclusive principles—unity and individuality.

Māra Zālīte

The ambivalent nature of Europe expresses itself in the persona of Faust.
Spirituality and the Holy Inquisition. The concepts of freedom and
colonialism. Democracy and imperialism. Human rights and the Holocaust.
© Maxim Segienko/PHOTOMAX

Māra Zālīte
Latvia

Born the child of deported Latvians in Siberia in 1952, the author and writer Māra Zālīte became an important spokeswoman during the "Singing Revolution" that led to the restoration of Latvia's national independence. Indeed, in 1989 Latvian media hailed her as "woman of the year." Her dramatic work comprises six plays as well as eight libretti to rock operas and musicals. In 1993, for her libretto to the rock opera *Lāčplēsis*, she was awarded the Herder Prize by the Toepfer Foundation of Hamburg. From 1989 until 2000, Māra Zālīte was editor in chief of the monthly literary journal *Karogs*. She lives as a writer in Riga.

Further Reading:
Poems in *All Birds Know This: Selected Latvian Poetry*. Compiled by Kristina Sadovska, edited by Astride Ivaska and Mara Rumniece. Riga: Tapals Press, 2001.

Unfinished Thoughts

Fausta tēlā izpaužas Eiropas ambivalentā daba.
Garīgums un Svētā inkvizīcija. Brīvības idejas
un koloniālisms. Demokrātija un imperiālisms.
Cilvēktiesības un holokausts.

I. Europe. A Greek myth as metaphor

Europe, the daughter of a Phoenician ruler, is young and beautiful. In her purple dress embroidered in gold, without a care, she frolics by the sea. The fields are profuse with flowers. Narcissi and lilies. Violets and crocuses. An idyll. Portrayed by the writers of antiquity and, over time, converted into an impersonal myth. Europe is wonderful. Everything is splendid.

But then, one night Europe has a bad dream. Europe dreams that Asia, who has raised her, is at war with a country across the sea from her. The battle is over Europe. Asia loses. The young Phoenician does not find out what happens next because she wakes. The lovely cheek of Europe grows troubled. Her thoughts are preoccupied with the meaning of the dream she has seen. What could this dreadful dream augur? She should ask one of the sibyls, query one of the oracles. Try to think herself. But there is no time to think. An Event is approaching. Europe has never been able to think anything through to the end. There are always Events that interfere with contemplation.

Then Europe is abducted. The Great ruler of the Olympus, in the guise of a bull, sweeps Europe off her feet. The breath of the beast smells as sweet as ambrosia. Europe embraces the bull's head and kisses his golden fur. Zeus, in the guise of a bull, releases Europe's base instincts and carries her away on his back. To steal her virginity. Take her by force to be his wife. He rapes her. But Europe is intoxicated with the sweet smell of ambrosia. The breath of her violator. Europe has kissed the golden fur of the bull. Her violator's fur. In the dark new ties form between the victim and the rapist. An exchange? A collaboration? A symbiosis?

The myth does say that nothing has happened but is always happening. The semantics of a myth are always unclear. Like the bad dream of Europe. A myth poses riddles.

The only thing that can be said for certain is that a myth repeats itself. Repeats itself again and again. In the Greek myth Europe is raped by a white bull. As time passes the bull—totalitarian power— assumes different colors. In the twentieth century—brown and red. Trampled under the hooves of the bull—the ideals of humanity, culture, and reason. The bull has gold horns. On his forehead—a red star. On his forehead—a swastika. There is a desire to idealize abducted Europe. So young. So beautiful. Narcissi and lilies. Violets and crocuses. The world before it fell into sin. Yes, what Latvia was before occupation.

During fifty years under the Communist regime the Baltic nations yearned for the abducted Europe. They, themselves, were a part of this abducted Europe. The part not raped is behind a wall. There everything is as good as it was—Europe frolics in her splendid dress. By the sea. In a field profuse with flowers. The bad dream? The captivating breath of the bull? There is no time for contemplation.

There is time, however, for idealization. Of abducted Europe. A yearning for a humane existence, freedom, and respect for the individual. For a Europe inside oneself. For a Europe—the one behind the wall. There is a fervent desire to belong to it. To an orderly, harmonious world. To deeply internalize the classical heritage of Europe. Shakespeare. Cervantes. Goethe. Molière. Hugo ... Spirituality, humanism, civilization, democracy—the splendid garb of Europe. Lack of air experienced in a Communist reality makes one take deep breaths of this idealized Europe. Distilled, extracted, clean. The main Event is spiritual survival. With an oxygen mask. With Europe as a means of anesthesia. There is no time to think. To know is not possible.

It is better not to know that European leftist intellectuals sang odes to the Soviet Union. As millions were slaughtered in the GULAG. It is better not to know the significant contribution of European intellectuals to the destruction of the peoples and cultures of the Soviet Empire. Of the two-hundred nationalities that lived on the territory of the USSR, less than a half succeeded in retaining their language, culture, and lifestyle. No one calls this genocide. Rare species of plants and animals—now that is a totally different thing. Europe does concern itself with these. The intoxicating smell of the ambrosia of the bull? The experience of suffering and violence, the energy generated by resistance, create a forceful cultural energy field, assign depth to art and generate a wide public resonance. It is good not to know. Not to know the marginalization and neuroticism of the culture of Europe. Better not to see the intercourse of Europe and the bull. It is better to dream an obscure dream. Not to think thoughts through to the end.

II. The Cross and the Sword

"The Chronicle of Henricus" (*Indriķa hronika*) is a historical document dating from the thirteenth century that describes the Crusades proclaimed by Pope Innocent III in 1199 against Livonia, now Latvia, and Estonia. "The Chronicle of Henricus," the rock opera, is based on this historical document. Produced by the National Theatre of Latvia, it has enjoyed several seasons of success. The music is by Jānis Lūsēns; the libretto and the text are by the author of this essay.

The Christianization of Livonia. The Baltics become a part of the Christian cultural milieu of the West. The boundaries drawn between Rome and Byzantium at that time have been retained to this day. Latvia's accession to the European Union is a balancing act on the same boundaries. On its crevasses. Wounds. Problems.

The cross and the sword are quite similar as geometric shapes. The vertical of the cross. The vertical of the sword. The horizontal line of the cross is longer than the characteristic horizontal line of the hilt of a sword. The vertical is masculine. God. Father. Global market. The horizontal is feminine. Mother. Language. Earth. Homeland.[1]

In Germany the concept "homeland" has fallen into disuse. It is discredited and no longer politically correct. In Germany the word gets caught in the throat. Germany has gorged herself on the word. The small, oppressed nations have not had enough of the word. They are starving for it. For a homeland, a mother tongue, an identity— which totalitarianism, both brown and red, has stolen from them. For small nations it is their daily bread—their sustenance. They suffer from a lack of the horizontal. They see the sword. Not the cross. They remember that "New Europe" is a term first used by the Nazis.

Too simple? Too complicated. Events. Events. No time to think. Harmonization of legislation. Standardization. Unification. The same laws for those who have lived in surfeit as for those who are starving.

In the Greek myth, the traditional epithet for Europe is "platace" — "Polyphonous." Polymorphous—diverse. National territories are small cultural preserves—sanctuaries for diverse forms of expression and content. The survival of ethnic cultures is a guarantee of diversity. The horizontal. Market economy and globalism shorten the horizontal. They turn the cross into a sword. De-integrate nations as carriers of the diverse cultures of Europe. The masculine vertical fears the feminine horizontal. Sin. Celibacy. Burning of witches. "Our Father in Heaven" ... Our Mother—the Earth. A human child needs both a Father and a Mother. The crucifix. Son of a human. Child of a human. At the point where the vertical and the horizontal of the cross meet— the crux.

In the rock opera "Chronicle of Henricus" (*Indriķa hronika*) the daughter of the Latvian ruler is expecting a child. It is a child of rape. Born of the seed of the enemy. The King wants to kill the child. But the child is the only possible continuation for the royal line. The King, therefore, reconciles himself to the birth, but he waits for the birth of an avenger. A son. One who will grow up, rule, divide, and hate. He will take revenge for all the wrongs that have been suffered. There is a feeling of great disappointment and betrayal when the child is born. It is a girl.

O, for the gentleness of forgiveness. Can forgiveness be given if it has not been asked for? A child, a girl, a new concept. The enemy is no longer external. Now it is internalized, merged. Was it ever external?

III. Margaret and Faust

It is true that there is nothing specifically German in the theme and problem of Faust. It is a human drama, wherein Faust represents humanity. Today Goethe again has become actual. Within the context of the development of Europe and the search for a new identity. Within the context of an exploited and transformed nature. Within the context of an eroding sense of what is human existence. The concept of Faust as a hero has taken a strange detour. Faust is larger than large, a great and true hero. Only Mephistopheles, that nasty Mephistopheles, is bent on ruining everything! The ruler is good; it is the courtiers who do not allow the people to breathe. The general secretary of the party is good; it is only his subordinates who interfere with the realization of sunny party ideals. Communism as an idea is good; it is only the people implementing it who have contaminated it. When Goethe created Mephistopheles as Faust's alter ego, Faust's shadow, could he have foreseen the surprising emancipation the image of this character would experience as a result of audience perception. An intriguing opportunity to externalize evil.

The image of Faust characterizes the essence of Europe. To understand the socio-psychological genesis of Goethe's hero and its influence, which has remained unchanged to this day, means to understand the great drama of Europe and its tragic delusions that have resulted in two totalitarian regimes. The ambivalent nature of Europe expresses itself in the persona of Faust. Spirituality and the Holy Inquisition. The concepts of freedom and colonialism. Democracy and imperialism. Human rights and the Holocaust.

Faustian plans for revamping the world are ones with which the superpowers of both the East and the West identify. On the other hand, Gretel—this seemingly peripheral, limited, and naïve figure (as she is in the interpretation of many) is the one with which, unfortunately, small nations, cultures, and languages, are able to identify.

In my play *Margaret*, we find Gretel in her prison cell twenty-five years (perhaps 250 years?) after Goethe (Or Faust? Or Mephistopheles? Or after a choir of angels?). In any case, twenty-five years pass until we again encounter Margaret—a grown-up and fully matured woman, no longer the small, naïve Gretel. The advocate arrives because finally the trial has begun (!) for this person who, from a legal point of view, has only been arrested. She has been charged with criminal offences. The charges are serious—poisoning of her mother, murder of her child, and conspiracy in the death of her brother. Only slowly it is revealed that the catalyst in all of what has happened is Faust. In the play all that has occurred is portrayed from the point of view of Margaret. It is, after all, important to give Margaret a voice. Margaret speaks. The advocate keeps strictly to the "case materials"—namely, the text of Goethe's *Faust*. Margaret, in poisoning her mother, has destroyed her past. In drowning her child she has robbed herself of a future. In betraying Valentine, her brother, she has destroyed an idealist. What remains? An irrational love of Faust. The bull's ambrosial breath. Its suggestion of strength. The body of the beast covered in golden fur. Margaret—abducted Europe. Faust—the bull.

As it turns out, the advocate, offspring of contemporary democracy and civilization, is the child of Gretel and Faust. (No, he did not drown, he has been saved! Yes, a miracle!) A son. A human being. A child. An orphan. The young advocate sees Faust as the source of all evil. Margaret slowly wakes from Faust's spell. Then, in some nuance, some small gesture, Margaret sees a frightening similarity between her son and his father. The son hates his father and is not aware of their similarity. He is not aware of the Faust in himself.

Europe's awareness is not clear. The focus on Margaret is an attempt to revise and cleanse the concept of Europe. The advocate, in interrogating Margaret, asks about the "other." We sense that he means Mephistopheles. There has been no other Margaret swears. Faust acted alone. The "other" is a substance that is to be found in our own cells and tissues.

There is no time to think things through. An Event is approaching. The advocate is invited to work for the European Parliament. Globalization, cultural standardization, and cultural imperialism. A transformation of the world—not included in it, the transformation of awareness, soul, and morality—the Faustian discourse. The horizontal? The eternally feminine? In it the wealth of Europe is buried, its diversity of cultures and polyphony of languages. Thus, Europe herself is threatened.

No longer is Europe the young and virginal Phoenician. No longer is she the young and naïve Gretel. Europe is experienced. Europe dreams. In her dream someone wants to steal one of her languages, one of her cultures. Then another, and yet another. But, it is only a bad dream. What happens next Europe does not find out. She wakes.

— *Translated by Margita Gailitis*

1 Since the English language does not have a case system this masculine/feminine polarization is not as obvious. In Latvian and German, as well as other languages, in which case systems exist, the examples given in the text distinctly fall into the masculine and feminine categories.

Körber-STIFTUNG
Forum für Impulse

édition Körber-STIFTUNG

BERGEDORFER
GESPRÄCHSKREIS
Bergedorf Round Table

BegegnungsCentrum
HAUS
im Park
Citizen's Center »Haus im Park«

USable
The Transatlantic Idea Contest

Boy
Gobert
Preis
Boy Gobert Prize

Democracy thrives on social dialogue and the collective search for solutions. As a forum for new ideas and impulses the Körber-Foundation seeks with its projects to involve citizens actively in social discourses.

The private, non-profit-making foundation provides a forum for involvement in politics, education, science and international communication. Citizens who take part in competitions and round table discussions organised by the foundation benefit in many ways: they can pass on knowledge, identify problems and initiate activities. These kinds of stimulus form the Körber-Foundation's contribution to the everyday culture of democracy.

Deutsch-
Türkischer
Dialog
German-Turkish Dialog

KÖRBER
FotoAward
Körber-Photo-Award

Eustory
History Network for Young Europeans

theater
haus im park
Theatre »Haus im Park«

Geschichtswettbewerb
des Bundespräsidenten
Jugendliche forschen vor Ort
The Federal President's History Competition.
Students researching on site

Deutscher Studienpreis
Der Wettbewerb für junge Forschung
German Students Award
The Competition for Young Researchers

KÖRBER-PREIS
FÜR DIE EUROPÄISCHE
WISSENSCHAFT
Körber European Science Award